THE NINTH DOCTOR

VOL 3: OFFICIAL SECRETS

"Readers new to the Ninth Doctor are in for a treat, and fans of Eccleston's era will not be disappointed!"
KASTERBOROUS

"Perfectly captures the voice and energy of the original Team TARDIS... 9 out of 10."
NEWSARAMA

"The dialogue, especially between the TARDIS crew, is excellent!"
NERDLY

"Fans of the Ninth Doctor and team will find this comic to be a satisfying continuation of their adventures!"
KABOOOOOM

"Scott, Melo and Lesko take you back in time, but with a modern punch and a distinctly Ninth Doctor growl!"
WARPED FACTOR

"The creative team have most definitely created something that any Whovian should enjoy!"
SNAP POW

"A fun and engaging read that should more than please fans of the series."
NERDS UNCHAINED

"An absolute joy to read!"
BLOGTOR WHO

"Doctor Who fans will love it for sure, and they will be captivated by this story."
GEEKS OF DOOM

TITAN COMICS

SENIOR COMICS EDITOR
Andrew James

ASSISTANT EDITORS
Jessica Burton,
Amoona Saohin

COLLECTION DESIGNER
Andrew Leung

TITAN COMICS EDITORIAL
Tom Williams, Lauren McPhee

PRODUCTION SUPERVISOR
Maria Pearson

PRODUCTION CONTROLLER
Peter James

**SENIOR PRODUCTION
CONTROLLER**
Jackie Flook

ART DIRECTOR
Oz Browne

SENIOR SALES MANAGER
Steve Tothill

PRESS OFFICER
Will O'Mullane

COMICS BRAND MANAGER
Chris Thompson

ADS & MARKETING ASSISTANT
Tom Miller

**DIRECT SALES & MARKETING
MANAGER** Ricky Claydon

COMMERCIAL MANAGER
Michelle Fairlamb

HEAD OF RIGHTS
Jenny Boyce

PUBLISHING MANAGER
Darryl Tothill

PUBLISHING DIRECTOR
Chris Teather

OPERATIONS DIRECTOR
Leigh Baulch

EXECUTIVE DIRECTOR
Vivian Cheung

PUBLISHER
Nick Landau

For rights information contact jenny.boyce@titanemail.com

Special thanks to Steven Moffat, Brian Minchin, Mandy Thwaites, Matt Nicholls,
James Dudley, Edward Russell, Derek Ritchie, Scott Handcock, Kirsty Mullan, Kate
Bush, Julia Nocciolino, and Ed Casey, for their invaluable assistance.

BBC WORLDWIDE

DIRECTOR OF EDITORIAL GOVERNANCE
Nicolas Brett

**DIRECTOR OF CONSUMER
PRODUCTS AND PUBLISHING**
Andrew Moultrie

HEAD OF UK PUBLISHING
Chris Kerwin

PUBLISHER
Mandy Thwaites

PUBLISHING CO-ORDINATOR
Eva Abramik

DOCTOR WHO: THE NINTH DOCTOR
VOL 3: OFFICIAL SECRETS
HB ISBN: 9781785861116 SB ISBN: 9781785861123
Published by Titan Comics, a division of
Titan Publishing Group, Ltd. 144 Southwark Street,
London, SE1 0UP.

A CIP catalogue record for this title is available from the British Library.
First edition: July 2017.

10 9 8 7 6 5 4 3 2 1

Printed in China.

Titan Comics does not read or accept unsolicited DOCTOR WHO
submissions of ideas, stories or artwork.

ALISTAIR LETHBRIDGE-STEWART APPEARS COURTESY OF **CANDY JAR** BOOKS,
WITH THANKS TO HANNAH HAISMAN, HENRY LINCOLN, AND ANDY FRANKHAM-
ALLEN. VISIT *WWW.LETHBRIDGESTEWART.CO.UK* FOR MORE!

www.titan-comics.com

DOCTOR WHO

THE NINTH DOCTOR

VOL 3: OFFICIAL SECRETS

WRITER: CAVAN SCOTT

ARTISTS: ADRIANA MELO & CRIS BOLSON

COLORIST: MARCO LESKO

LETTERS: RICHARD STARKINGS AND COMICRAFT'S JIMMY BETANCOURT

ALISTAIR LETHBRIDGE-STEWART CREATED BY **MERVYN HAISMAN** AND **HENRY LINCOLN**

DOCTOR WHO

THE NINTH DOCTOR

THE DOCTOR

Last of the Time Lords of Gallifrey, sole survivor of the Time War. Beginning to have his rough edges sanded off by Rose, and to trust the scoundrel Jack. Recently put the contents of his brain up for auction to prove a point. That *definitely* won't come back to bite him.

CAPTAIN JACK

A roguish ex-Time Agent from the 51st century, and an interstellar con man. Brash, brave and willing to hit on anything with a pulse, Jack has now joined the TARDIS crew. Happy to keep running from con to con, will Jack be forced at last to face his future... and his missing, carefully-edited past?

ROSE TYLER

Became the Doctor's companion when she helped save London from the Autons. She's been the spark of humanity that is helping him heal from the Time War. She is also the one who keeps him in check. Recently gained (and was subsequently cured of) superpowers!

PREVIOUSLY...

The Doctor, Rose, and Jack are slowly-but-surely turning into a tight-knit TARDIS crew. Their last adventure took them to modern-day San Francisco, to answer a mysterious call of help from none other than... Mickey Smith! The city's population, including his wife, Martha, were gaining powers and turning into gargoyles. Rose quickly became infected, too – and started to fly! The Doctor and Mickey managed to solve the root cause of the problem – but they accidentally sent one of the gargoyles back in time in the process! Now the Doctor, Rose, and Jack are in hot pursuit...

These adventures occur between 'The Doctor Dances' and 'Boom Town'.

When you've finished reading this collection, please email your thoughts to doctorwhocomic@titanemail.com

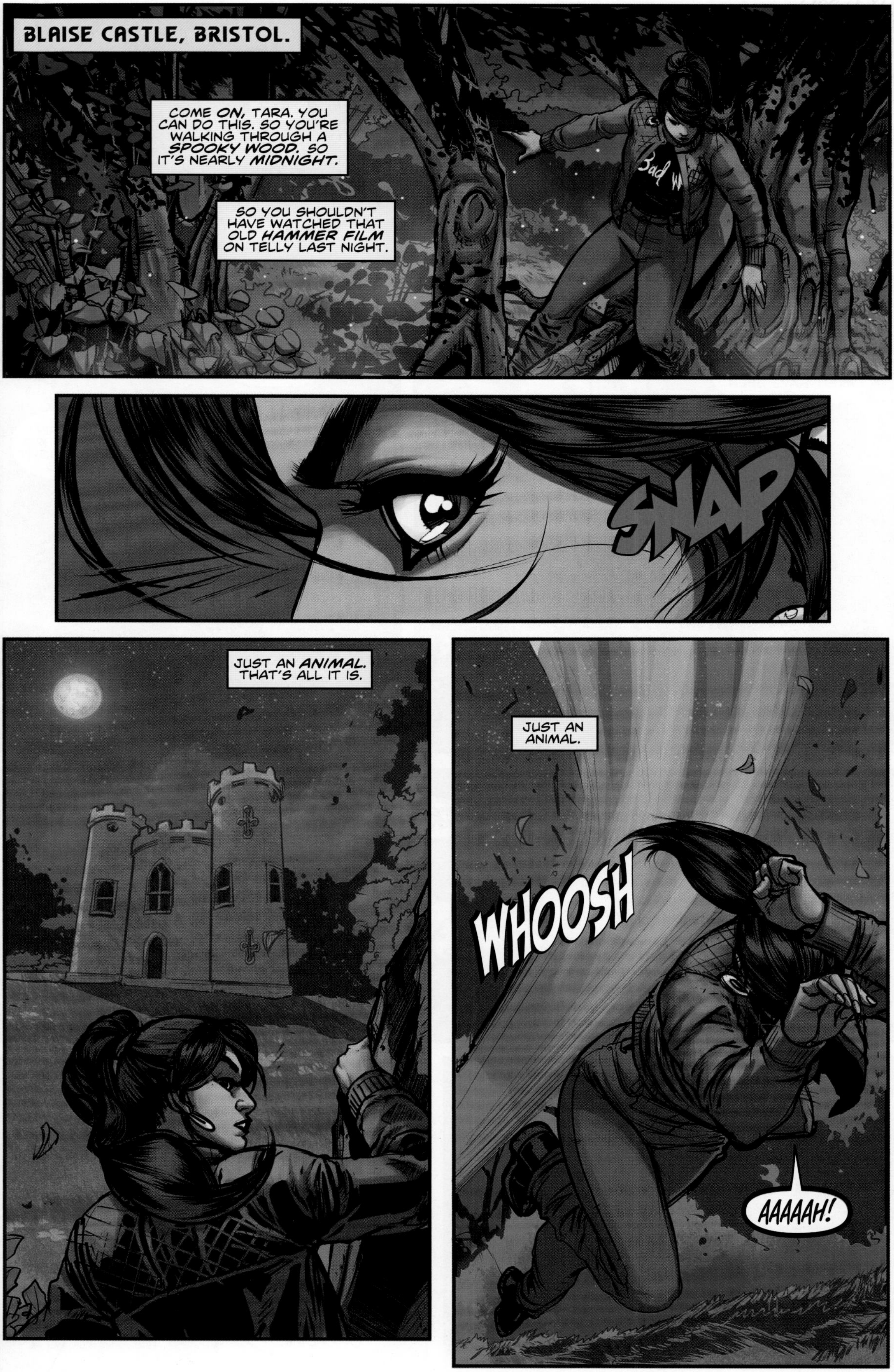
BLAISE CASTLE, BRISTOL.
COME ON, TARA. YOU CAN DO THIS. SO YOU'RE WALKING THROUGH A SPOOKY WOOD. SO IT'S NEARLY MIDNIGHT.
SO YOU SHOULDN'T HAVE WATCHED THAT OLD HAMMER FILM ON TELLY LAST NIGHT.
SNAP
JUST AN ANIMAL. THAT'S ALL IT IS.
JUST AN ANIMAL.
WHOOSH
AAAAAH!

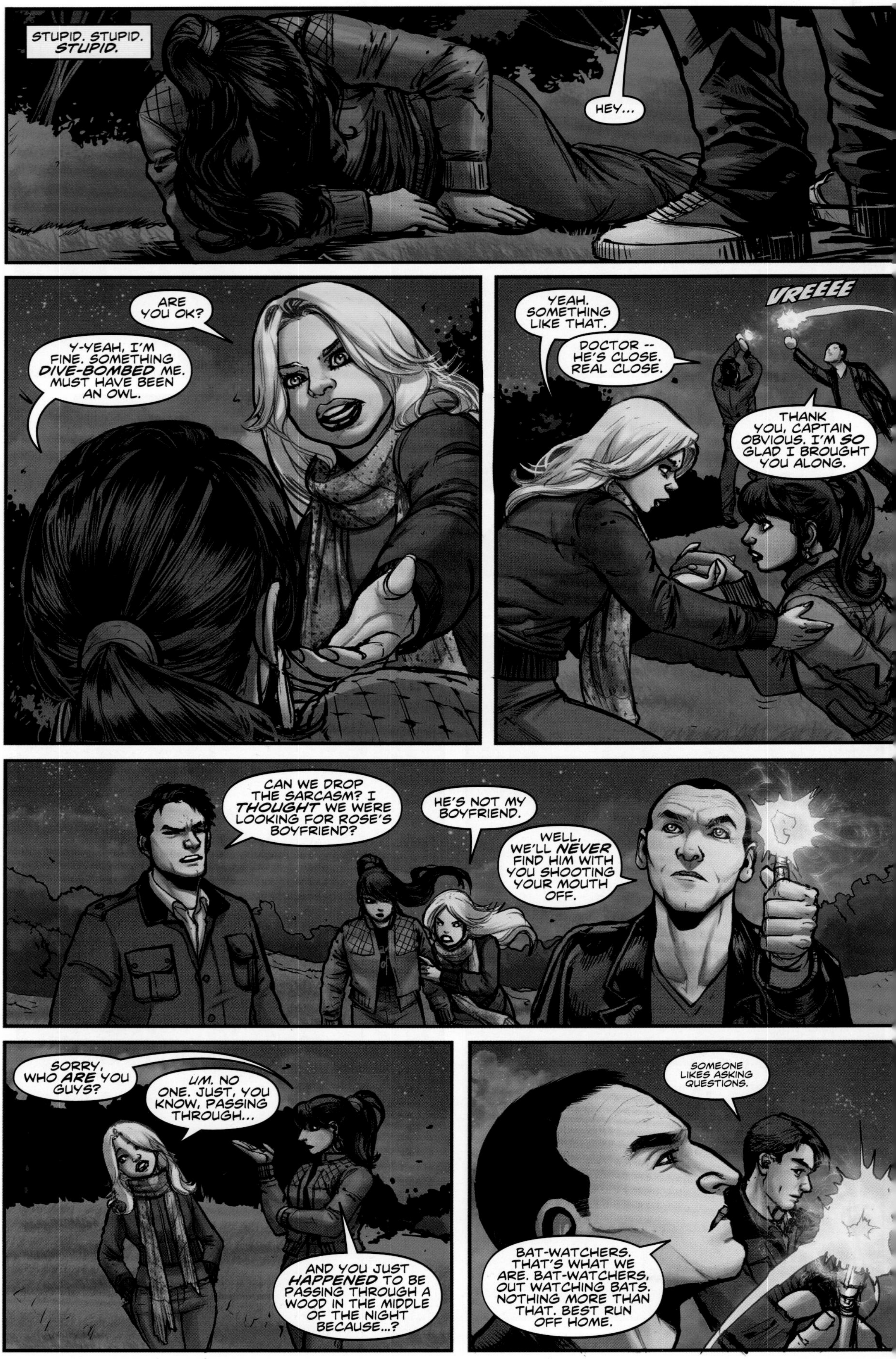

STUPID. STUPID. STUPID.
HEY...
ARE YOU OK?
Y-YEAH, I'M FINE. SOMETHING DIVE-BOMBED ME. MUST HAVE BEEN AN OWL.
YEAH. SOMETHING LIKE THAT.
DOCTOR -- HE'S CLOSE. REAL CLOSE.
VREEEE
THANK YOU, CAPTAIN OBVIOUS. I'M SO GLAD I BROUGHT YOU ALONG.
CAN WE DROP THE SARCASM? I THOUGHT WE WERE LOOKING FOR ROSE'S BOYFRIEND?
HE'S NOT MY BOYFRIEND.
WELL, WE'LL NEVER FIND HIM WITH YOU SHOOTING YOUR MOUTH OFF.
SORRY, WHO ARE YOU GUYS?
UM. NO ONE. JUST, YOU KNOW, PASSING THROUGH...
AND YOU JUST HAPPENED TO BE PASSING THROUGH A WOOD IN THE MIDDLE OF THE NIGHT BECAUSE...?
SOMEONE LIKES ASKING QUESTIONS.
BAT-WATCHERS. THAT'S WHAT WE ARE. BAT-WATCHERS, OUT WATCHING BATS. NOTHING MORE THAN THAT. BEST RUN OFF HOME.

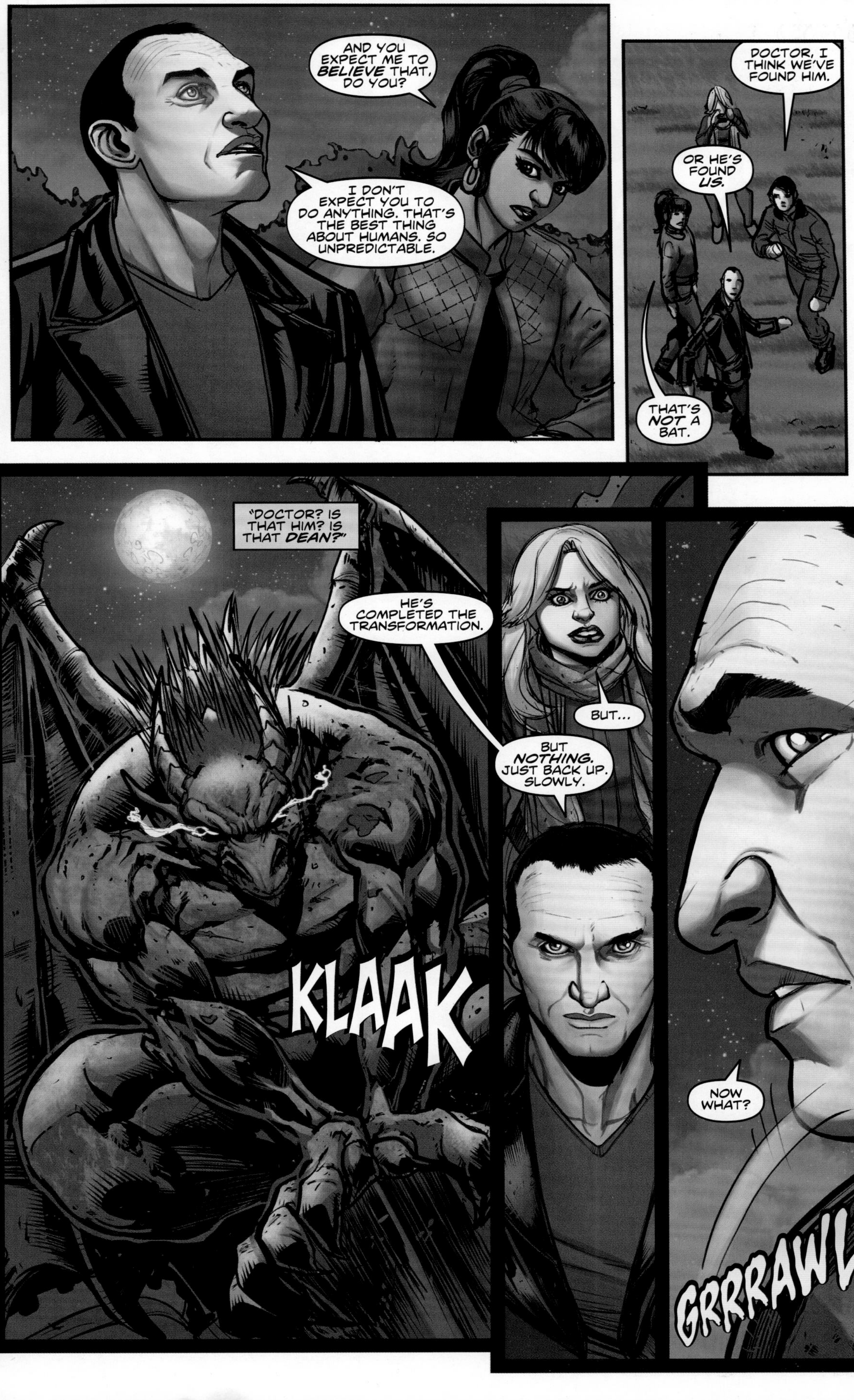
AND YOU EXPECT ME TO BELIEVE THAT, DO YOU?
I DON'T EXPECT YOU TO DO ANYTHING. THAT'S THE BEST THING ABOUT HUMANS. SO UNPREDICTABLE.
DOCTOR, I THINK WE'VE FOUND HIM.
OR HE'S FOUND US.
THAT'S NOT A BAT.
"DOCTOR? IS THAT HIM? IS THAT DEAN?"
HE'S COMPLETED THE TRANSFORMATION.
BUT...
BUT NOTHING. JUST BACK UP. SLOWLY.
KLAAK
NOW WHAT?
GRRRAWL

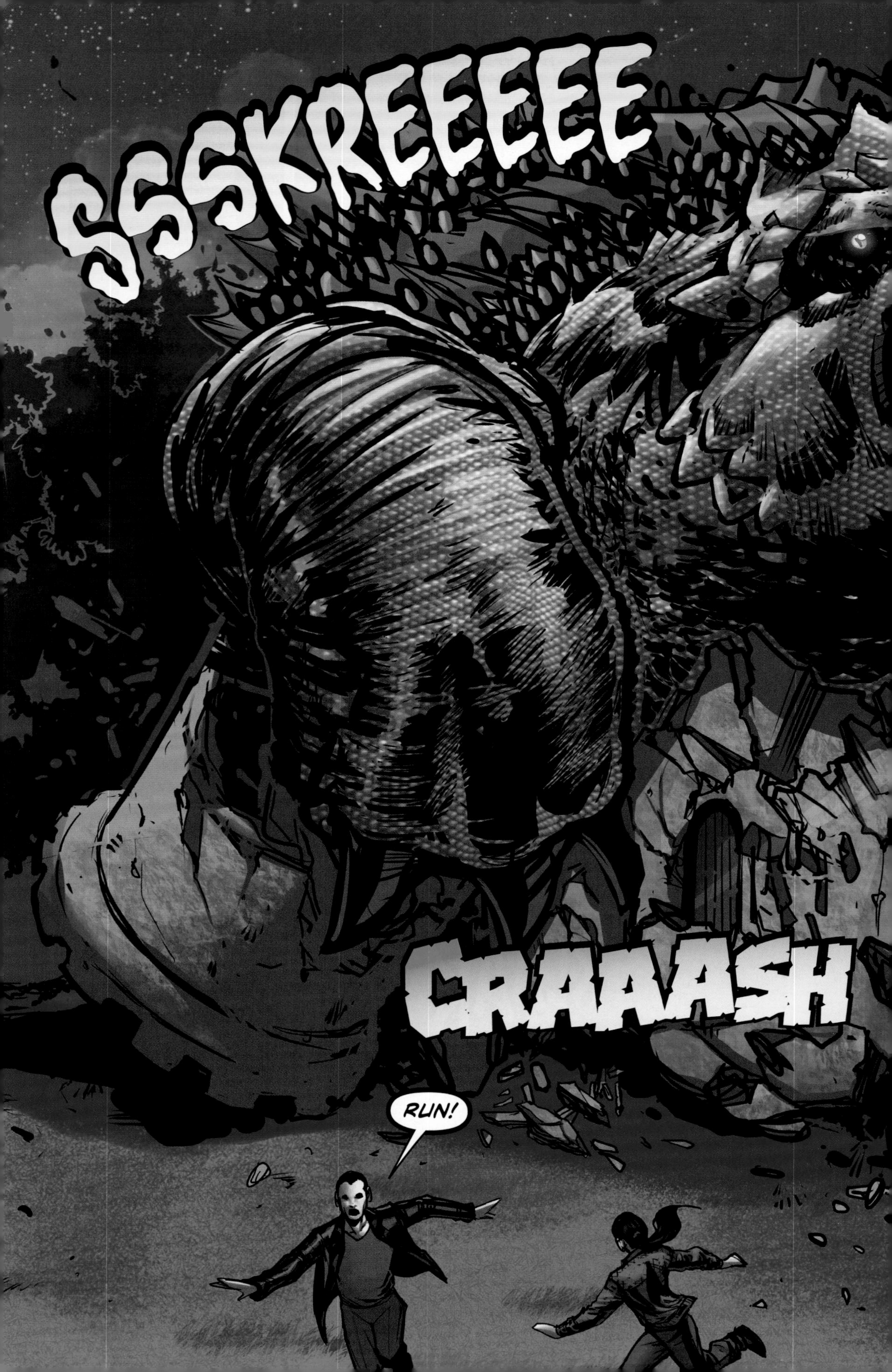
SSSKREEEEEE
CRAAASH
RUN!

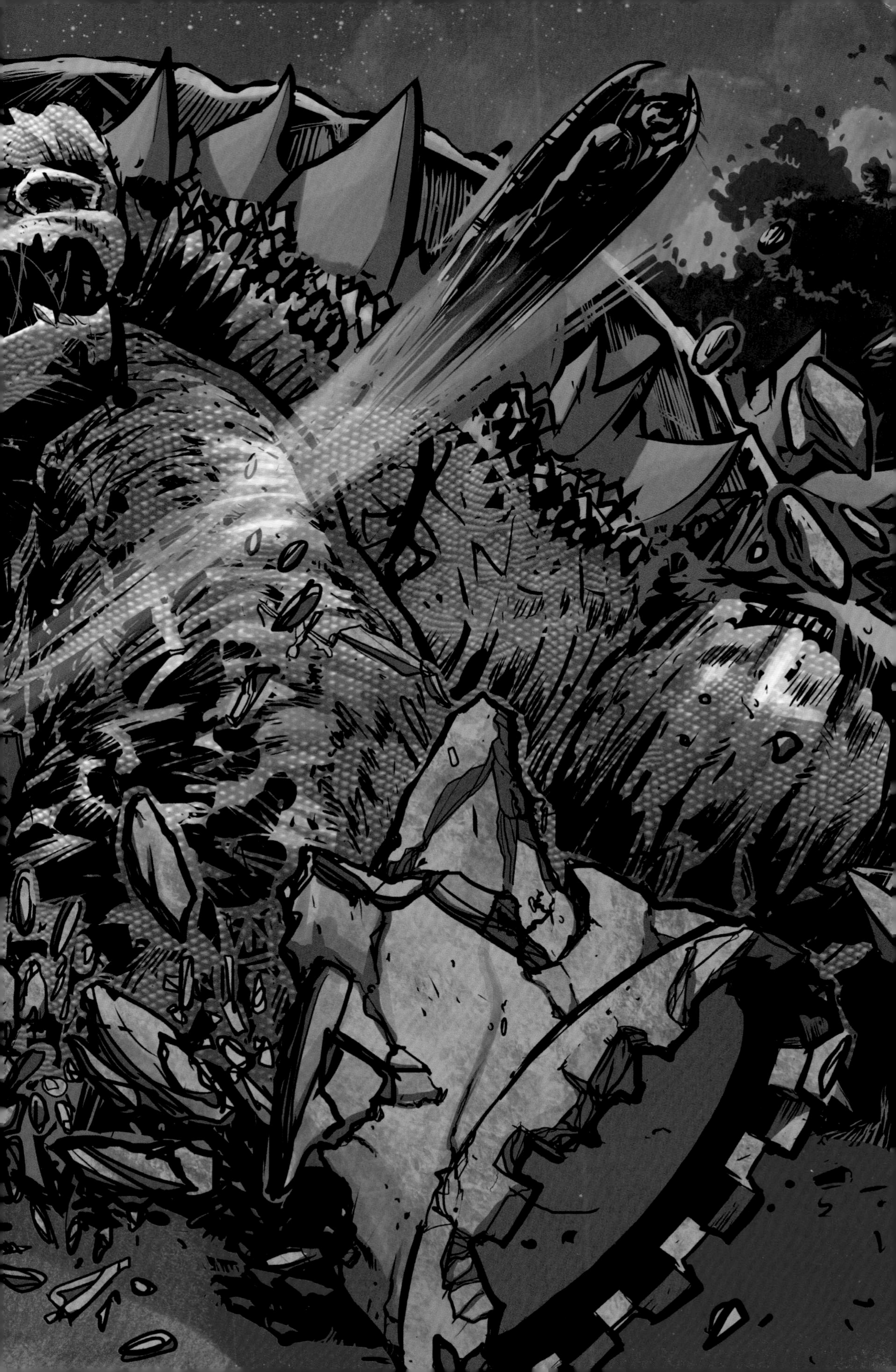

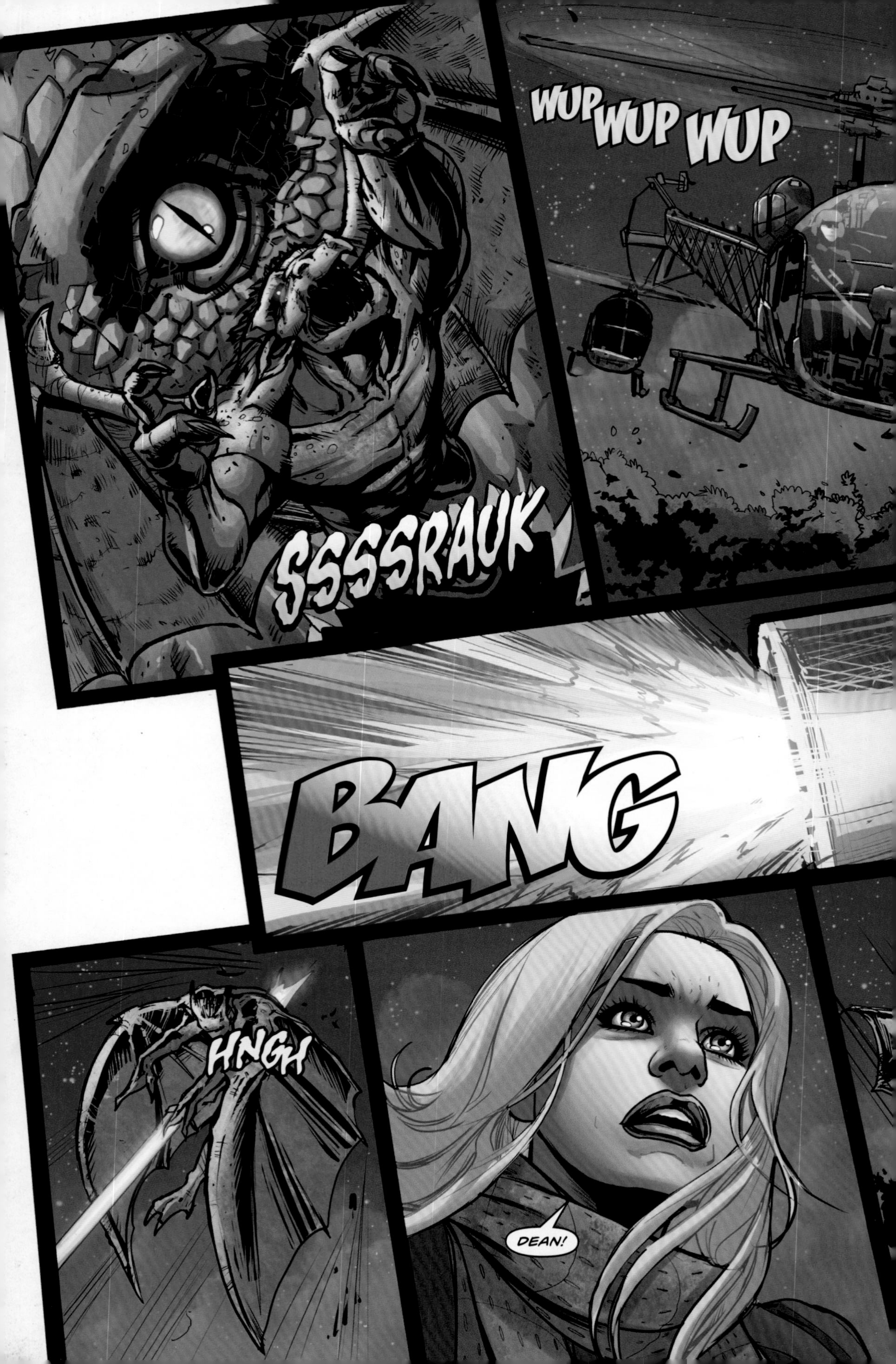
SSSSRAUK
WUP WUP WUP
BANG
HNGH
DEAN!

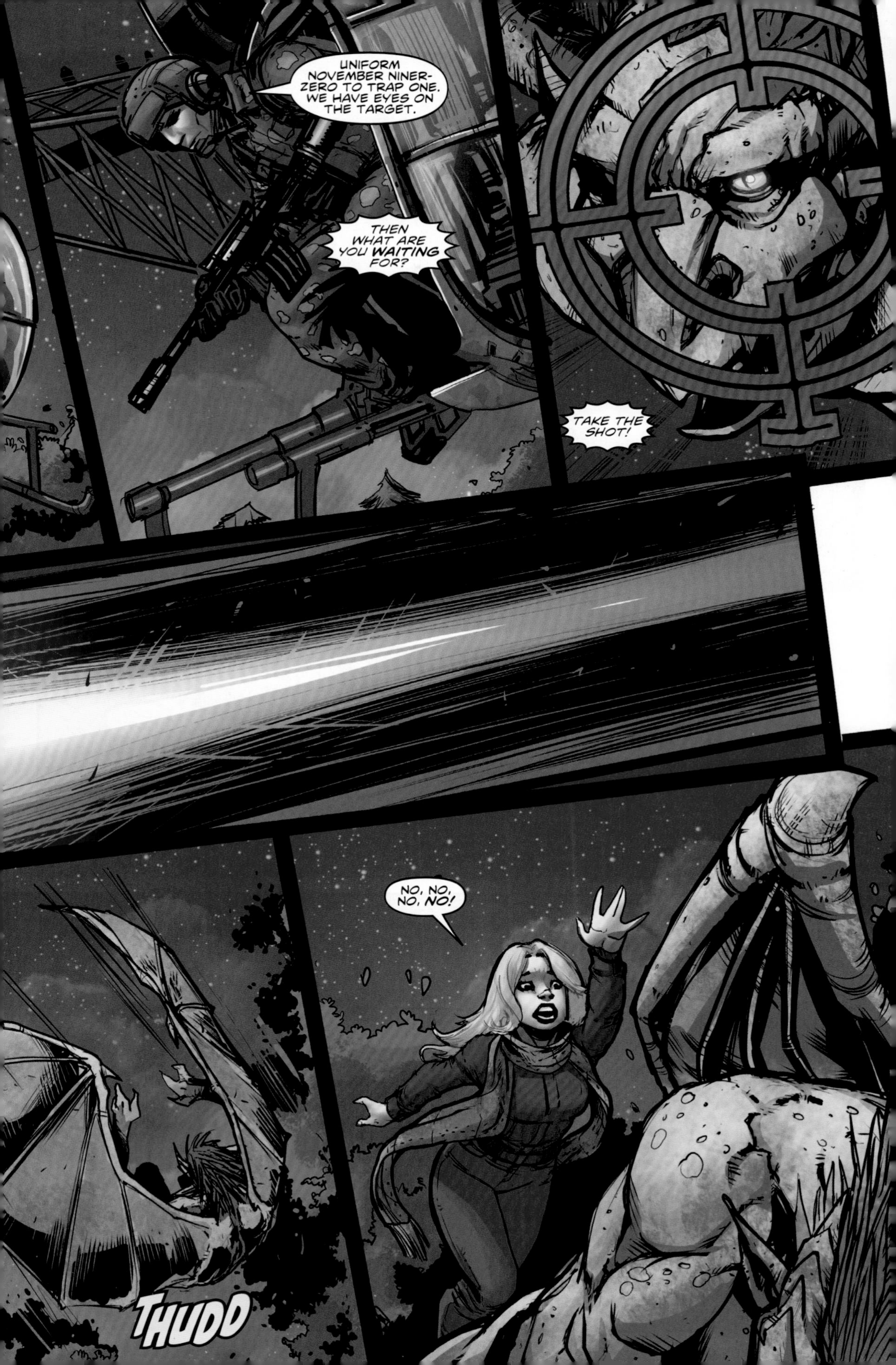
UNIFORM NOVEMBER NINER-ZERO TO TRAP ONE. WE HAVE EYES ON THE TARGET.
THEN WHAT ARE YOU WAITING FOR?
TAKE THE SHOT!
NO, NO, NO, NO!
THUDD

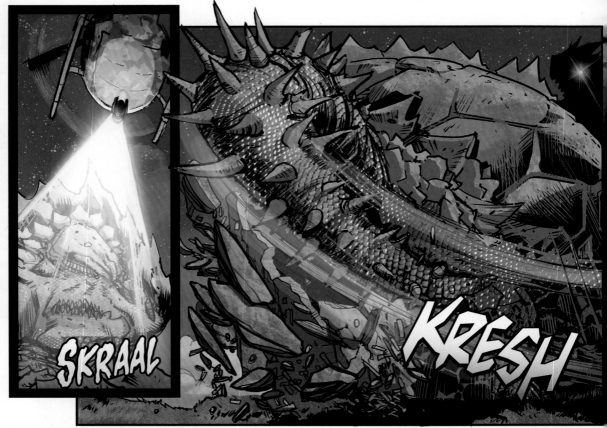

SKRAAL

KRESH

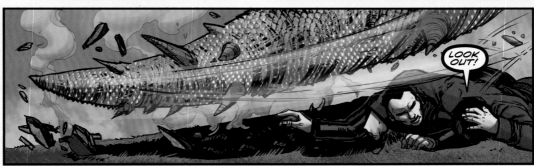

LOOK OUT!

DOCTOR. WHAT *IS* THAT THING?

WHAT IS IT? IT'S...

...GONE.

BUT THAT'S *IMPOSSIBLE.*

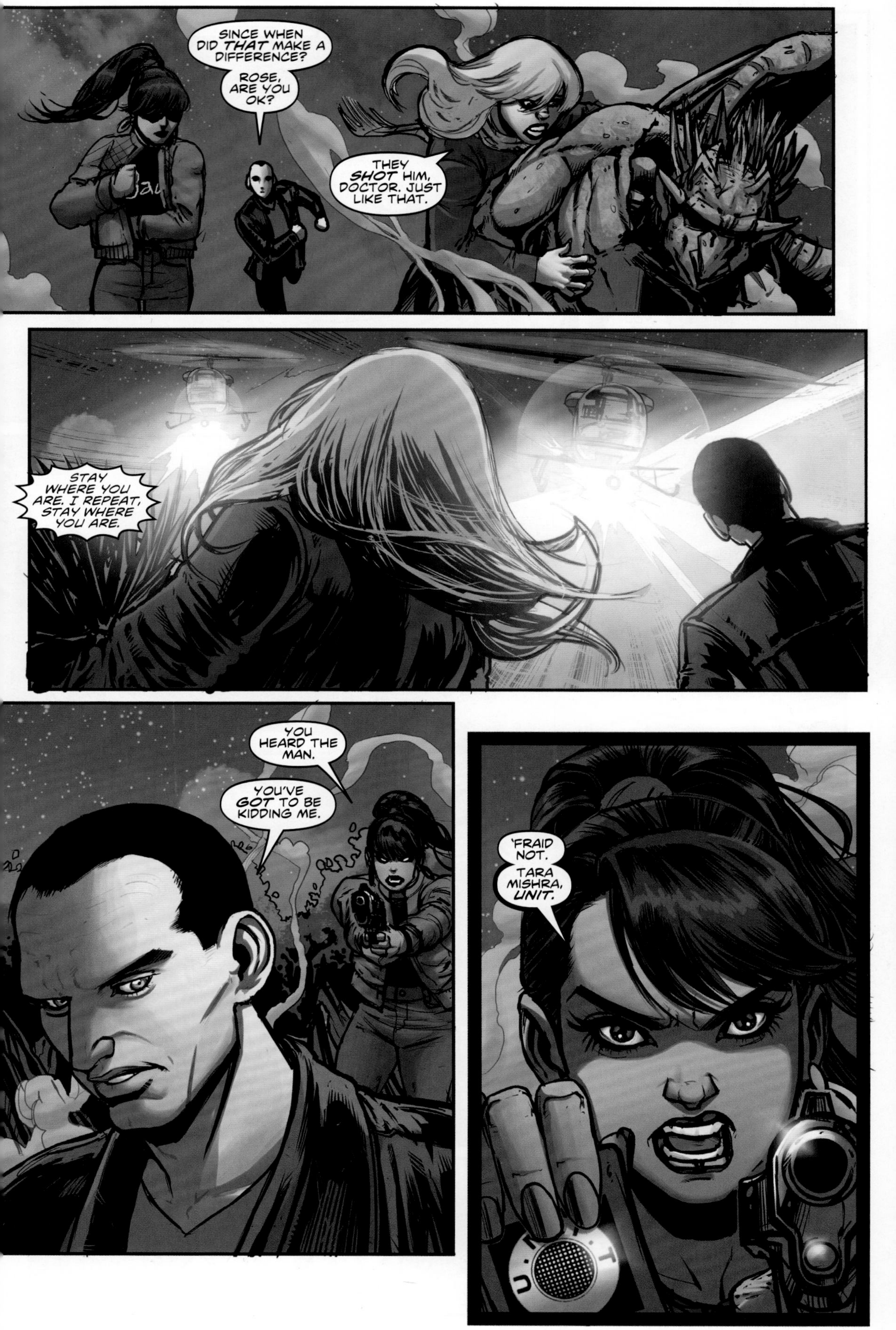
SINCE WHEN DID *THAT* MAKE A DIFFERENCE?
ROSE, ARE YOU OK?
THEY *SHOT* HIM, DOCTOR. JUST LIKE THAT.
STAY WHERE YOU ARE. I REPEAT, STAY WHERE YOU ARE.
YOU HEARD THE MAN.
YOU'VE *GOT* TO BE KIDDING ME.
'FRAID NOT.
TARA MISHRA, *UNIT*.

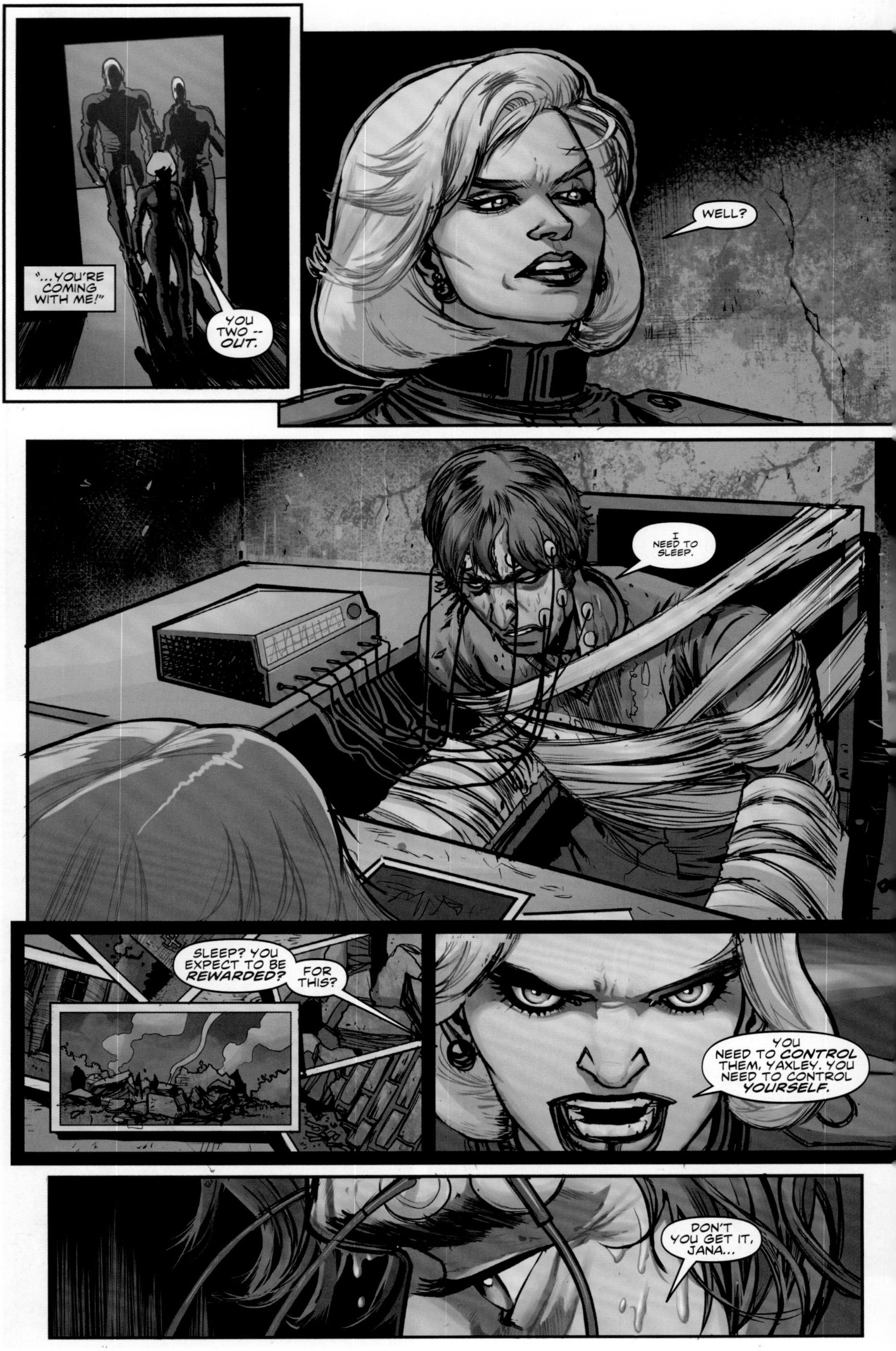
"...YOU'RE COMING WITH ME!"
YOU TWO -- OUT.
WELL?
I NEED TO SLEEP.
SLEEP? YOU EXPECT TO BE REWARDED?
FOR THIS?
YOU NEED TO CONTROL THEM, YAXLEY. YOU NEED TO CONTROL YOURSELF.
DON'T YOU GET IT, JANA...

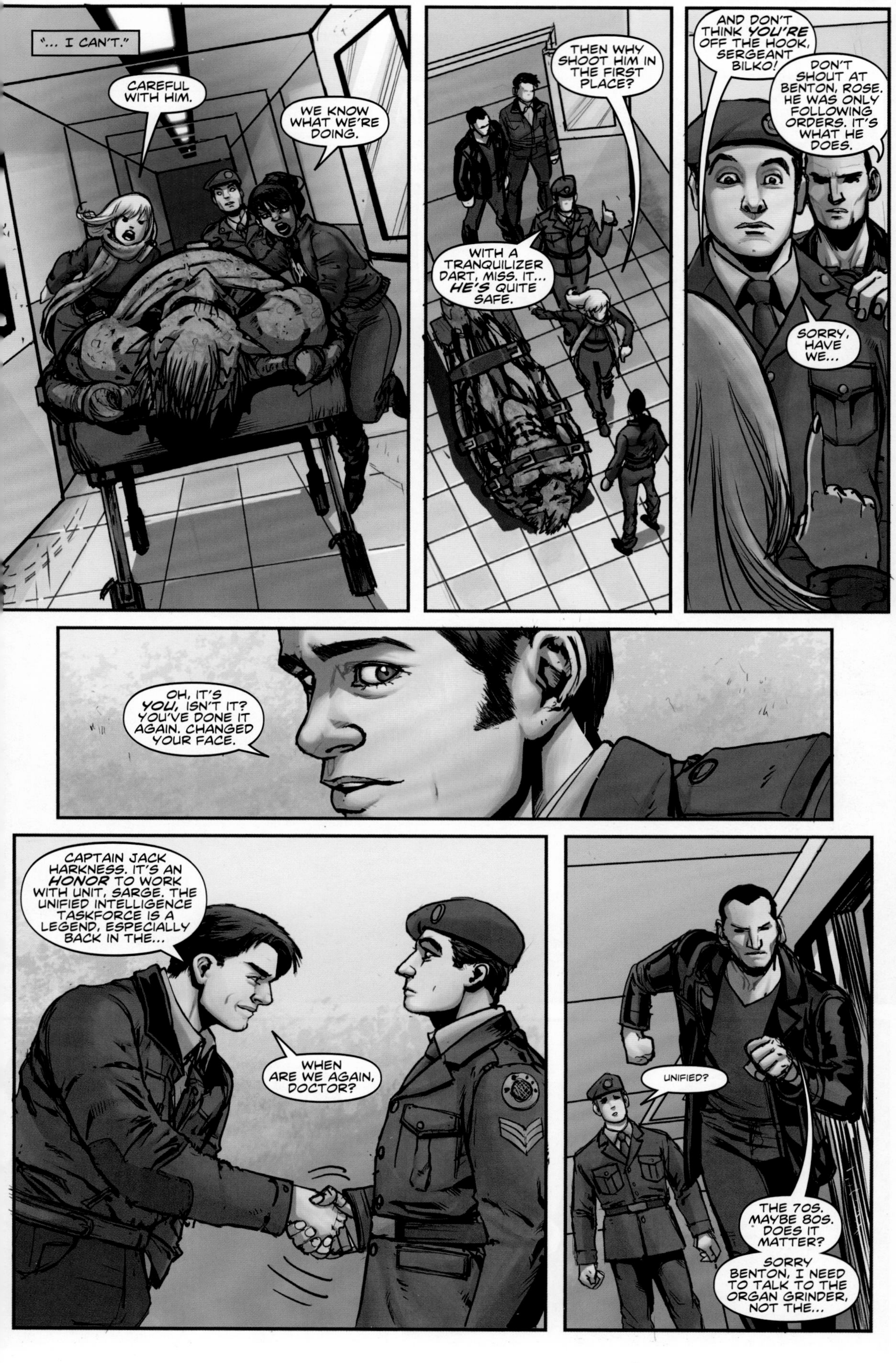
"... I CAN'T."
CAREFUL WITH HIM.
WE KNOW WHAT WE'RE DOING.
THEN WHY SHOOT HIM IN THE FIRST PLACE?
WITH A TRANQUILIZER DART, MISS. IT... HE'S QUITE SAFE.
AND DON'T THINK YOU'RE OFF THE HOOK, SERGEANT BILKO!
DON'T SHOUT AT BENTON, ROSE. HE WAS ONLY FOLLOWING ORDERS. IT'S WHAT HE DOES.
SORRY, HAVE WE...
OH, IT'S YOU, ISN'T IT? YOU'VE DONE IT AGAIN. CHANGED YOUR FACE.
CAPTAIN JACK HARKNESS. IT'S AN HONOR TO WORK WITH UNIT, SARGE. THE UNIFIED INTELLIGENCE TASKFORCE IS A LEGEND, ESPECIALLY BACK IN THE...
WHEN ARE WE AGAIN, DOCTOR?
UNIFIED?
THE 70S. MAYBE 80S. DOES IT MATTER?
SORRY BENTON, I NEED TO TALK TO THE ORGAN GRINDER, NOT THE...

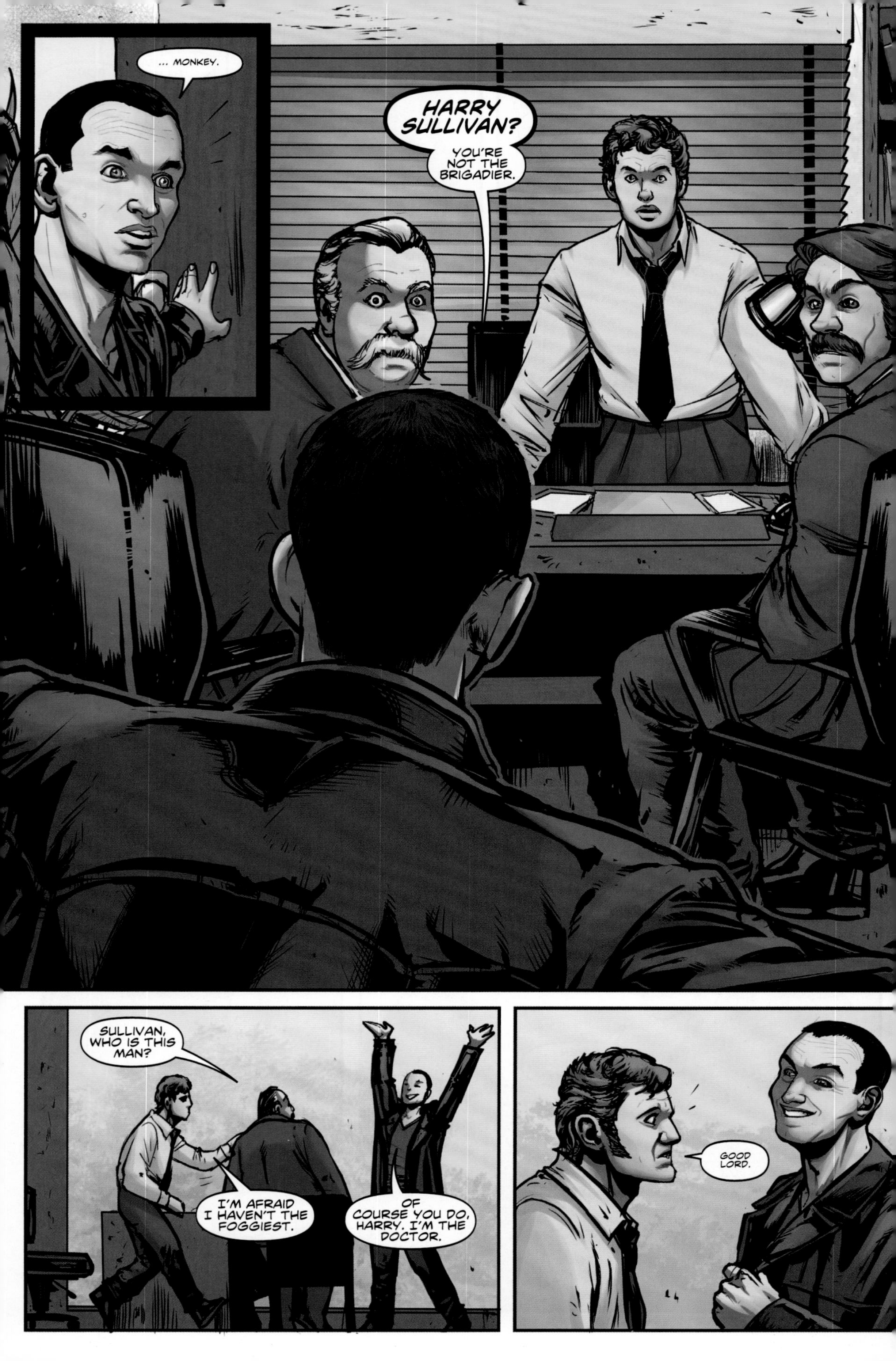

... MONKEY.
HARRY SULLIVAN?
YOU'RE NOT THE BRIGADIER.
SULLIVAN, WHO IS THIS MAN?
I'M AFRAID I HAVEN'T THE FOGGIEST.
OF COURSE YOU DO, HARRY. I'M THE DOCTOR.
GOOD LORD.

M-MINISTER, MAY I INTRODUCE... ER... UNIT'S SCIENTIFIC ADVISOR.

HELLO!

SCIENTIFIC ADVISOR? ON WHOSE AUTHORITY?

SO, YOU'RE THE DOCTOR, EH? I WAS HOPING WE'D RUN INTO EACH OTHER. WE HAVE A LOT TO DISCUSS.

WE DO?

OF COURSE. WHATEVER UNIT'S PAYING YOU, I'LL DOUBLE IT.

SORRY, THEY DON'T PAY ME AT ALL. I DO IT FOR LOVE, MR...?

DOCTOR, THIS IS JASPER CORRIGAN, HEAD OF ALBION DEFENSE.

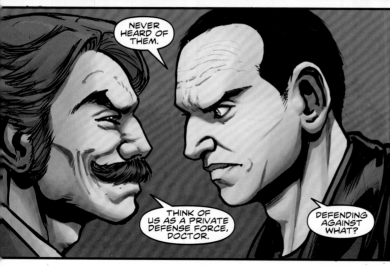

NEVER HEARD OF THEM.

THINK OF US AS A PRIVATE DEFENSE FORCE, DOCTOR.

DEFENDING AGAINST WHAT?

ALIENS, OF COURSE.

I HOPE YOUR 'SCIENTIFIC ADVISOR' CAN SHED SOME LIGHT ON WHAT'S HAPPENING, DR. SULLIVAN.

24 HOURS.

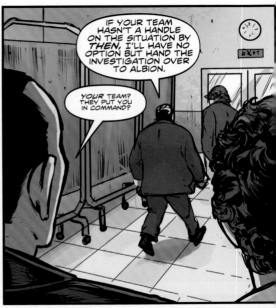

IF YOUR TEAM HASN'T A HANDLE ON THE SITUATION BY *THEN*, I'LL HAVE NO OPTION BUT HAND THE INVESTIGATION OVER TO ALBION.

YOUR TEAM? THEY PUT YOU IN COMMAND?

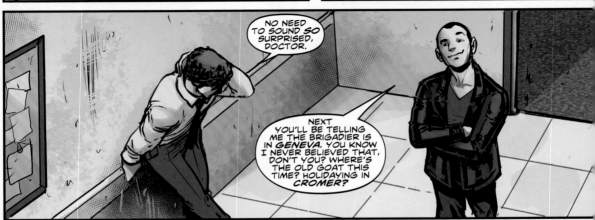

NO NEED TO SOUND *SO* SURPRISED, DOCTOR.

NEXT YOU'LL BE TELLING ME THE BRIGADIER IS IN *GENEVA*. YOU KNOW I NEVER BELIEVED THAT, DON'T YOU? WHERE'S THE OLD GOAT THIS TIME? HOLIDAYING IN *CROMER*?

YES, ALL VERY FUNNY, DOCTOR. YOU WALTZ IN WITHOUT A BY OR LEAVE, DISRUPTING *MY* MEETING.

HAVE YOU *ANY* IDEA HOW CLOSE THE MINISTER IS TO MOTH-BALLING *UNIT* ONCE AND FOR ALL?

NO, OF *COURSE* YOU HAVEN'T. BECAUSE YOU'RE TOO BUSY SWANNING ABOUT THE UNIVERSE, *SWAPPING FACES WILLY-NILLY*, TO CARE ABOUT WHAT HAPPENS BACK HERE.

THEN TELL ME HARRY. TELL ME ABOUT THE *MONSTERS*.

MA'AM. MA'AM, YOU CAN'T GO IN THERE.

I CAN GO WHERE I LIKE.

NOW WHAT?

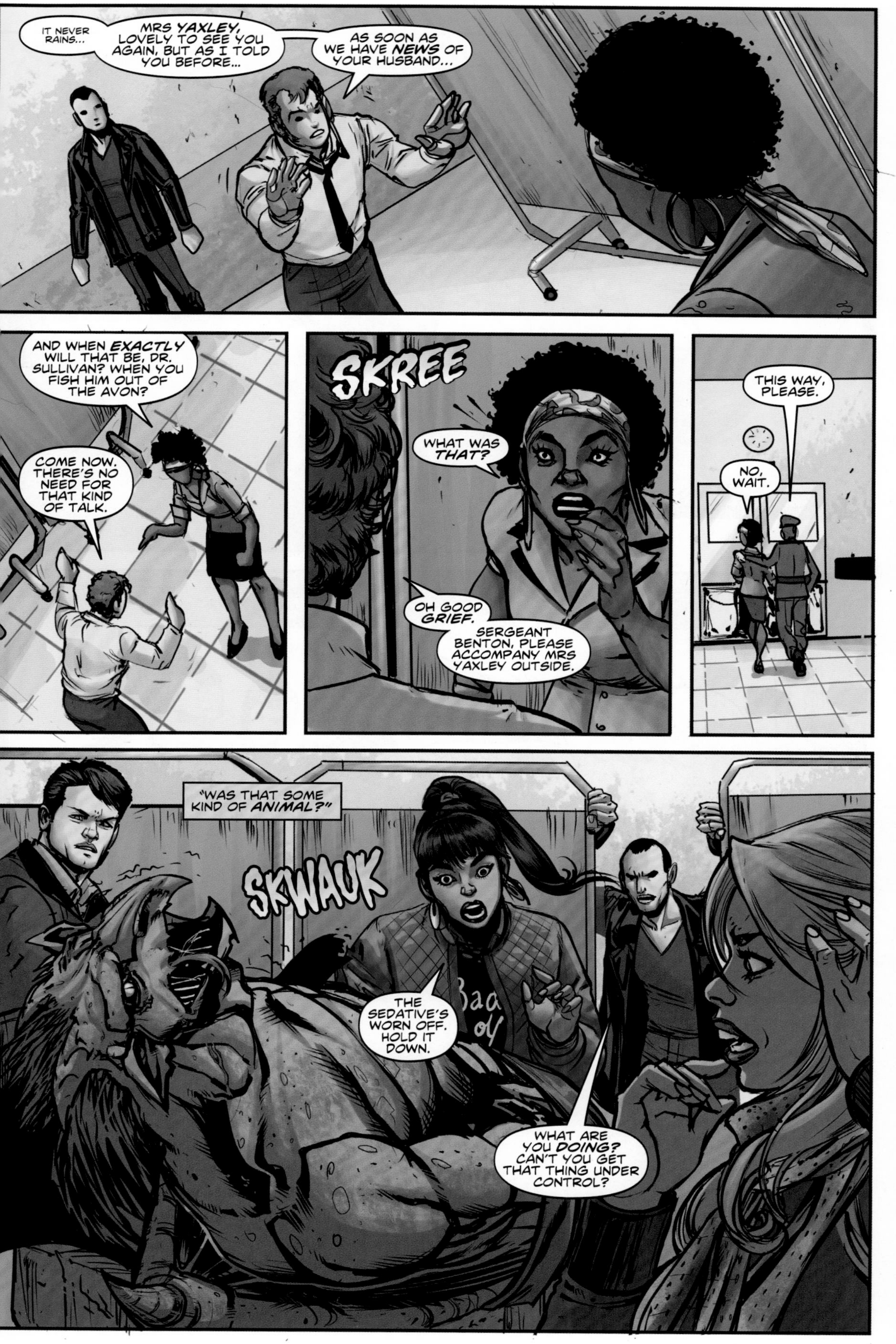
IT NEVER RAINS...
MRS YAXLEY, LOVELY TO SEE YOU AGAIN, BUT AS I TOLD YOU BEFORE...
AS SOON AS WE HAVE NEWS OF YOUR HUSBAND...
AND WHEN EXACTLY WILL THAT BE, DR. SULLIVAN? WHEN YOU FISH HIM OUT OF THE AVON?
COME NOW. THERE'S NO NEED FOR THAT KIND OF TALK.
SKREE
WHAT WAS THAT?
OH GOOD GRIEF.
SERGEANT BENTON, PLEASE ACCOMPANY MRS YAXLEY OUTSIDE.
THIS WAY, PLEASE.
NO, WAIT.
"WAS THAT SOME KIND OF ANIMAL?"
SKWAUK
THE SEDATIVE'S WORN OFF. HOLD IT DOWN.
WHAT ARE YOU DOING? CAN'T YOU GET THAT THING UNDER CONTROL?

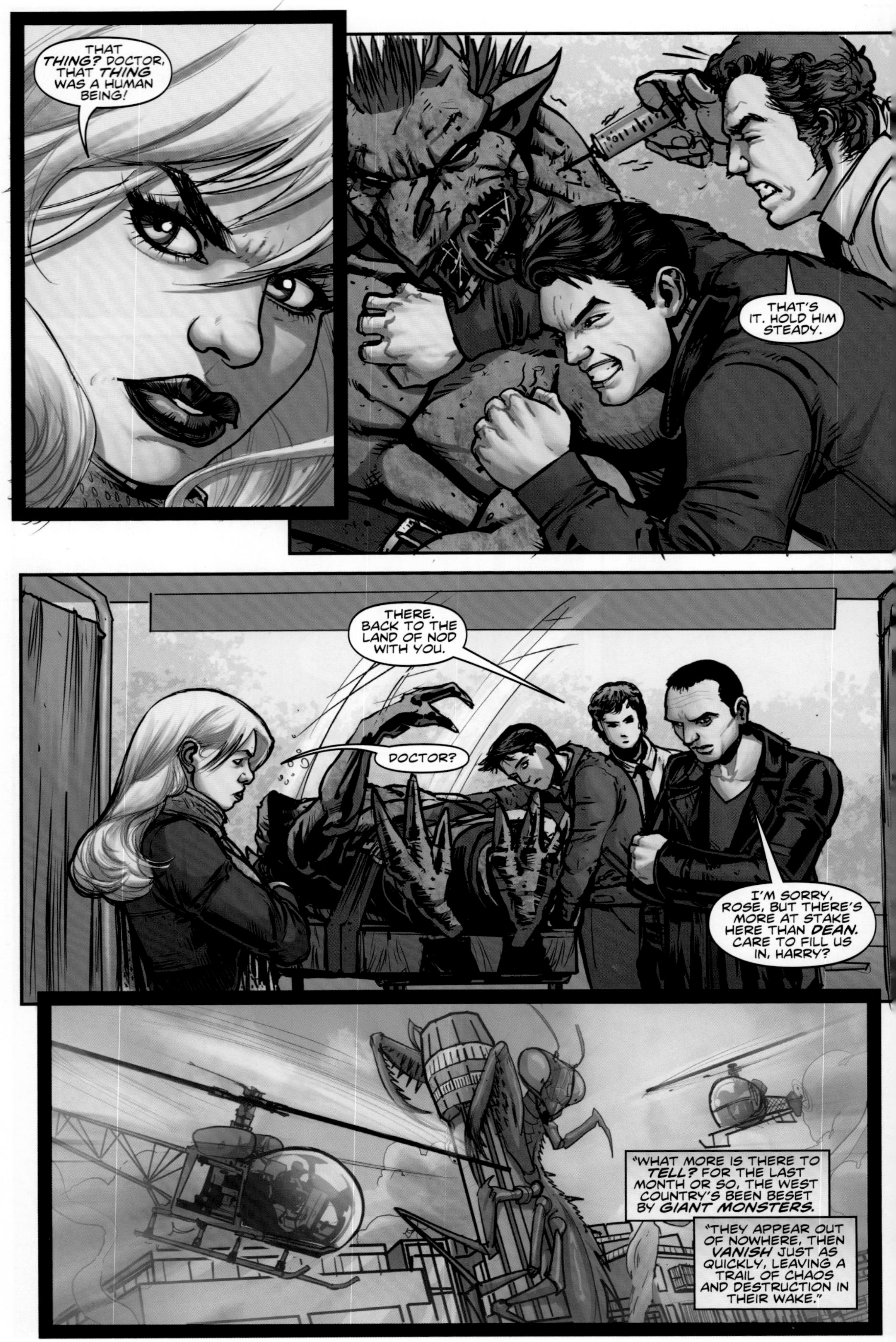

THAT THING? DOCTOR, THAT THING WAS A HUMAN BEING!
THAT'S IT. HOLD HIM STEADY.
THERE. BACK TO THE LAND OF NOD WITH YOU.
DOCTOR?
I'M SORRY, ROSE, BUT THERE'S MORE AT STAKE HERE THAN DEAN. CARE TO FILL US IN, HARRY?
"WHAT MORE IS THERE TO TELL? FOR THE LAST MONTH OR SO, THE WEST COUNTRY'S BEEN BESET BY GIANT MONSTERS.
"THEY APPEAR OUT OF NOWHERE, THEN VANISH JUST AS QUICKLY, LEAVING A TRAIL OF CHAOS AND DESTRUCTION IN THEIR WAKE."

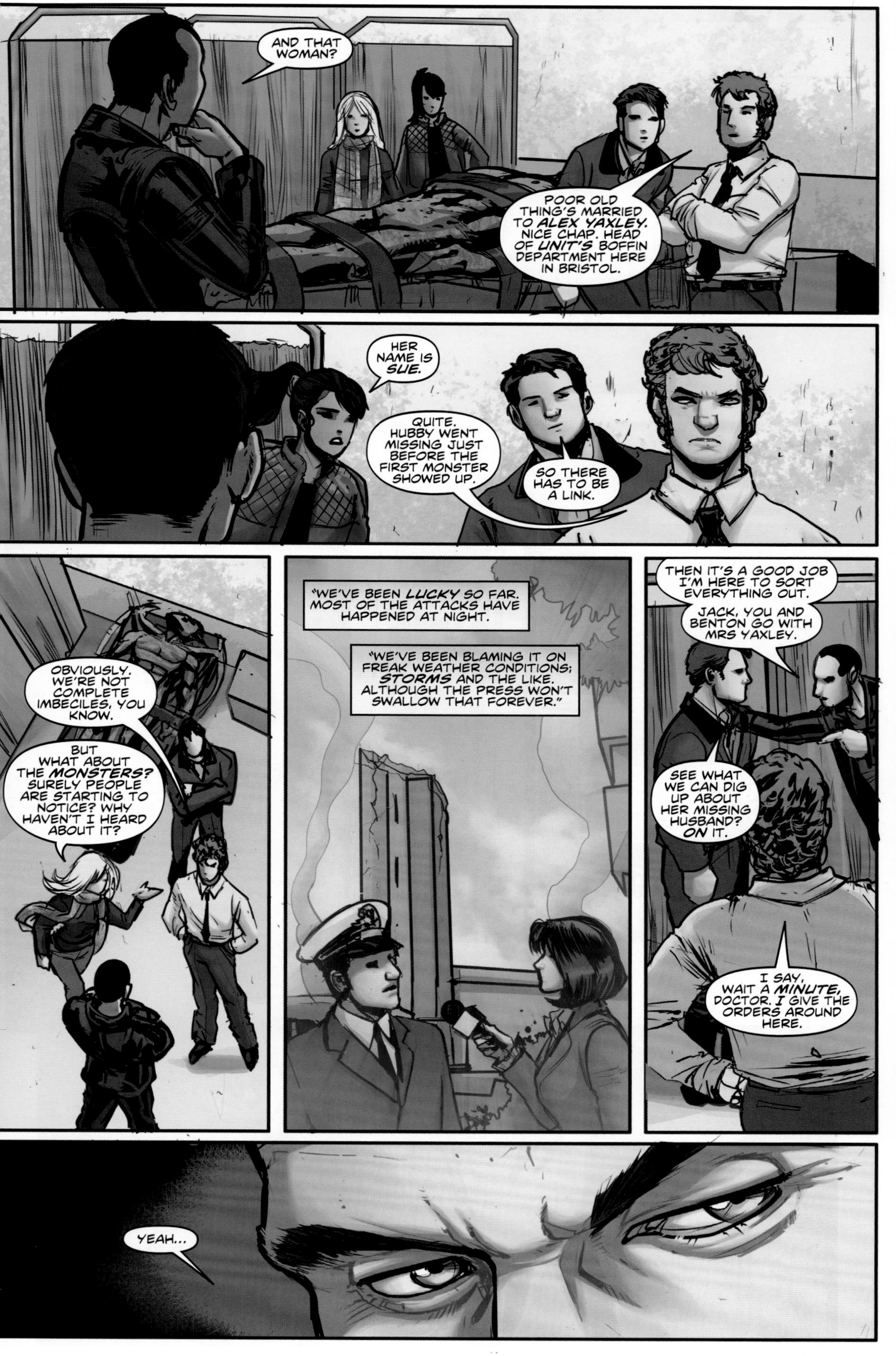
AND THAT WOMAN?
POOR OLD THING'S MARRIED TO ALEX YAXLEY. NICE CHAP. HEAD OF UNIT'S BOFFIN DEPARTMENT HERE IN BRISTOL.
HER NAME IS SUE.
QUITE. HUBBY WENT MISSING JUST BEFORE THE FIRST MONSTER SHOWED UP.
SO THERE HAS TO BE A LINK.
OBVIOUSLY. WE'RE NOT COMPLETE IMBECILES, YOU KNOW.
BUT WHAT ABOUT THE MONSTERS? SURELY PEOPLE ARE STARTING TO NOTICE? WHY HAVEN'T I HEARD ABOUT IT?
"WE'VE BEEN LUCKY SO FAR. MOST OF THE ATTACKS HAVE HAPPENED AT NIGHT.
"WE'VE BEEN BLAMING IT ON FREAK WEATHER CONDITIONS; STORMS AND THE LIKE. ALTHOUGH THE PRESS WON'T SWALLOW THAT FOREVER."
THEN IT'S A GOOD JOB I'M HERE TO SORT EVERYTHING OUT.
JACK, YOU AND BENTON GO WITH MRS YAXLEY.
SEE WHAT WE CAN DIG UP ABOUT HER MISSING HUSBAND? ON IT.
I SAY, WAIT A MINUTE, DOCTOR. I GIVE THE ORDERS AROUND HERE.
YEAH...

"... HOW'S THAT WORKING OUT FOR YOU?"

THANKS FOR WATCHING JOSH.

HE'S NO BOTHER, MY LOVE. ANYTIME.

CAPTAIN. SERGEANT. THIS IS MY SON, JOSHUA.

PLEASED TO MEET YOU, JOSH.

ARE YOU HERE ABOUT MY DAD?

"YES, WE ARE. WANT TO SHOW ME AROUND?"

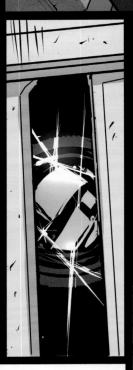

ARE YOU SEEING THIS, ALEX? YOUR FAMILY IS IN DANGER.

WHAT ARE YOU GOING TO DO ABOUT IT?

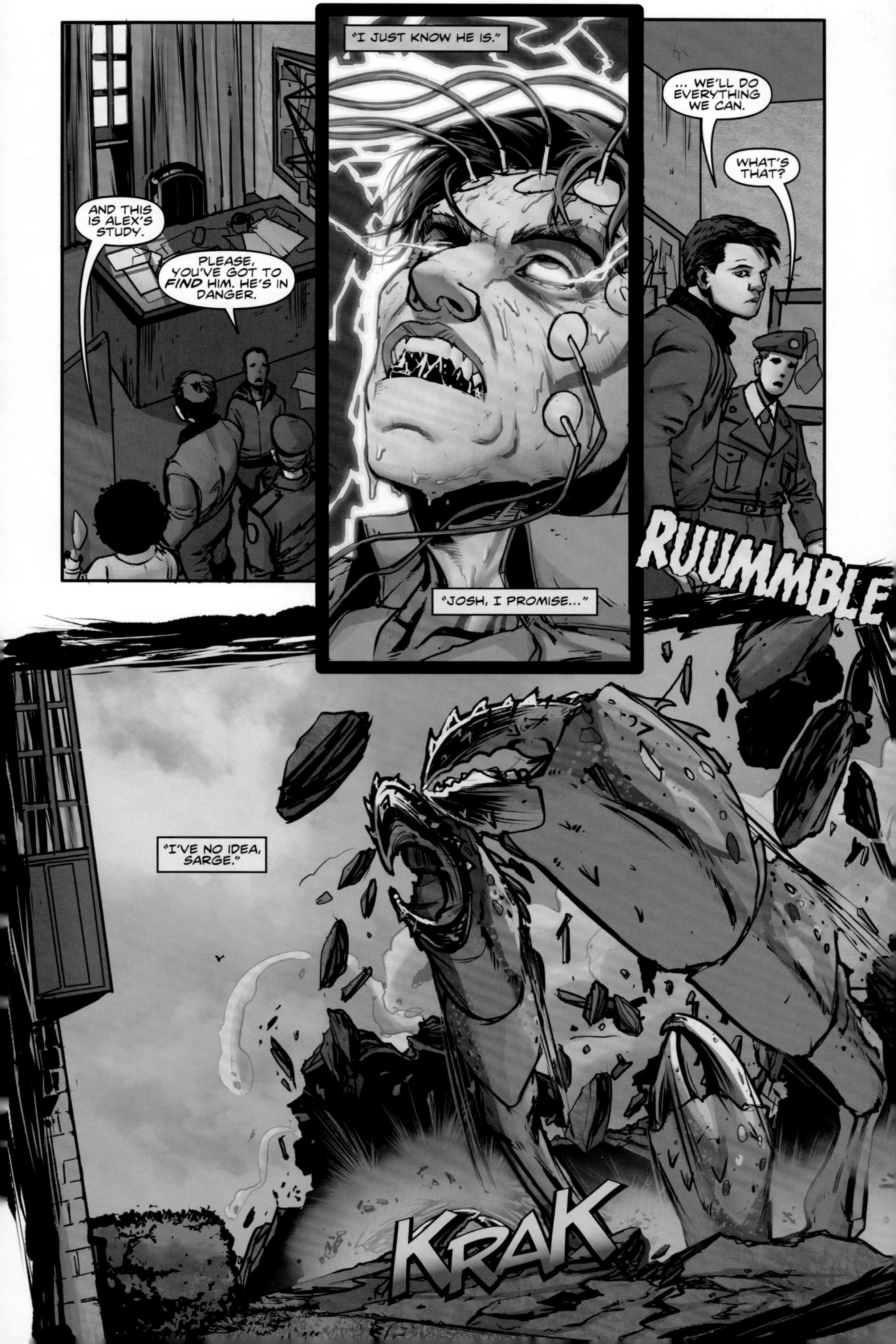
AND THIS IS ALEX'S STUDY.
PLEASE, YOU'VE GOT TO FIND HIM. HE'S IN DANGER.
"I JUST KNOW HE IS."
"JOSH, I PROMISE..."
... WE'LL DO EVERYTHING WE CAN.
WHAT'S THAT?
RUUMMBLE
"I'VE NO IDEA, SARGE."
KRAK

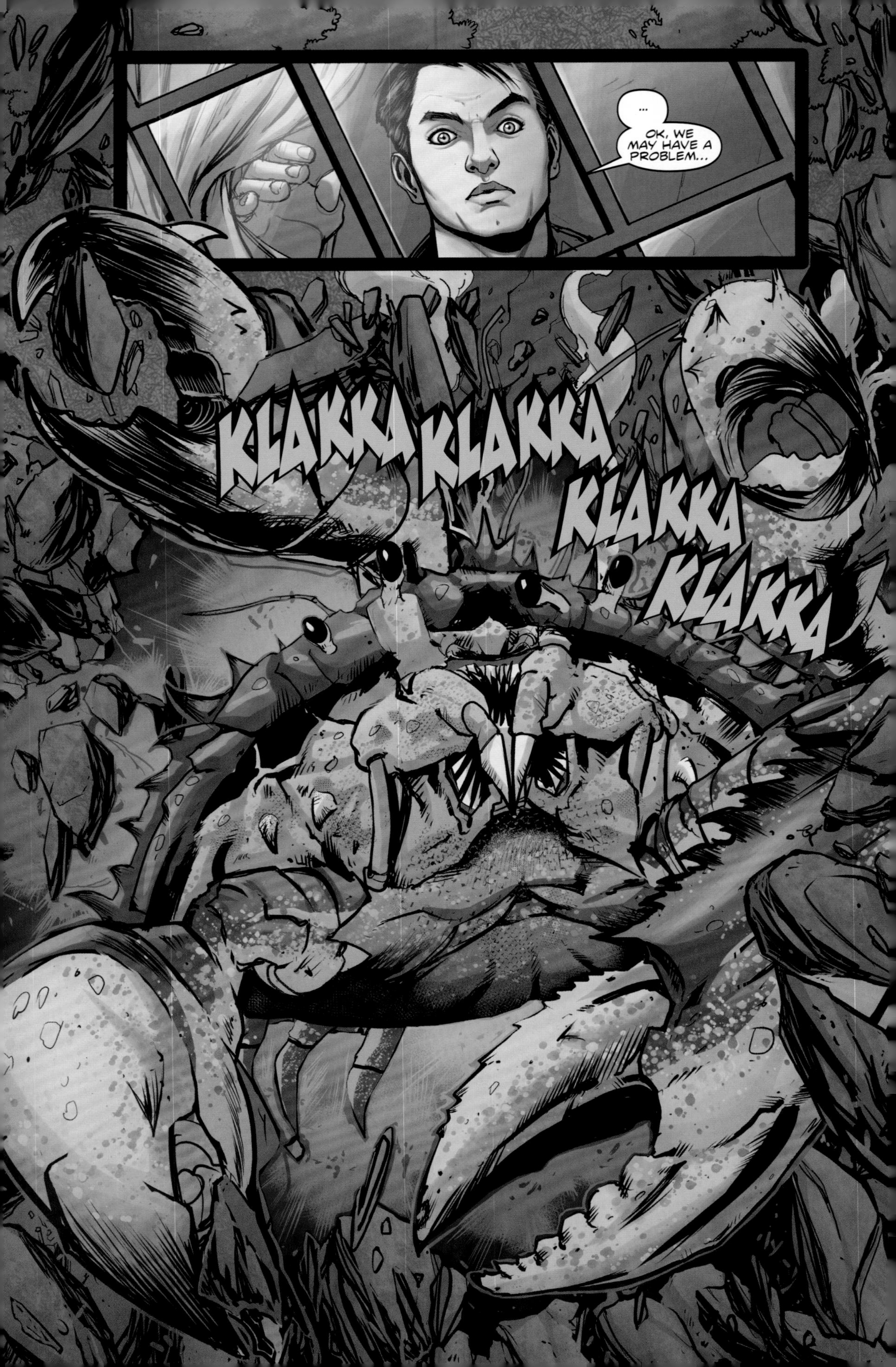
...
OK, WE MAY HAVE A PROBLEM...
KLAKKA KLAKKA KLAKKA KLAKKA

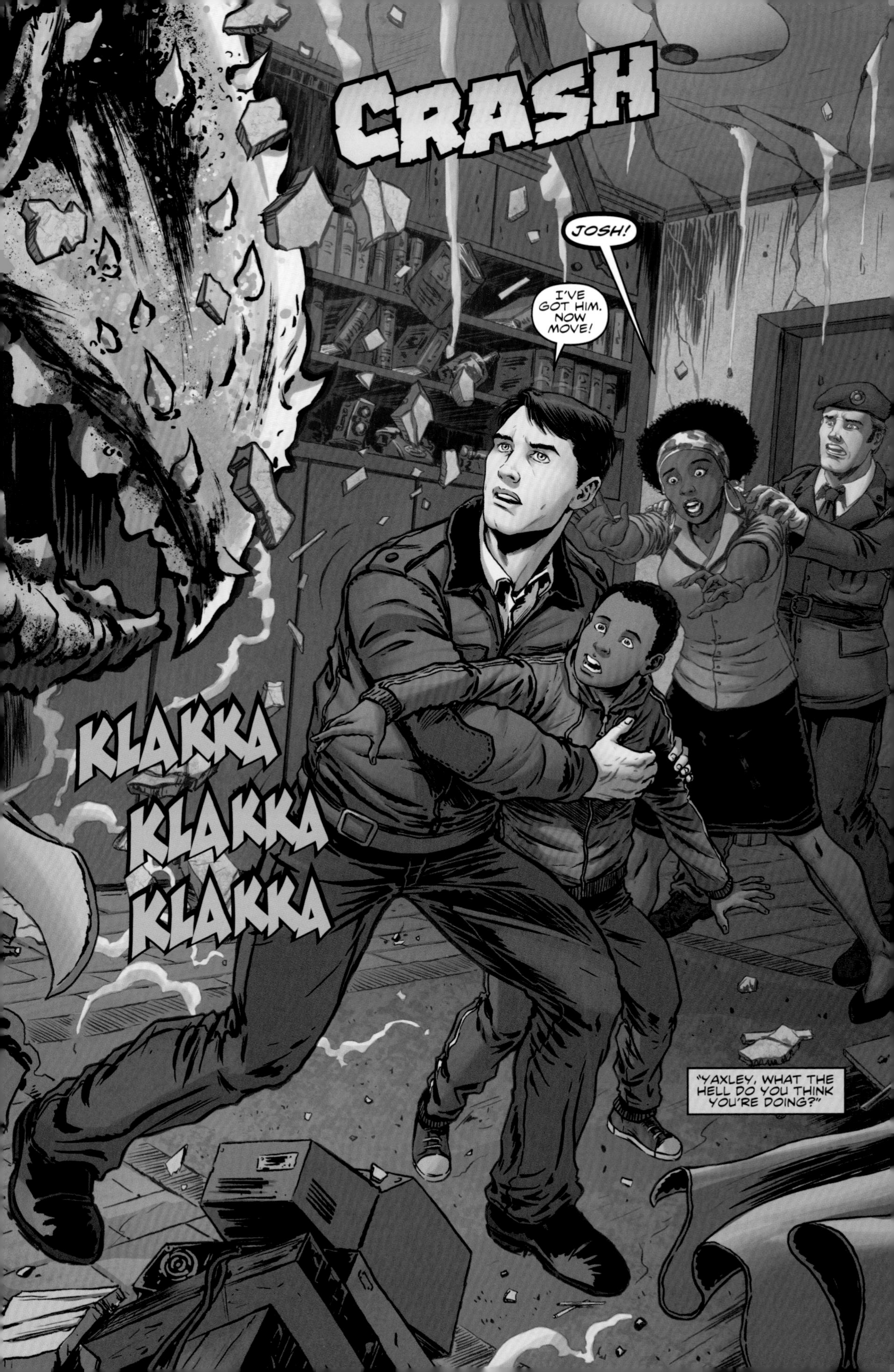
CRASH
JOSH!
I'VE GOT HIM. NOW MOVE!
KLAKKA
KLAKKA
KLAKKA
"YAXLEY, WHAT THE HELL DO YOU THINK YOU'RE DOING?"

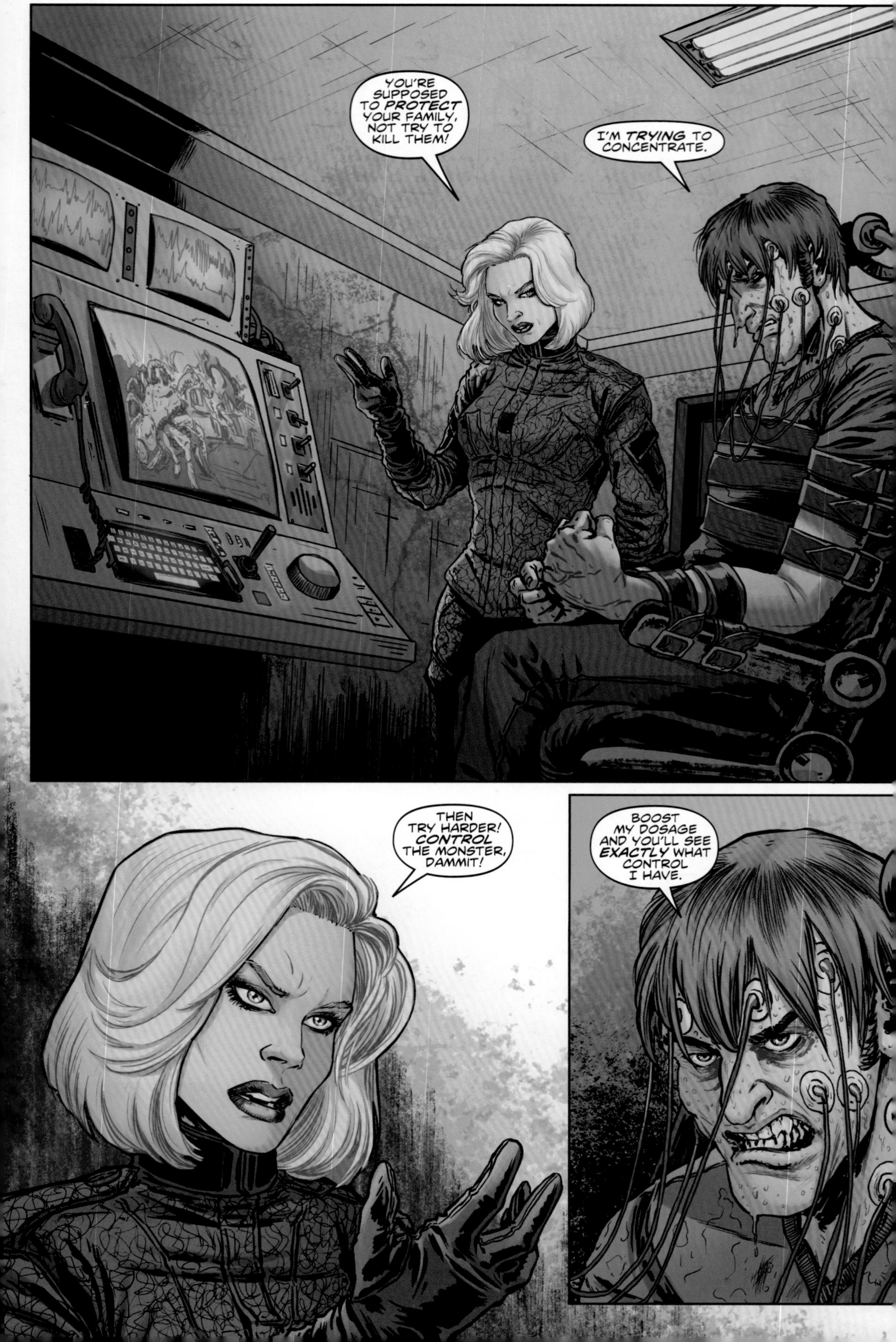
YOU'RE SUPPOSED TO *PROTECT* YOUR FAMILY, NOT TRY TO KILL THEM!
I'M *TRYING* TO CONCENTRATE.
THEN TRY HARDER! *CONTROL* THE MONSTER, DAMMIT!
BOOST MY DOSAGE AND YOU'LL SEE *EXACTLY* WHAT CONTROL I HAVE.

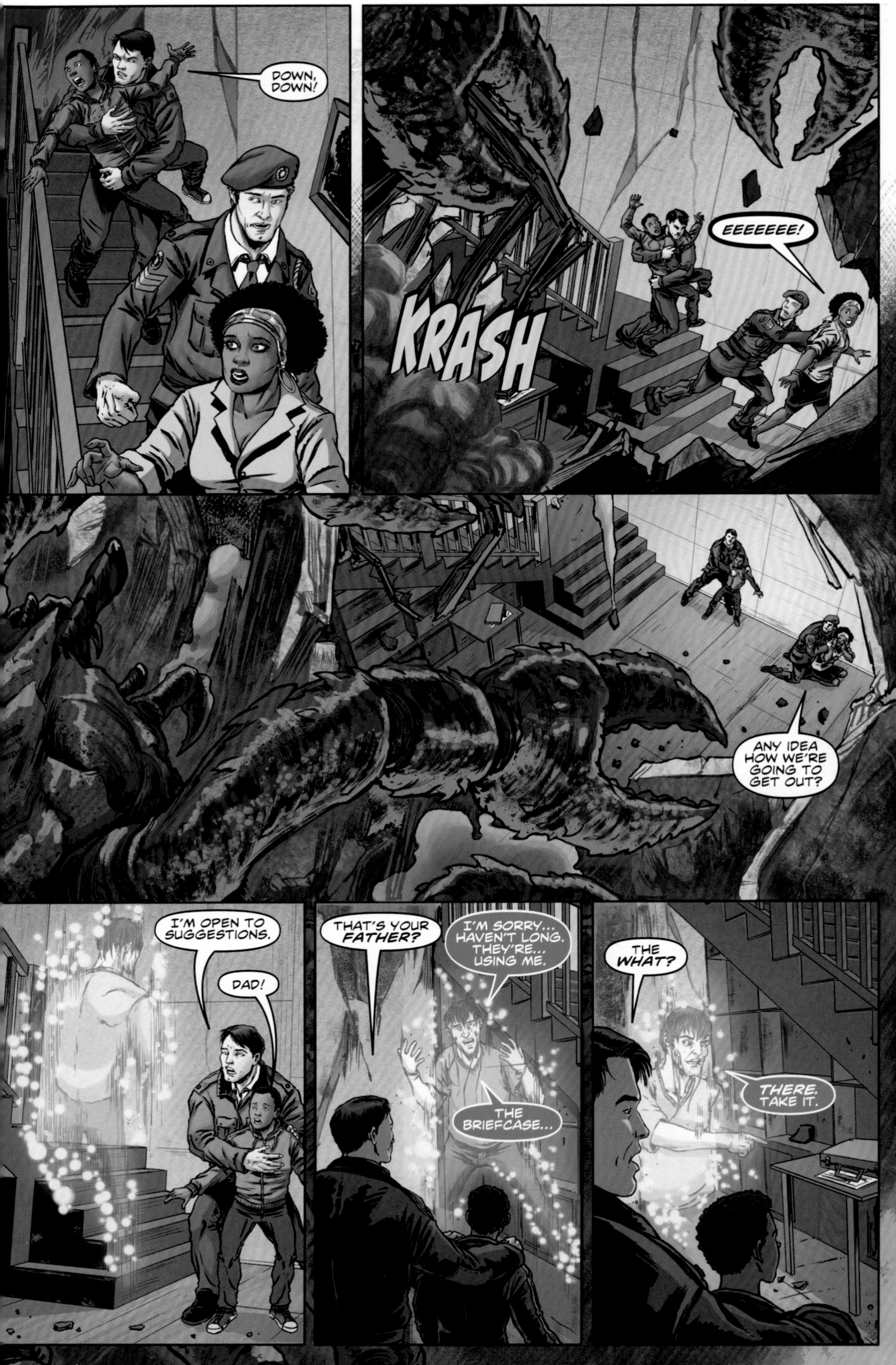
DOWN, DOWN!
KRASH
EEEEEEE!
ANY IDEA HOW WE'RE GOING TO GET OUT?
I'M OPEN TO SUGGESTIONS.
DAD!
THAT'S YOUR FATHER?
I'M SORRY... HAVEN'T LONG. THEY'RE... USING ME.
THE BRIEFCASE...
THE WHAT?
THERE. TAKE IT.

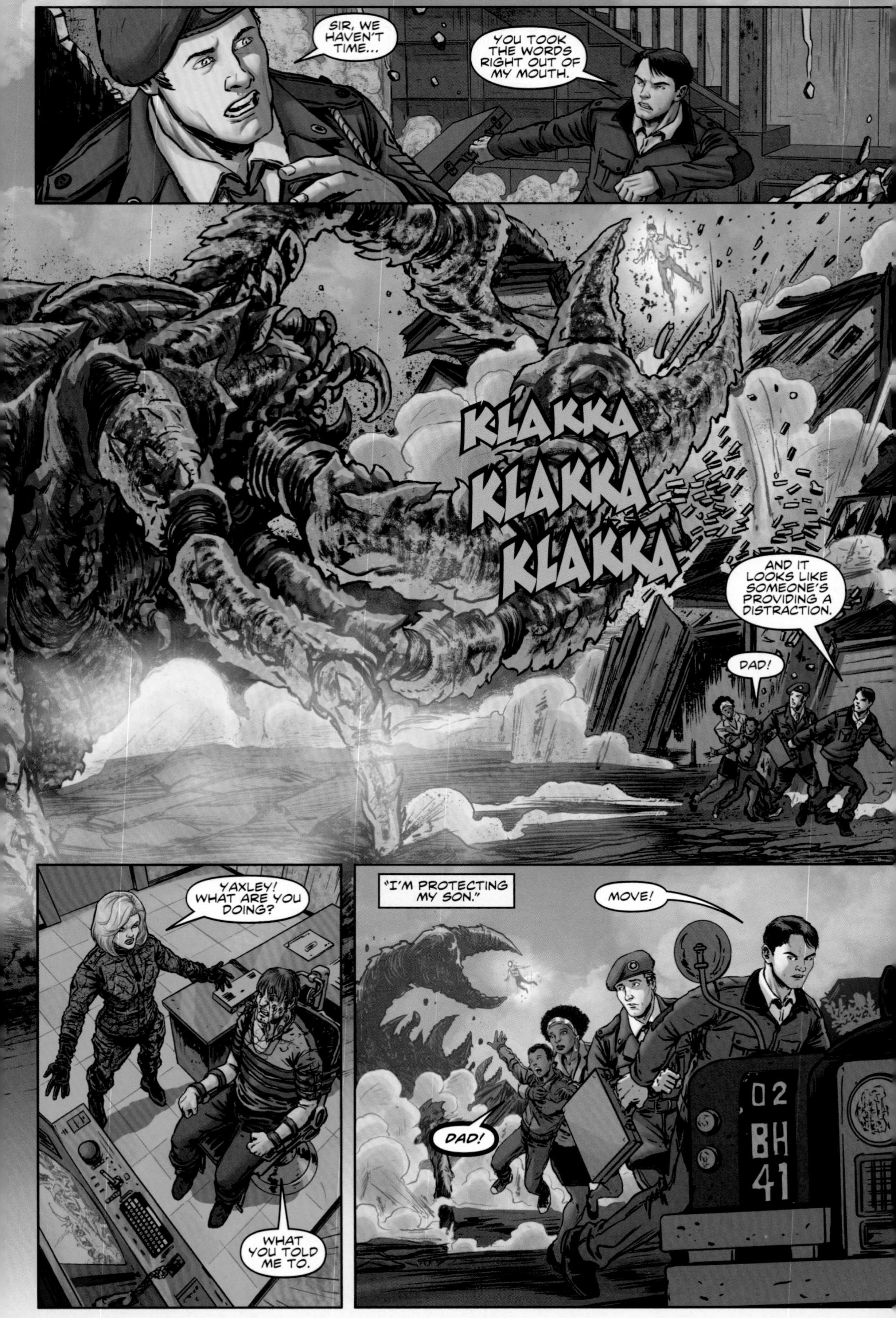
SIR, WE HAVEN'T TIME...
YOU TOOK THE WORDS RIGHT OUT OF MY MOUTH.
KLAKKA KLAKKA KLAKKA
AND IT LOOKS LIKE SOMEONE'S PROVIDING A DISTRACTION.
DAD!
YAXLEY! WHAT ARE YOU DOING?
WHAT YOU TOLD ME TO.
"I'M PROTECTING MY SON."
MOVE!
DAD!
02 BH 41

GET THE KID IN!

JOSH, PLEASE. WE NEED TO GO.

BENTON, DRIVE!

NO, WE CAN'T! DAD NEEDS US!

VROOOM

"JOSH, I THINK YOUR DAD CAN HANDLE HIMSELF..."

"WHATEVER HE IS..."

SIR, THE MONSTER--

YEAH, I SEE IT, SARGE.

OR RATHER, I DON'T.

JUST LIKE BEFORE -- THERE ONE MINUTE, GONE THE NEXT.

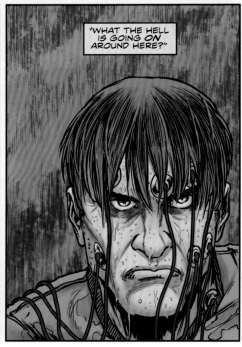

"WHAT THE HELL IS GOING ON AROUND HERE?"

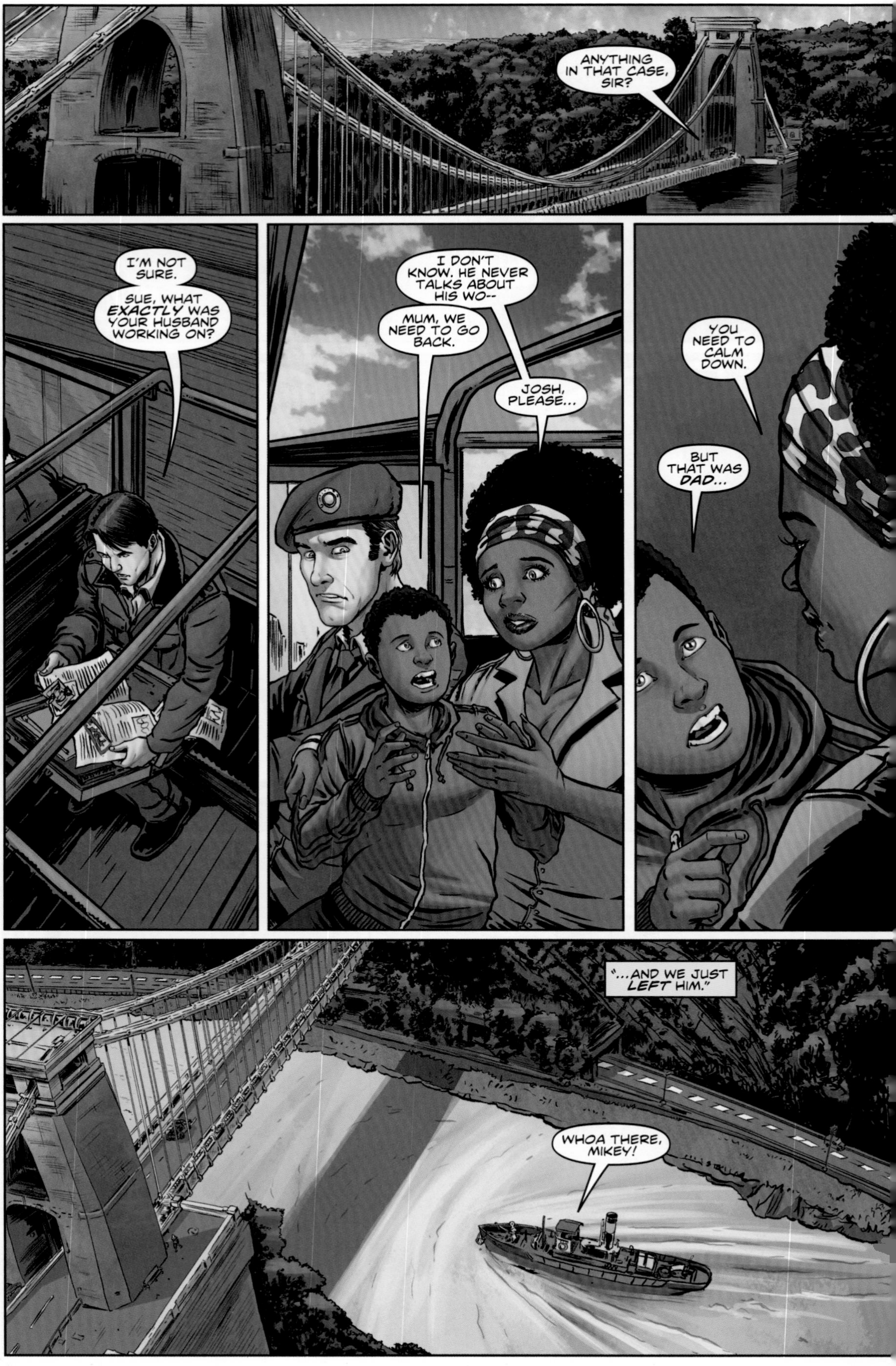
ANYTHING IN THAT CASE, SIR?
I'M NOT SURE.
SUE, WHAT *EXACTLY* WAS YOUR HUSBAND WORKING ON?
I DON'T KNOW. HE NEVER TALKS ABOUT HIS WO--
MUM, WE NEED TO GO BACK.
JOSH, PLEASE...
YOU NEED TO CALM DOWN.
BUT THAT WAS *DAD*...
"...AND WE JUST *LEFT* HIM."
WHOA THERE, MIKEY!

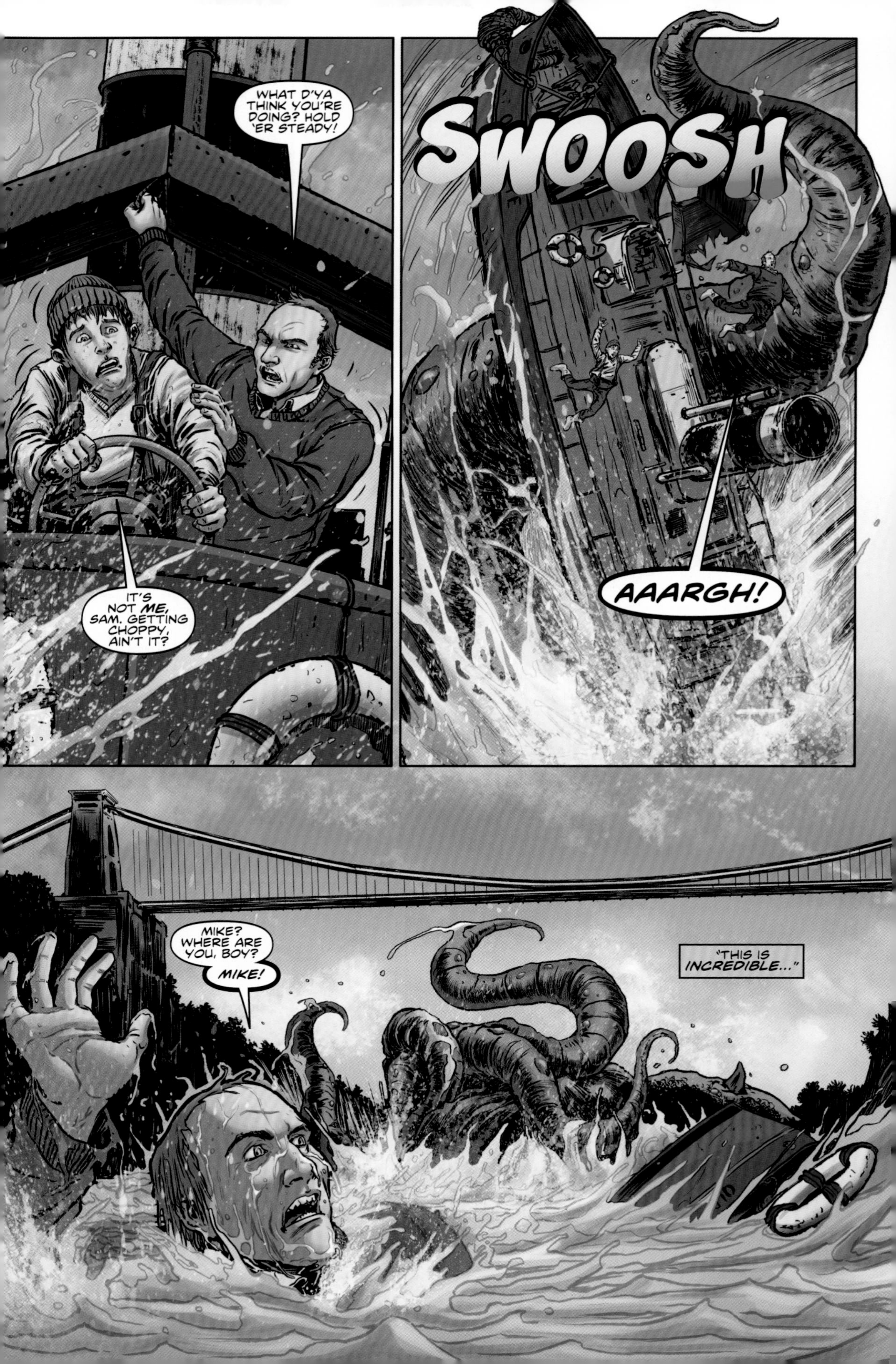
WHAT D'YA THINK YOU'RE DOING? HOLD 'ER STEADY!
IT'S NOT ME, SAM. GETTING CHOPPY, AIN'T IT?
SWOOSH
AAARGH!
MIKE? WHERE ARE YOU, BOY? MIKE!
"THIS IS INCREDIBLE..."

UNIT RESEARCH BASE, BRISTOL

... ITS HEART IS GOING LIKE THE CLAPPERS!

I'VE TOLD YOU -- HE'S A *HE*, NOT AN *IT*! HIS *NAME* IS DEAN.

NOT THAT THE DOCTOR SEEMS TO REMEMBER.

DEAN *WHO?*

THAT'S THE PROBLEM. I DON'T KNOW ANYTHING ABOUT HIM. NOT *REALLY*. WHO HE IS, WHERE HE COMES FROM. I DON'T EVEN KNOW WHAT HE DID FOR A *JOB*.

"WHERE DID YOU MEET HIM?"

"SAN FRANCISCO. THERE WERE THESE LIGHTS IN THE SKY, AND--"

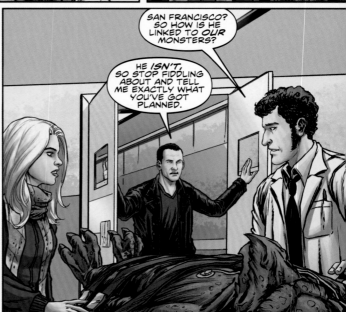

SAN FRANCISCO? SO HOW IS HE LINKED TO *OUR* MONSTERS?

HE *ISN'T*, SO STOP FIDDLING ABOUT AND TELL ME EXACTLY WHAT YOU'VE GOT PLANNED.

HOW DO YOU MEAN, OLD BOY?

HARRY, I'VE BEEN ALL OVER THIS SO-CALLED RESEARCH BASE OF YOURS AND HAVE YET TO SEE ANYTHING EVEN *REMOTELY* USEFUL.

WHY THE BRIGADIER THOUGHT IT WAS A GOOD IDEA LEAVING YOU IN CHARGE IS BEYOND ME.

DOCTOR, *PLEASE.* WE KNOW WHAT WE'RE DOING. HERE, TAKE A LOOK AT THIS!

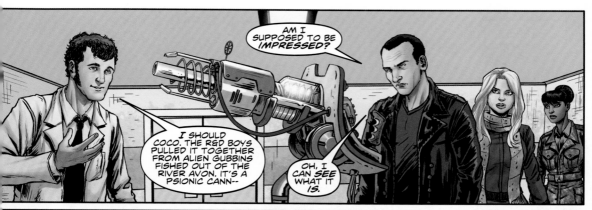

AM I SUPPOSED TO BE IMPRESSED?

I SHOULD COCO. THE R&D BOYS PULLED IT TOGETHER FROM ALIEN GUBBINS FISHED OUT OF THE RIVER AVON. IT'S A PSIONIC CANN--

OH, I CAN *SEE* WHAT IT *IS.*

IT'S A *GUN*, HARRY. A DIRTY GREAT GUN. YOU'VE GONE AND INVENTED ANOTHER WEAPON. *JUST* WHAT WE NEED.

AND I SUPPOSE YOU HAVE A BETTER IDEA!

IF HE *DOES*, I'D LIKE TO HEAR IT.

SIR, YOU'RE *BACK!*

BRIGADIER ALISTAIR GORDON LETHBRIDGE-STEWART. WHAT TIME DO YOU CALL *THIS?*

I COULD SAY THE SAME ABOUT YOU, DOCTOR. IF THAT'S WHO YOU *REALLY ARE.*

OH, IT'S ME ALRIGHT. LIKE A BAD PENNY.

AND *NORTHERN* IT SEEMS.

DON'T START.

PERISH THE THOUGHT. NOW, IF YOU'VE *QUITE* FINISHED INSULTING MY STAFF...

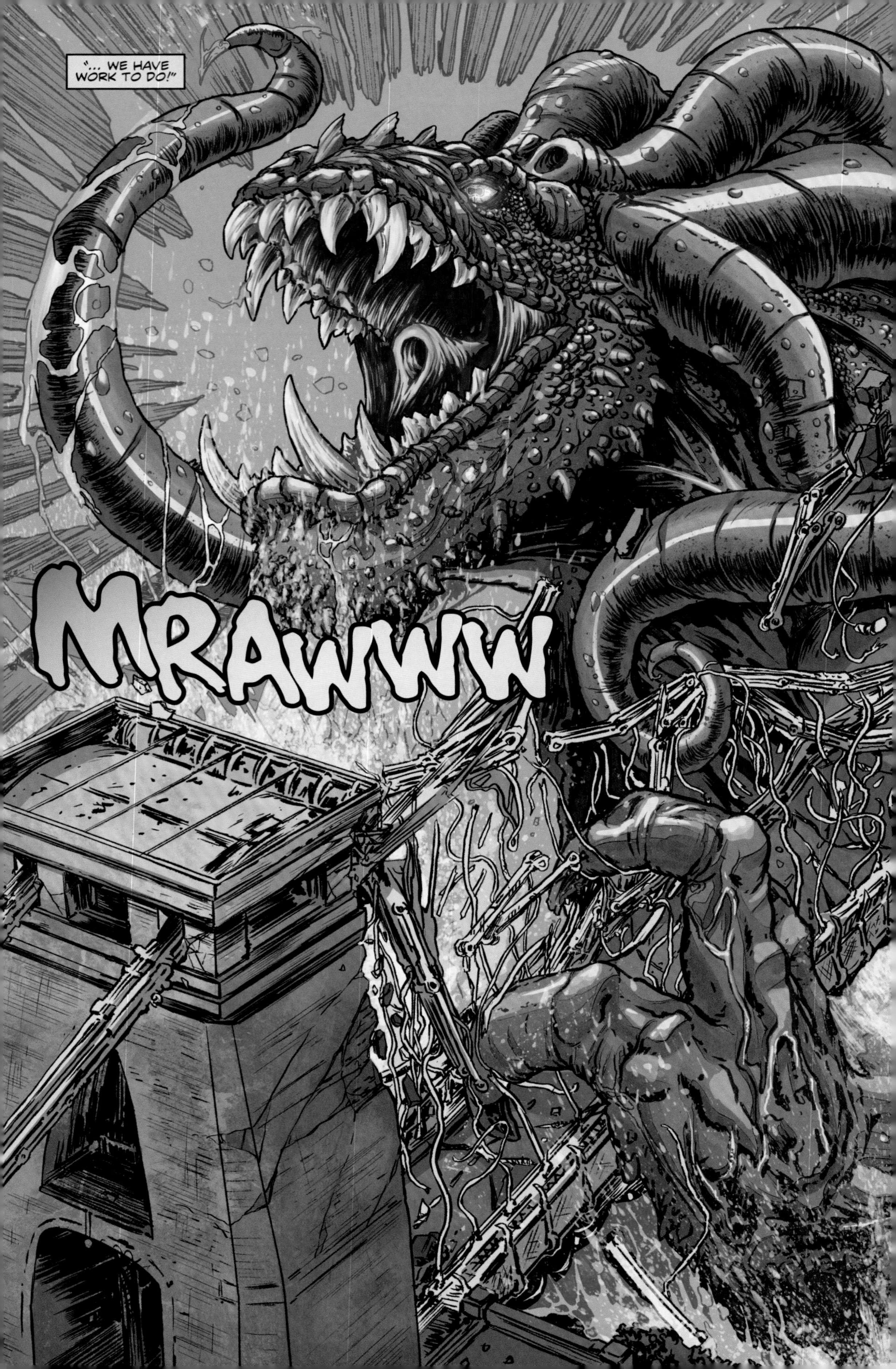
"... WE HAVE WORK TO DO!"
MRAWWW

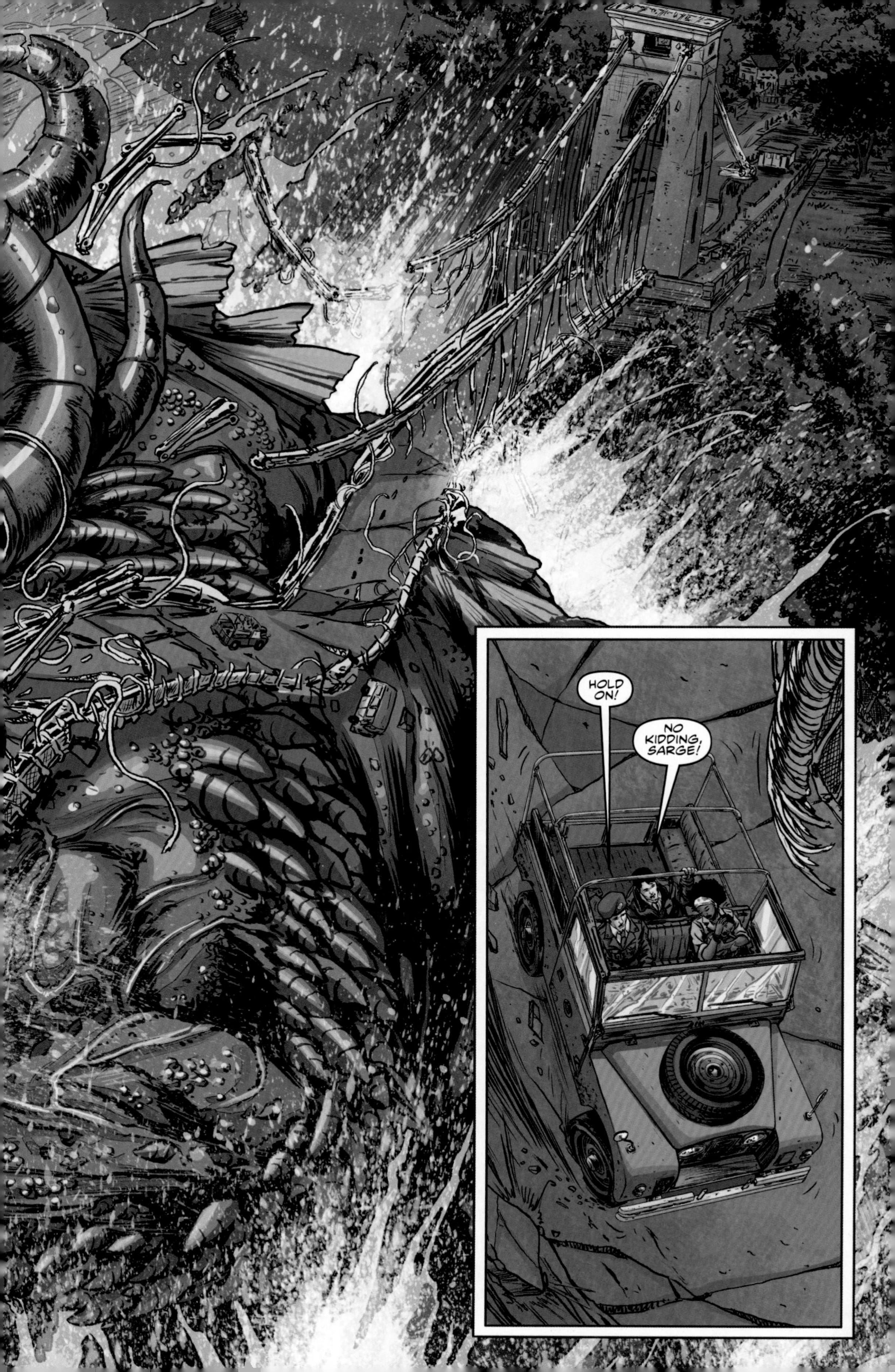
HOLD ON!
NO KIDDING, SARGE!

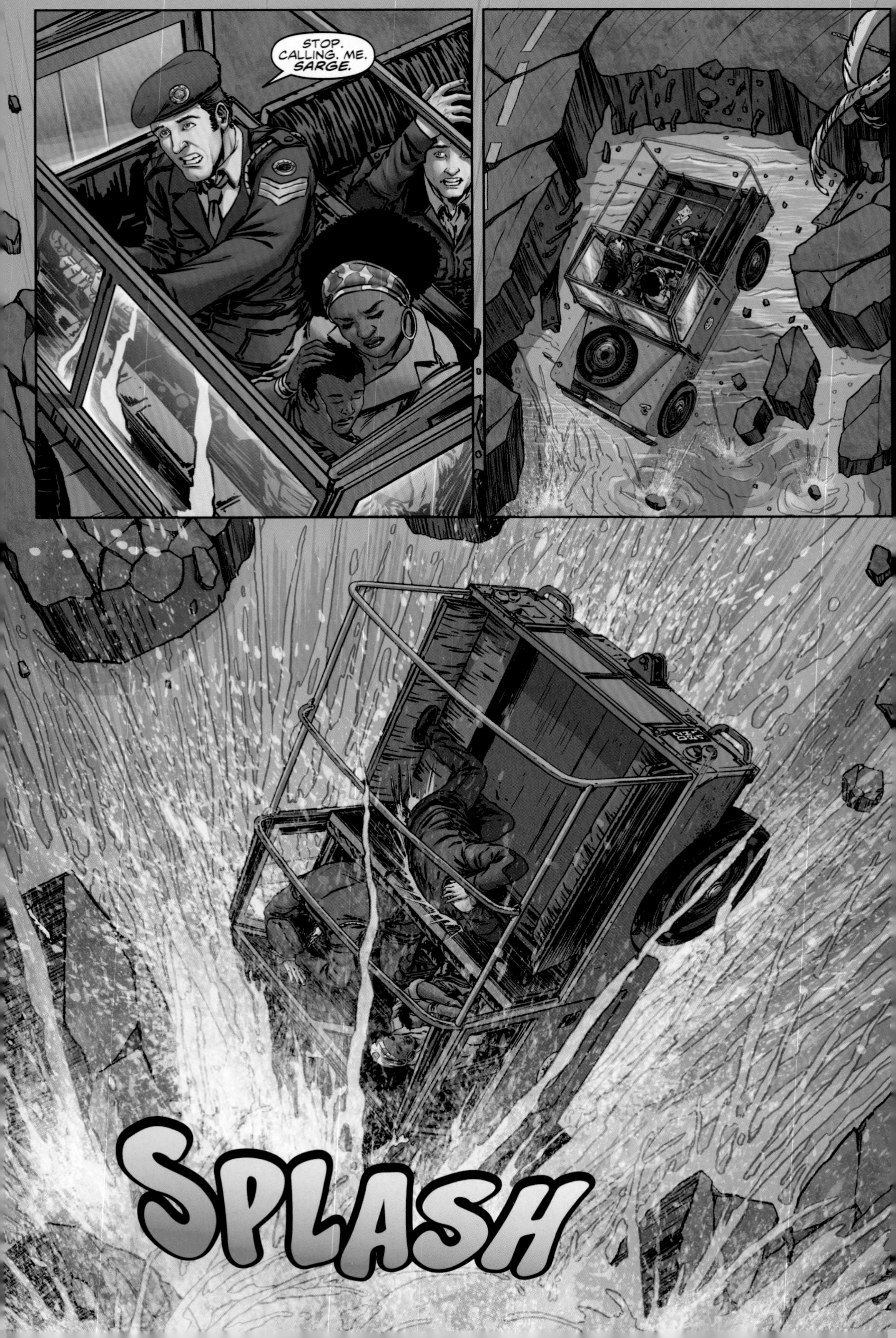
STOP. CALLING. ME. SARGE.
SPLASH

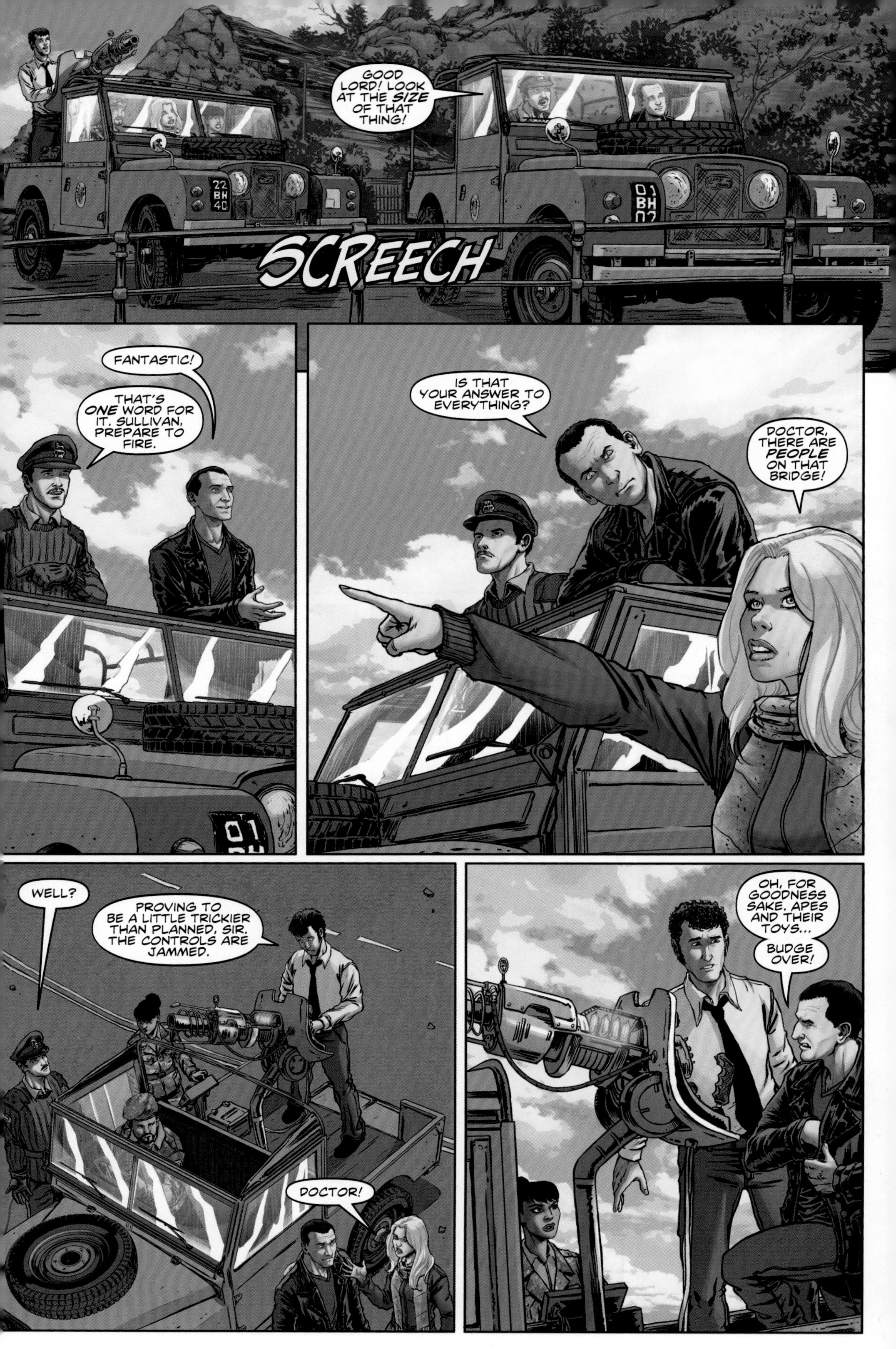

22 BH 40
GOOD LORD! LOOK AT THE SIZE OF THAT THING!
01 BH 07
SCREECH
FANTASTIC!
THAT'S ONE WORD FOR IT. SULLIVAN, PREPARE TO FIRE.
IS THAT YOUR ANSWER TO EVERYTHING?
DOCTOR, THERE ARE PEOPLE ON THAT BRIDGE!
WELL?
PROVING TO BE A LITTLE TRICKIER THAN PLANNED, SIR. THE CONTROLS ARE JAMMED.
DOCTOR!
OH, FOR GOODNESS SAKE. APES AND THEIR TOYS...
BUDGE OVER!

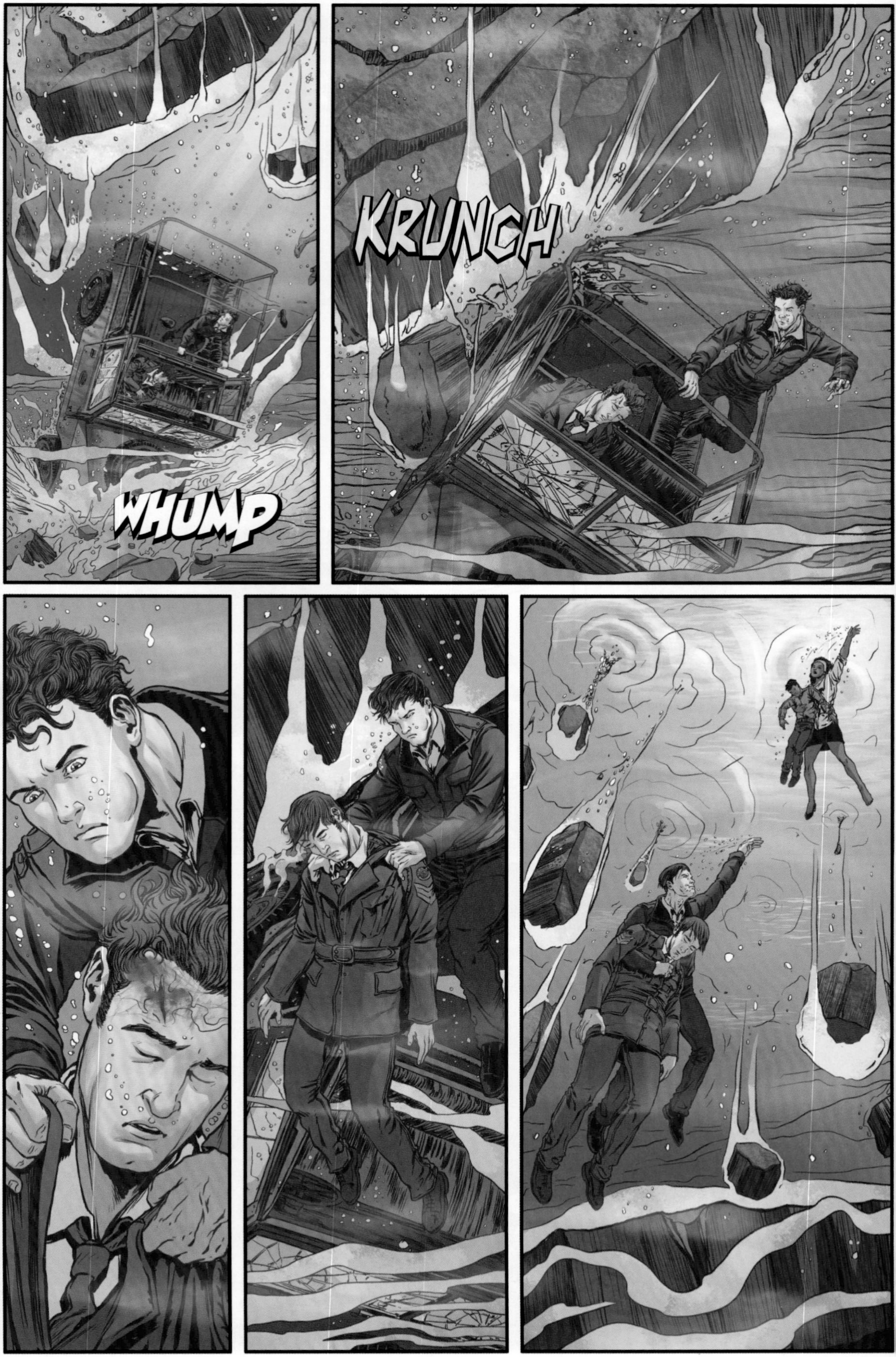
WHUMP
KRUNCH

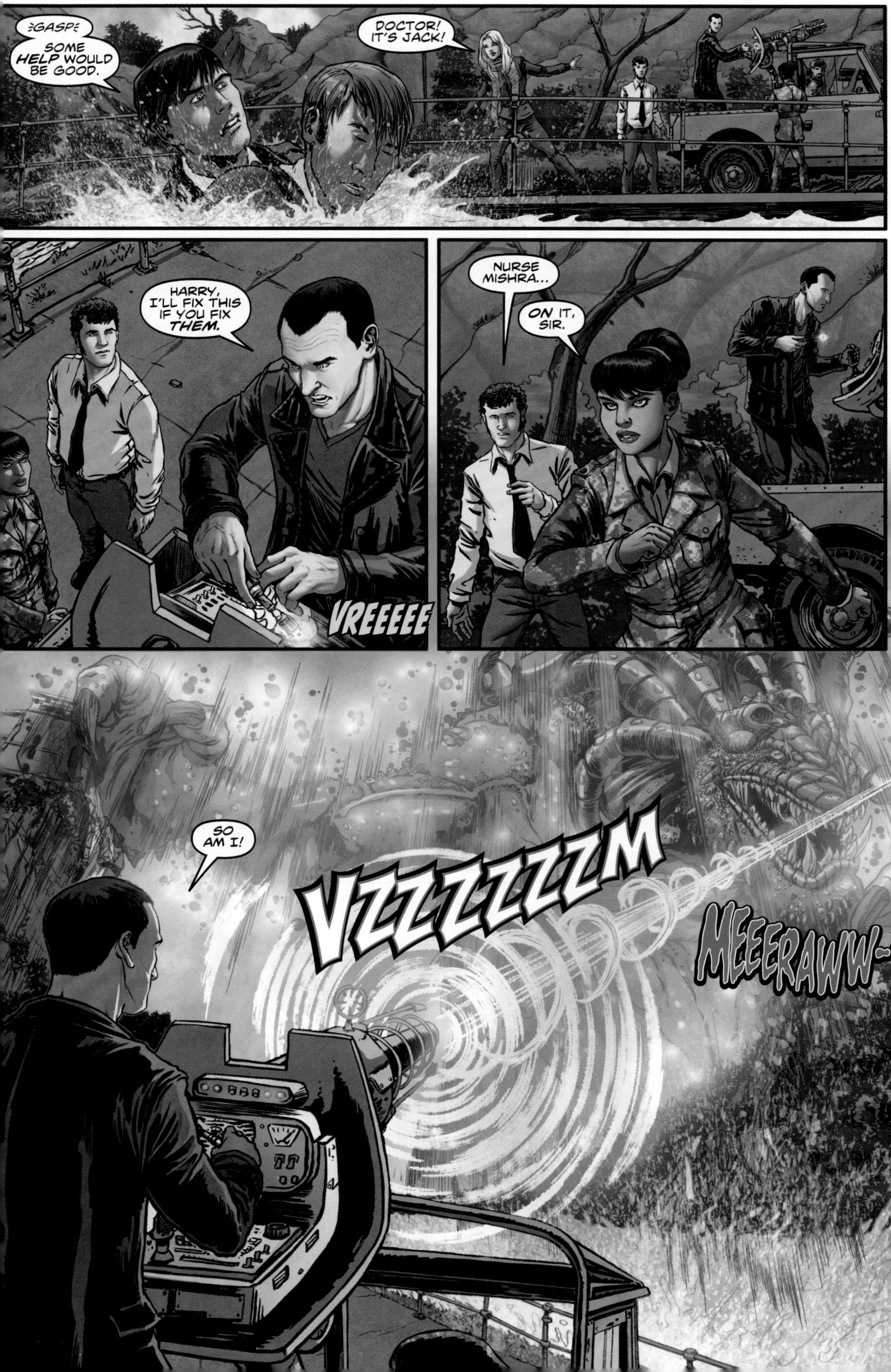
GASP
SOME HELP WOULD BE GOOD.
DOCTOR! IT'S JACK!
HARRY, I'LL FIX THIS IF YOU FIX THEM.
VREEEEE
NURSE MISHRA...
ON IT, SIR.
SO AM I!
VZZZZZZZM
MEEERAWW--

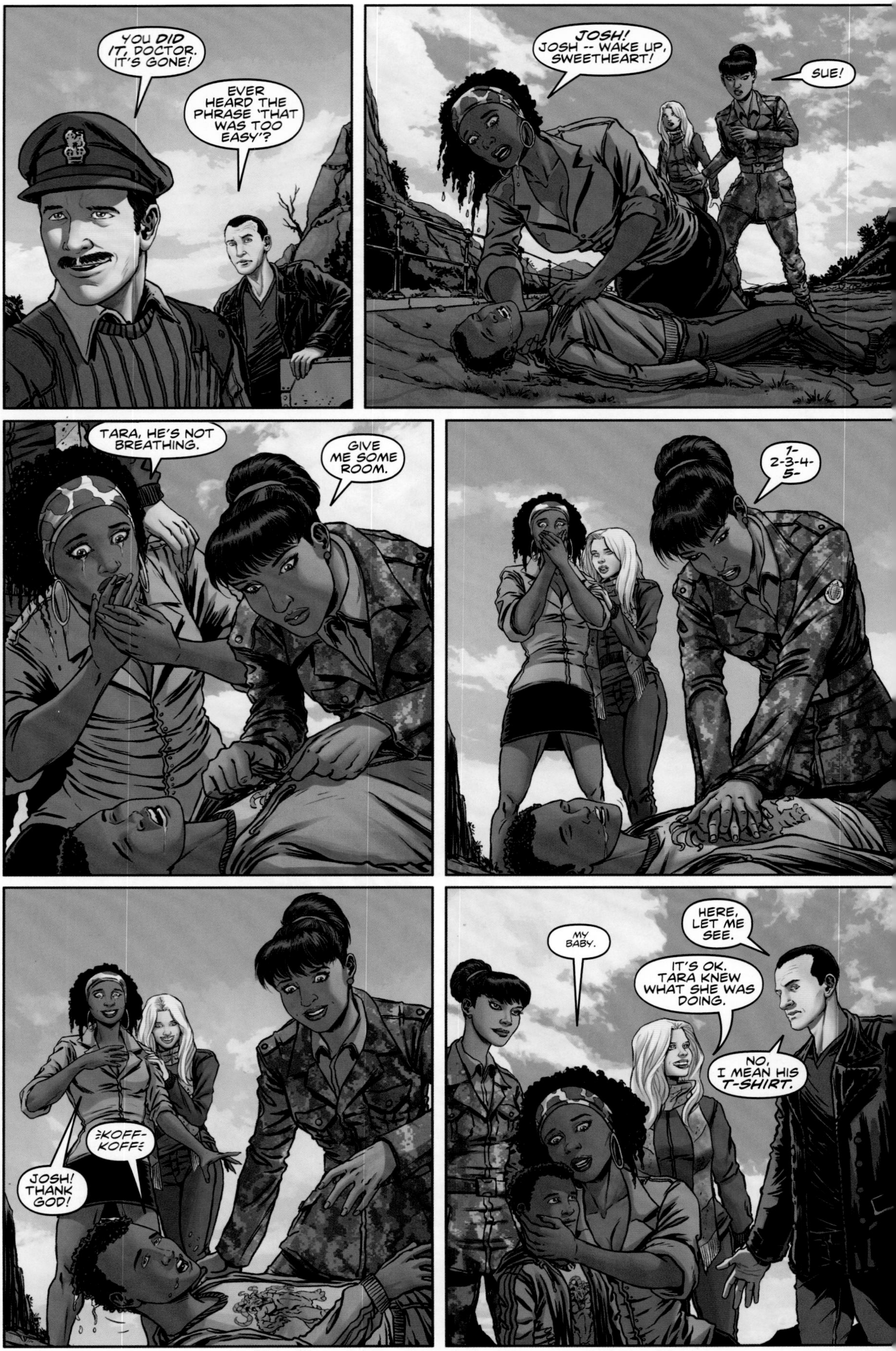
YOU DID IT, DOCTOR. IT'S GONE!
EVER HEARD THE PHRASE 'THAT WAS TOO EASY'?
JOSH! JOSH -- WAKE UP, SWEETHEART!
SUE!
TARA, HE'S NOT BREATHING.
GIVE ME SOME ROOM.
1- 2-3-4- 5-
KOFF-KOFF
JOSH! THANK GOD!
MY BABY.
HERE, LET ME SEE.
IT'S OK. TARA KNEW WHAT SHE WAS DOING.
NO, I MEAN HIS T-SHIRT.

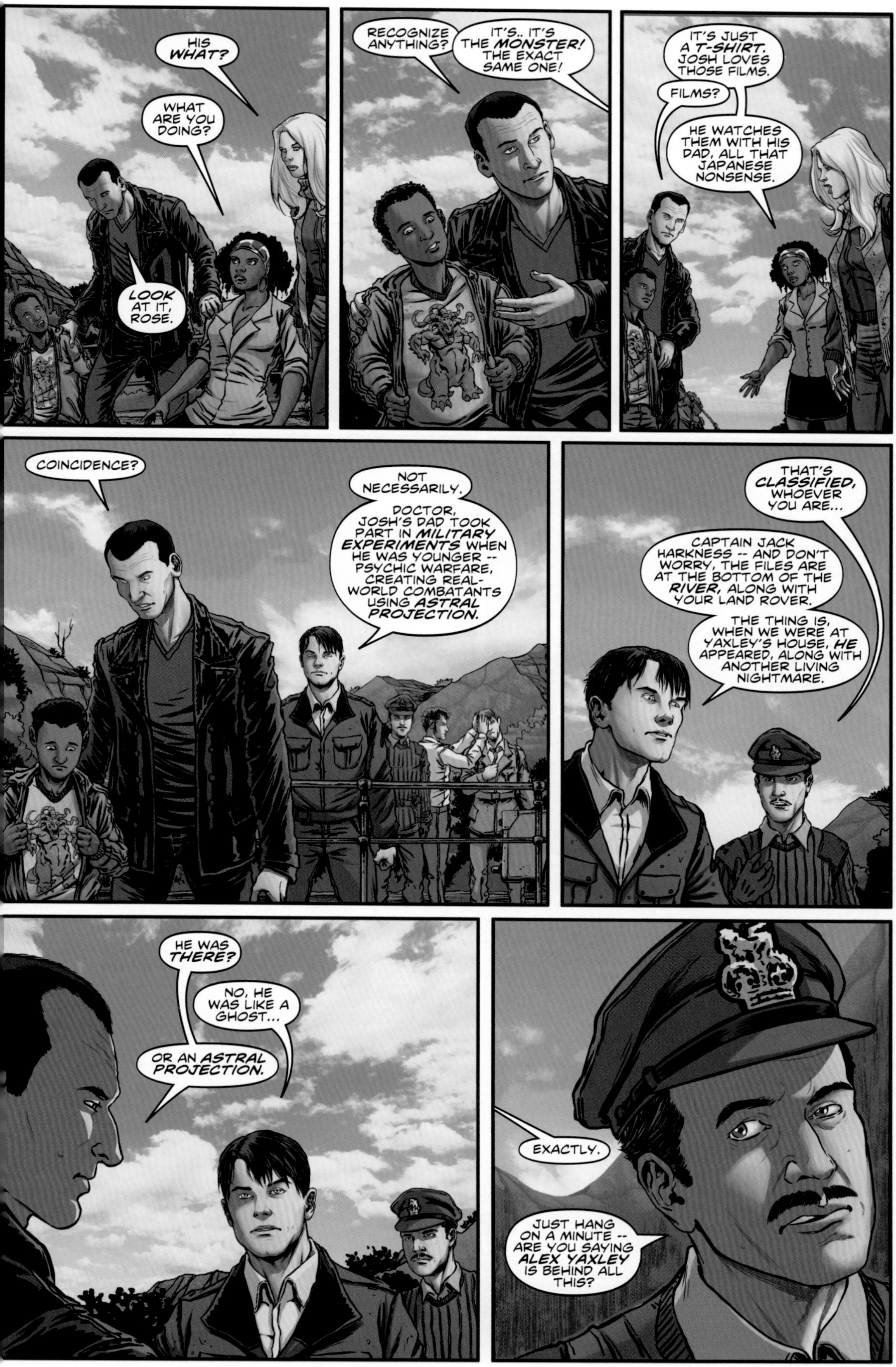
HIS WHAT?
WHAT ARE YOU DOING?
LOOK AT IT, ROSE.
RECOGNIZE ANYTHING?
IT'S.. IT'S THE MONSTER! THE EXACT SAME ONE!
IT'S JUST A T-SHIRT. JOSH LOVES THOSE FILMS.
FILMS?
HE WATCHES THEM WITH HIS DAD, ALL THAT JAPANESE NONSENSE.
COINCIDENCE?
NOT NECESSARILY.
DOCTOR, JOSH'S DAD TOOK PART IN MILITARY EXPERIMENTS WHEN HE WAS YOUNGER -- PSYCHIC WARFARE, CREATING REAL-WORLD COMBATANTS USING ASTRAL PROJECTION.
THAT'S CLASSIFIED, WHOEVER YOU ARE...
CAPTAIN JACK HARKNESS -- AND DON'T WORRY, THE FILES ARE AT THE BOTTOM OF THE RIVER, ALONG WITH YOUR LAND ROVER.
THE THING IS, WHEN WE WERE AT YAXLEY'S HOUSE, HE APPEARED, ALONG WITH ANOTHER LIVING NIGHTMARE.
HE WAS THERE?
NO, HE WAS LIKE A GHOST...
OR AN ASTRAL PROJECTION.
EXACTLY.
JUST HANG ON A MINUTE -- ARE YOU SAYING ALEX YAXLEY IS BEHIND ALL THIS?

"THAT HE'S SOMEHOW *CREATING* ALL THESE HORRORS?"

YAXLEY? YAXLEY, WAKE UP!

STILL OUT COLD.

BUT I DON'T UNDERSTAND. IF YOU'RE UNCONSCIOUS...

... HOW DID HE CONJURE UP A MONSTER IN THE AVON GORGE?

SIR!

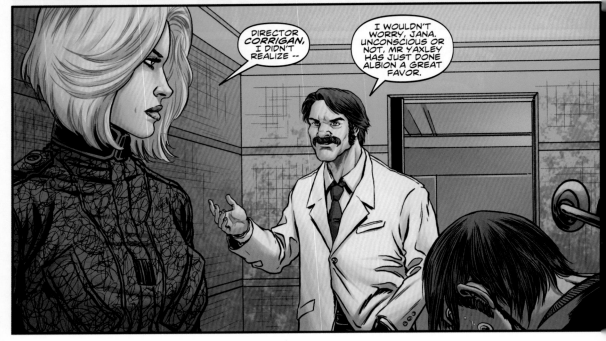

DIRECTOR *CORRIGAN*, I DIDN'T REALIZE --

I WOULDN'T WORRY, JANA. UNCONSCIOUS OR NOT, MR YAXLEY HAS JUST DONE ALBION A GREAT FAVOR.

HOW'S BENTON?

HE'LL SURVIVE. AS TOUGH AS OLD BOOTS THAT ONE.

WE'RE JUST LUCKY THE CANNON WORKED. NOT SO BAD FOR A 'DIRTY GREAT GUN', EH, DOCTOR?

THAT'S JUST *IT*, BRIGADIER. I'M NOT SURE IT DID-- *NOW* WHAT?

MINISTER, I--

SO, YOU'VE *FINALLY* DECIDED TO GRACE US WITH YOUR PRESENCE, BRIGADIER.

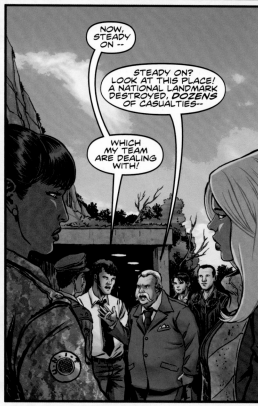

NOW, STEADY ON --

STEADY ON? LOOK AT THIS PLACE! A NATIONAL LANDMARK DESTROYED, *DOZENS* OF CASUALTIES--

WHICH MY TEAM ARE DEALING WITH!

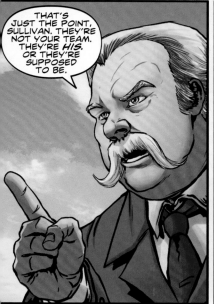

THAT'S JUST THE POINT, SULLIVAN. THEY'RE NOT YOUR TEAM. THEY'RE *HIS*. OR THEY'RE SUPPOSED TO BE.

IF THE BRIGADIER HAD *STAYED PUT* RATHER THAN SWANNING OFF TO GENEVA--

DO WE *REALLY* HAVE TO DO THIS NOW?

-- LEAVING A CRITICAL OPERATION IN THE HANDS OF A *BUFFOON* LIKE YOU.

FRANKLY, *UNIT* IS A JOKE--

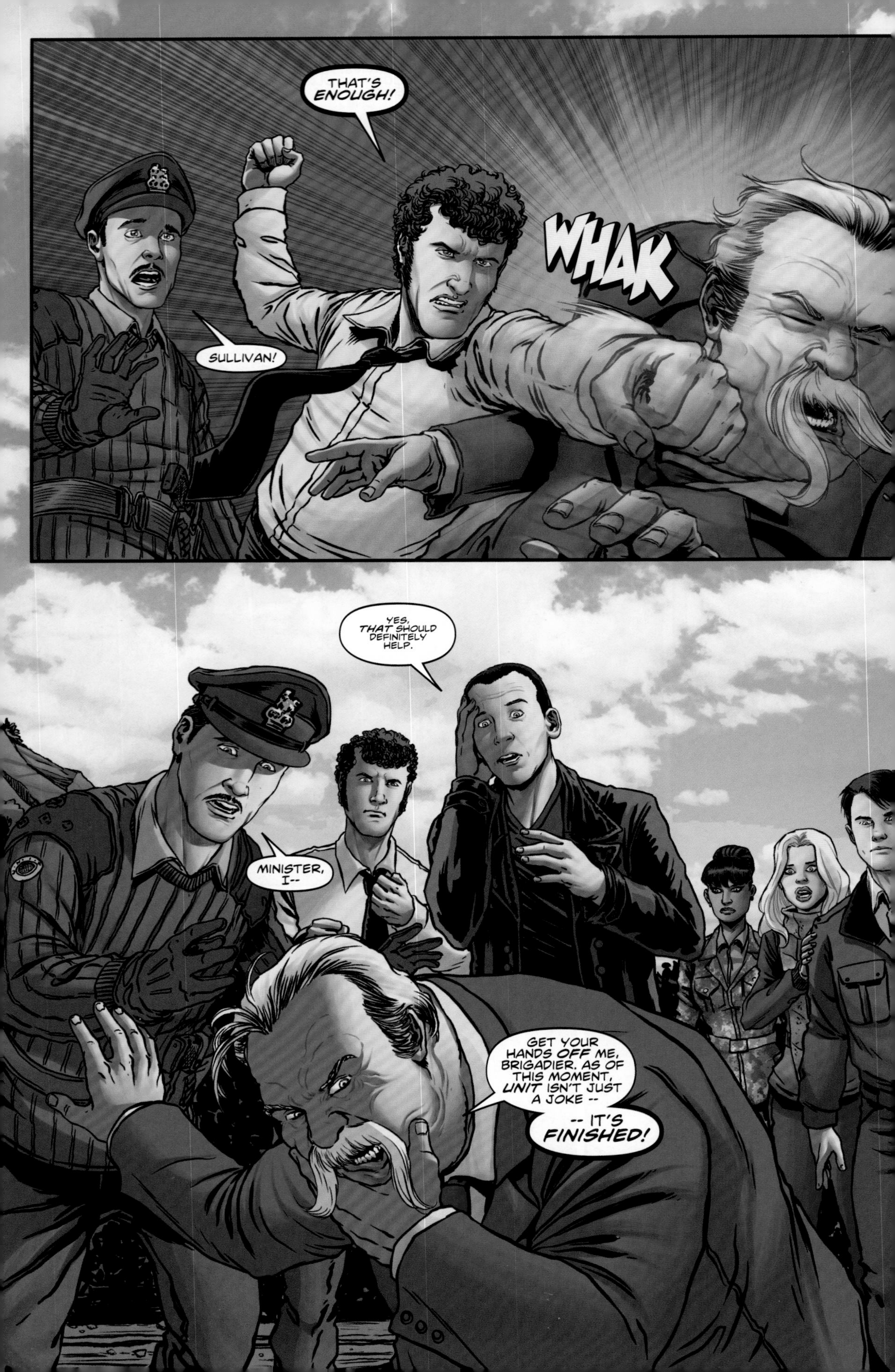
THAT'S ENOUGH!
SULLIVAN!
WHAK
YES, THAT SHOULD DEFINITELY HELP.
MINISTER, I--
GET YOUR HANDS OFF ME, BRIGADIER. AS OF THIS MOMENT, UNIT ISN'T JUST A JOKE --
-- IT'S FINISHED!

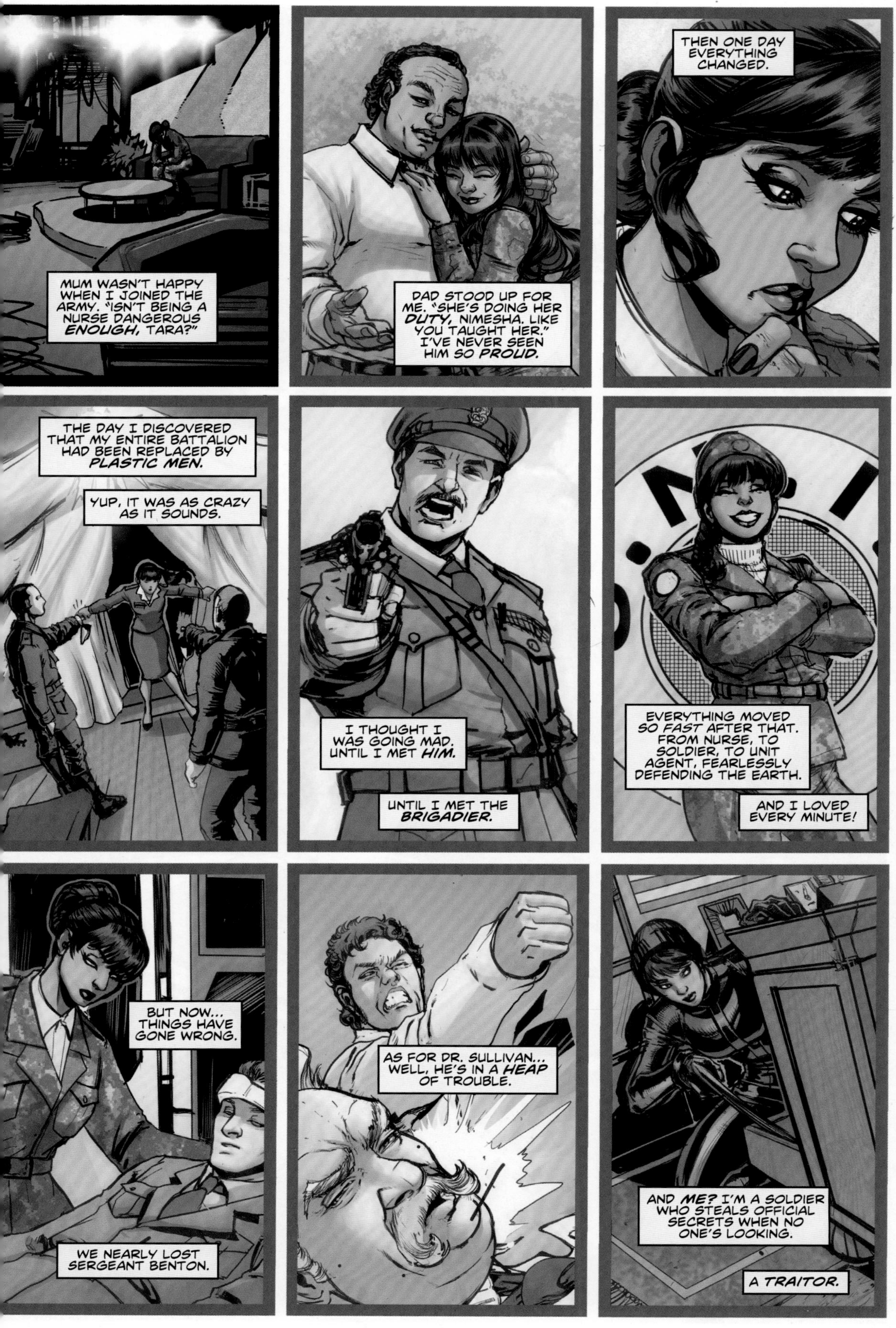
MUM WASN'T HAPPY WHEN I JOINED THE ARMY. "ISN'T BEING A NURSE DANGEROUS ENOUGH, TARA?"
DAD STOOD UP FOR ME. "SHE'S DOING HER DUTY, NIMESHA. LIKE YOU TAUGHT HER." I'VE NEVER SEEN HIM SO PROUD.
THEN ONE DAY EVERYTHING CHANGED.
THE DAY I DISCOVERED THAT MY ENTIRE BATTALION HAD BEEN REPLACED BY PLASTIC MEN.
YUP, IT WAS AS CRAZY AS IT SOUNDS.
I THOUGHT I WAS GOING MAD. UNTIL I MET HIM.
UNTIL I MET THE BRIGADIER.
EVERYTHING MOVED SO FAST AFTER THAT. FROM NURSE, TO SOLDIER, TO UNIT AGENT, FEARLESSLY DEFENDING THE EARTH.
AND I LOVED EVERY MINUTE!
BUT NOW... THINGS HAVE GONE WRONG.
WE NEARLY LOST SERGEANT BENTON.
AS FOR DR. SULLIVAN... WELL, HE'S IN A HEAP OF TROUBLE.
AND ME? I'M A SOLDIER WHO STEALS OFFICIAL SECRETS WHEN NO ONE'S LOOKING.
A TRAITOR.

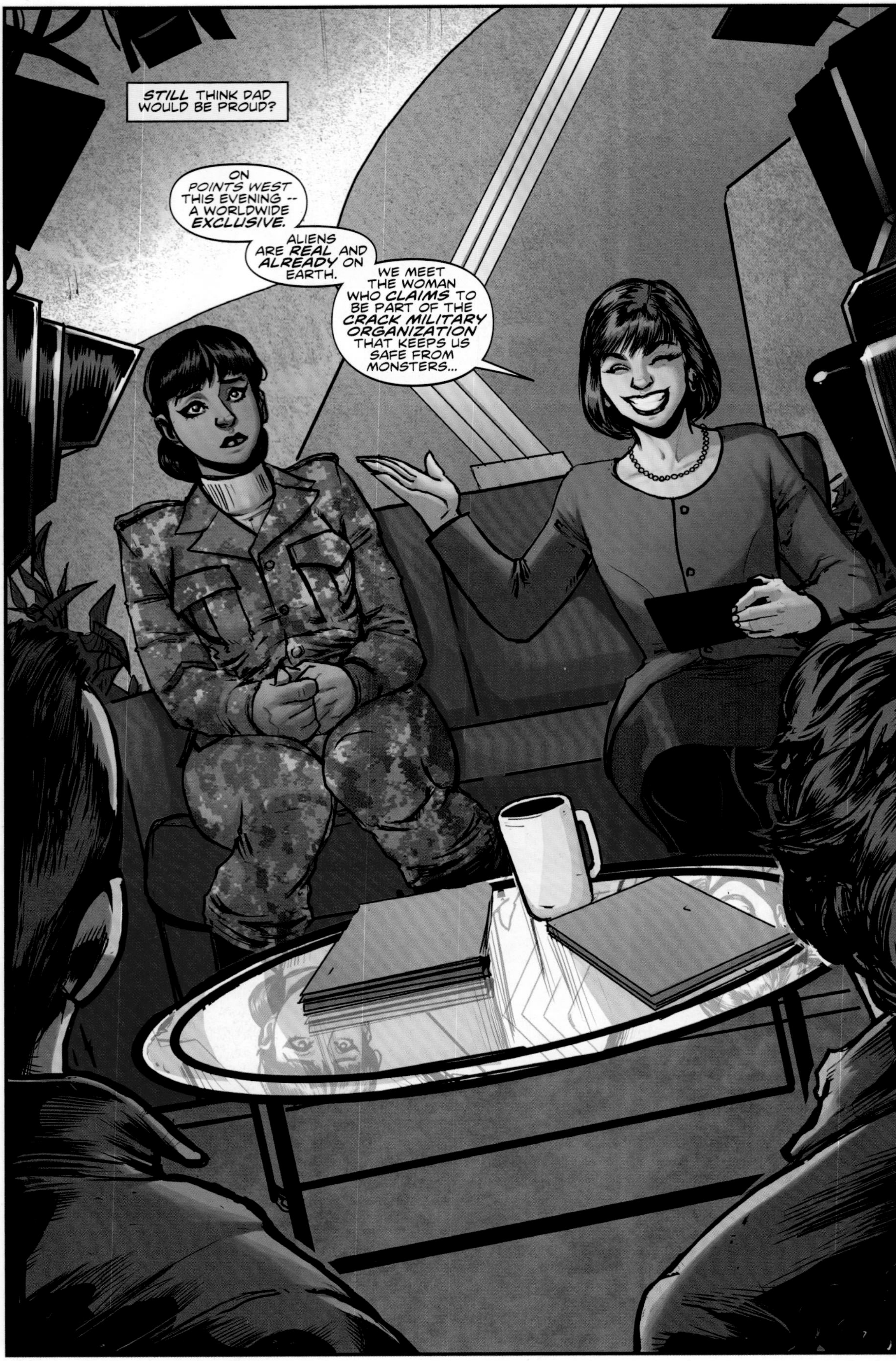
STILL THINK DAD WOULD BE PROUD?
ON POINTS WEST THIS EVENING -- A WORLDWIDE EXCLUSIVE.
ALIENS ARE REAL AND ALREADY ON EARTH.
WE MEET THE WOMAN WHO CLAIMS TO BE PART OF THE CRACK MILITARY ORGANIZATION THAT KEEPS US SAFE FROM MONSTERS...

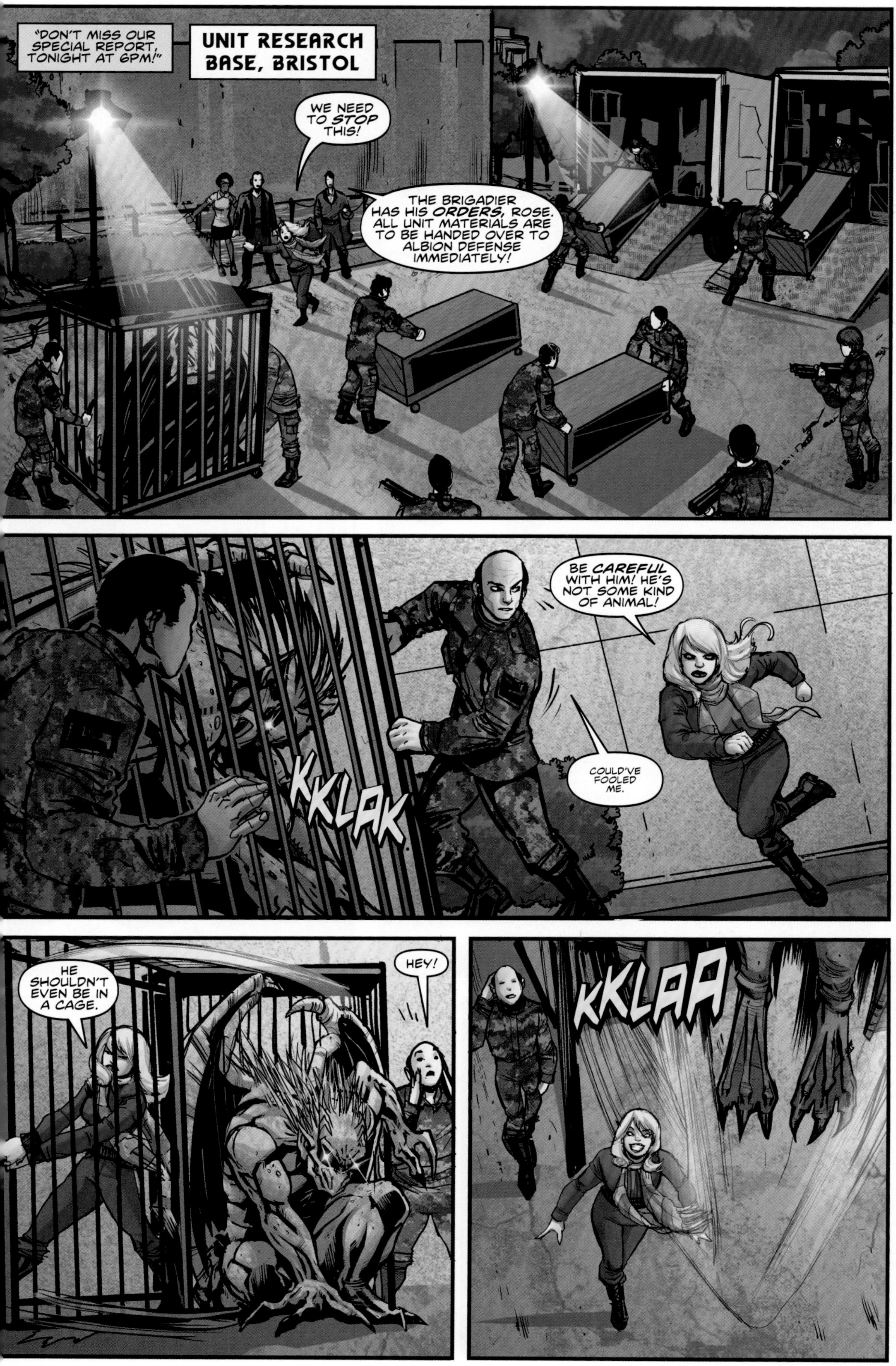
"DON'T MISS OUR SPECIAL REPORT, TONIGHT AT 6PM!"
UNIT RESEARCH BASE, BRISTOL
WE NEED TO STOP THIS!
THE BRIGADIER HAS HIS ORDERS, ROSE. ALL UNIT MATERIALS ARE TO BE HANDED OVER TO ALBION DEFENSE IMMEDIATELY!
BE CAREFUL WITH HIM! HE'S NOT SOME KIND OF ANIMAL!
KKLAK
COULD'VE FOOLED ME.
HE SHOULDN'T EVEN BE IN A CAGE.
HEY!
KKLAA

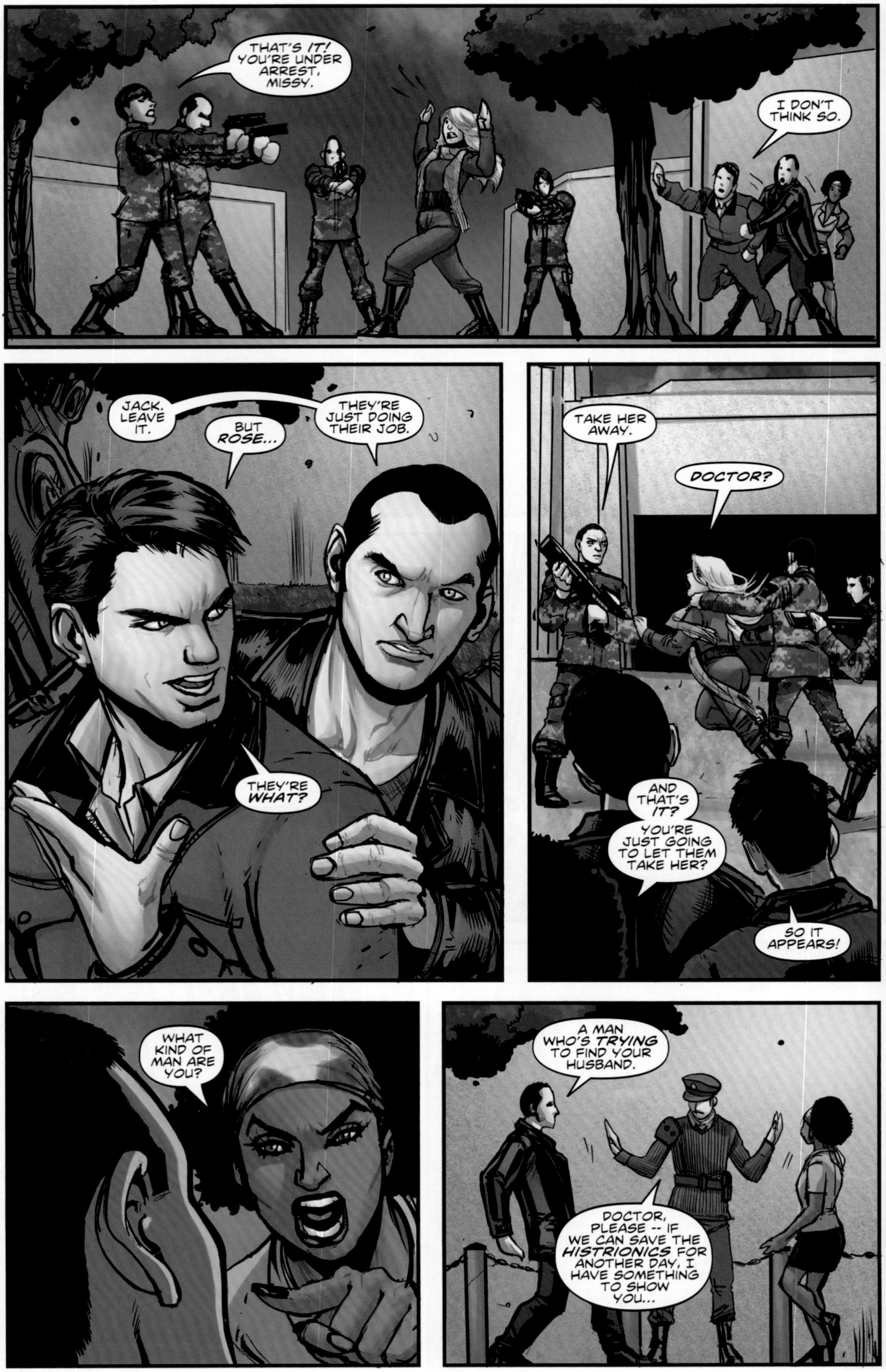
THAT'S IT! YOU'RE UNDER ARREST, MISSY.
I DON'T THINK SO.
JACK. LEAVE IT.
BUT ROSE...
THEY'RE JUST DOING THEIR JOB.
THEY'RE WHAT?
TAKE HER AWAY.
DOCTOR?
AND THAT'S IT? YOU'RE JUST GOING TO LET THEM TAKE HER?
SO IT APPEARS!
WHAT KIND OF MAN ARE YOU?
A MAN WHO'S TRYING TO FIND YOUR HUSBAND.
DOCTOR, PLEASE -- IF WE CAN SAVE THE HISTRIONICS FOR ANOTHER DAY, I HAVE SOMETHING TO SHOW YOU...

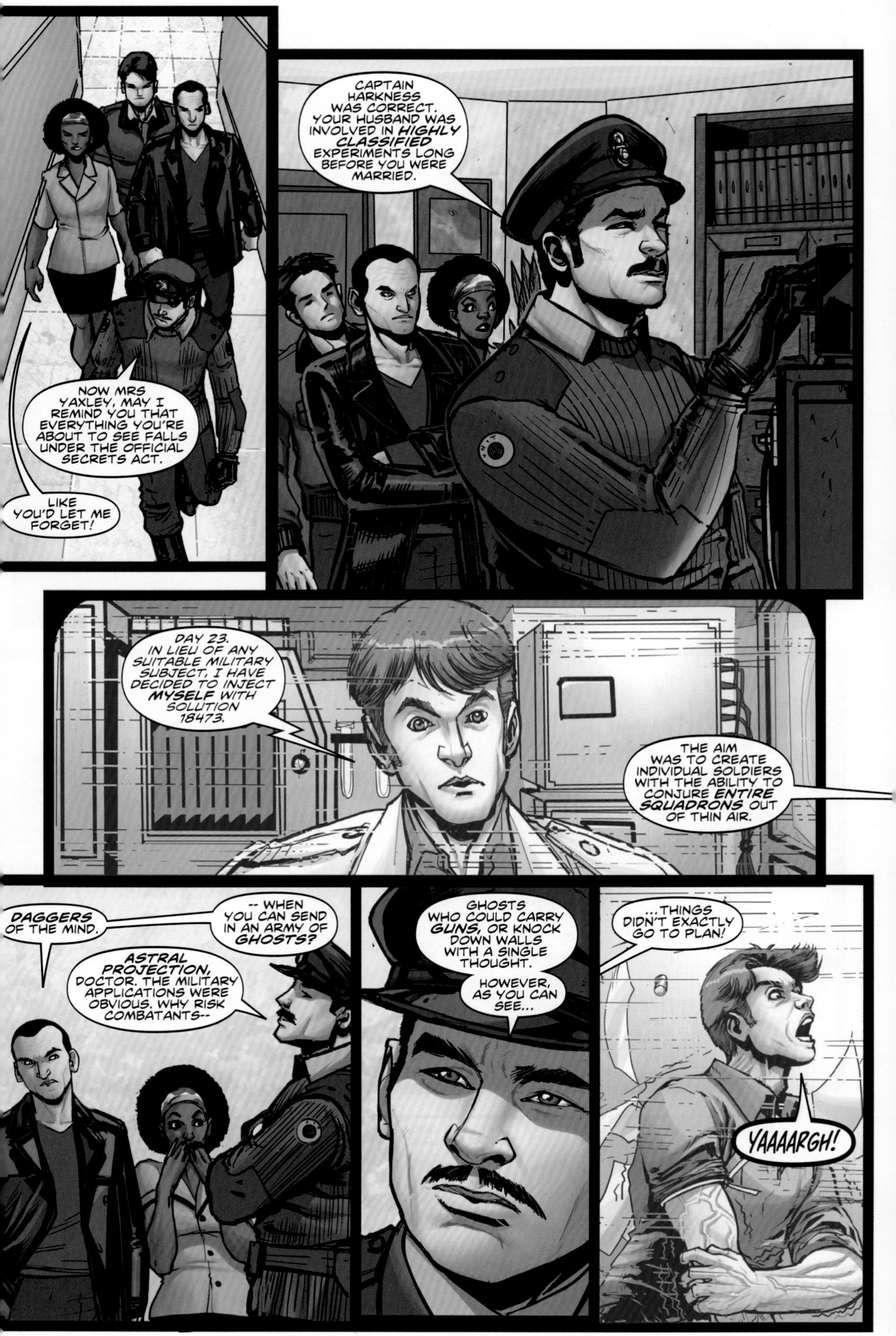
NOW MRS YAXLEY, MAY I REMIND YOU THAT EVERYTHING YOU'RE ABOUT TO SEE FALLS UNDER THE OFFICIAL SECRETS ACT.
LIKE YOU'D LET ME FORGET!
CAPTAIN HARKNESS WAS CORRECT. YOUR HUSBAND WAS INVOLVED IN HIGHLY CLASSIFIED EXPERIMENTS LONG BEFORE YOU WERE MARRIED.
DAY 23. IN LIEU OF ANY SUITABLE MILITARY SUBJECT, I HAVE DECIDED TO INJECT MYSELF WITH SOLUTION 18473.
THE AIM WAS TO CREATE INDIVIDUAL SOLDIERS WITH THE ABILITY TO CONJURE ENTIRE SQUADRONS OUT OF THIN AIR.
DAGGERS OF THE MIND.
ASTRAL PROJECTION, DOCTOR. THE MILITARY APPLICATIONS WERE OBVIOUS. WHY RISK COMBATANTS--
-- WHEN YOU CAN SEND IN AN ARMY OF GHOSTS?
GHOSTS WHO COULD CARRY GUNS, OR KNOCK DOWN WALLS WITH A SINGLE THOUGHT.
HOWEVER, AS YOU CAN SEE...
...THINGS DIDN'T EXACTLY GO TO PLAN!
YAAAARGH!

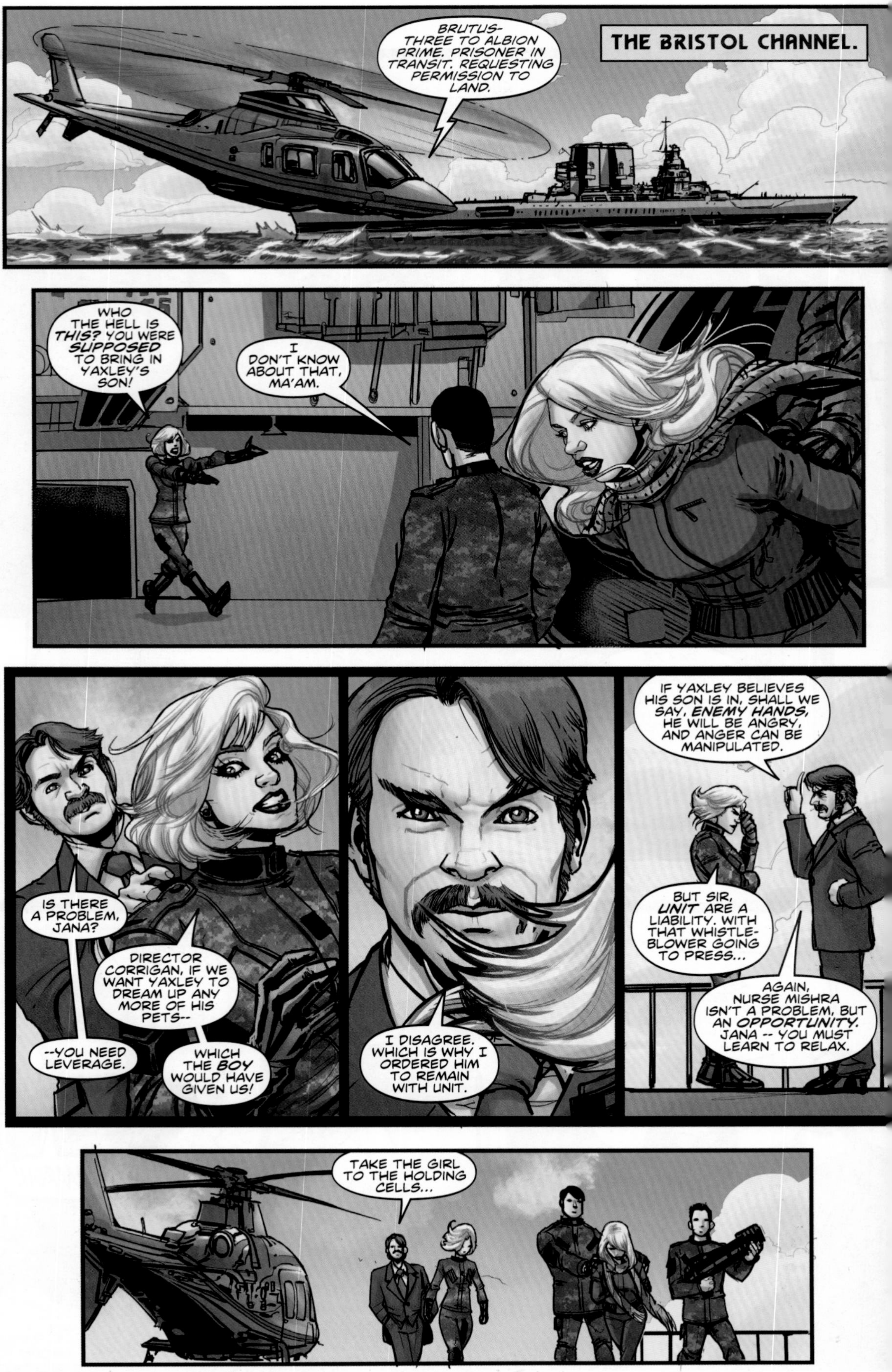
THE BRISTOL CHANNEL.
BRUTUS-THREE TO ALBION PRIME. PRISONER IN TRANSIT. REQUESTING PERMISSION TO LAND.
WHO THE HELL IS THIS? YOU WERE SUPPOSED TO BRING IN YAXLEY'S SON!
I DON'T KNOW ABOUT THAT, MA'AM.
IS THERE A PROBLEM, JANA?
DIRECTOR CORRIGAN, IF WE WANT YAXLEY TO DREAM UP ANY MORE OF HIS PETS--
--YOU NEED LEVERAGE.
WHICH THE BOY WOULD HAVE GIVEN US!
I DISAGREE. WHICH IS WHY I ORDERED HIM TO REMAIN WITH UNIT.
IF YAXLEY BELIEVES HIS SON IS IN, SHALL WE SAY, ENEMY HANDS, HE WILL BE ANGRY, AND ANGER CAN BE MANIPULATED.
BUT SIR, UNIT ARE A LIABILITY. WITH THAT WHISTLE-BLOWER GOING TO PRESS...
AGAIN, NURSE MISHRA ISN'T A PROBLEM, BUT AN OPPORTUNITY. JANA -- YOU MUST LEARN TO RELAX.
TAKE THE GIRL TO THE HOLDING CELLS...

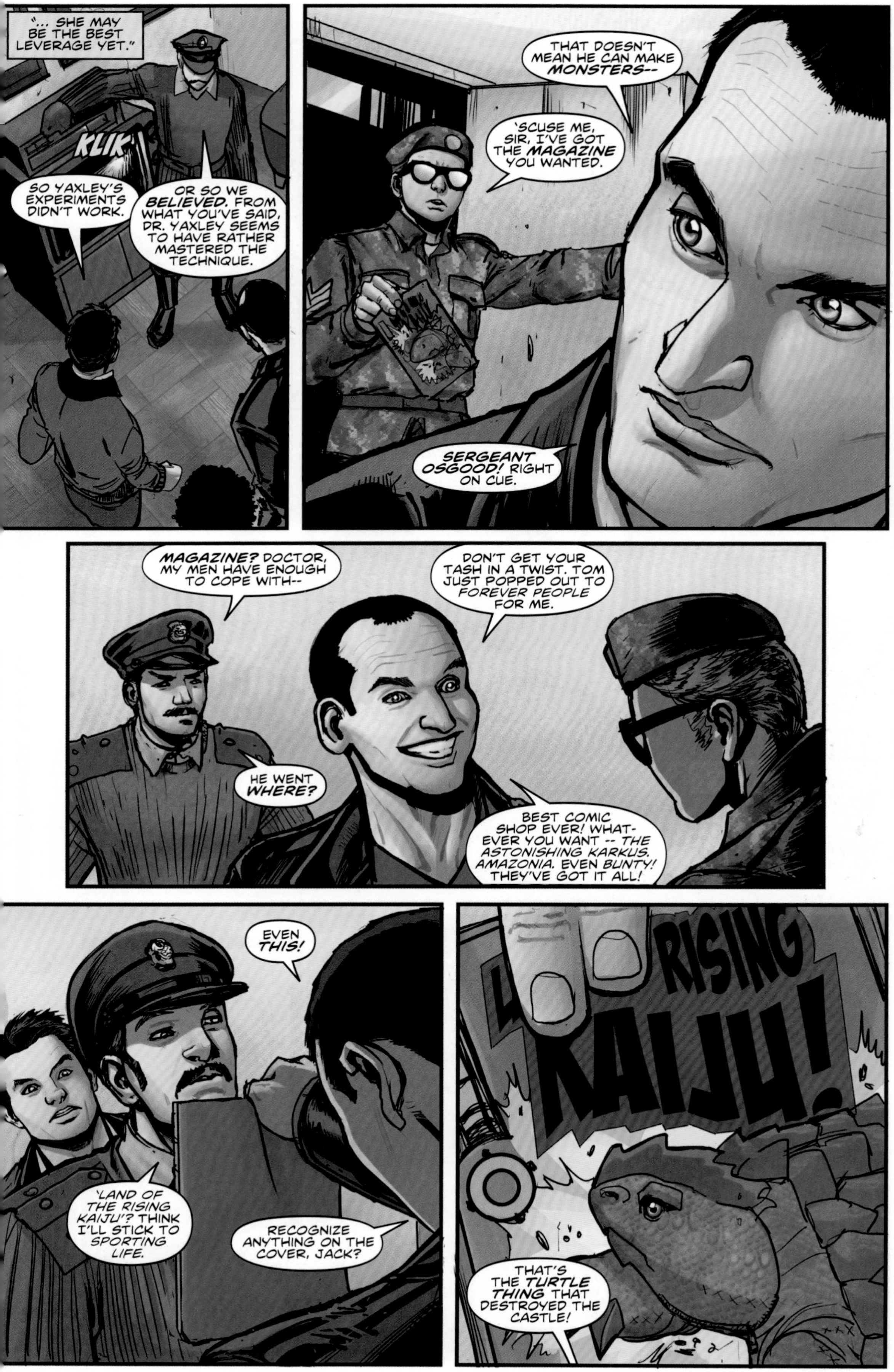
"... SHE MAY BE THE BEST LEVERAGE YET."
KLIK
SO YAXLEY'S EXPERIMENTS DIDN'T WORK.
OR SO WE BELIEVED. FROM WHAT YOU'VE SAID, DR. YAXLEY SEEMS TO HAVE RATHER MASTERED THE TECHNIQUE.
THAT DOESN'T MEAN HE CAN MAKE MONSTERS--
'SCUSE ME, SIR, I'VE GOT THE MAGAZINE YOU WANTED.
SERGEANT OSGOOD! RIGHT ON CUE.
MAGAZINE? DOCTOR, MY MEN HAVE ENOUGH TO COPE WITH--
DON'T GET YOUR TASH IN A TWIST. TOM JUST POPPED OUT TO FOREVER PEOPLE FOR ME.
HE WENT WHERE?
BEST COMIC SHOP EVER! WHAT-EVER YOU WANT -- THE ASTONISHING KARKUS. AMAZONIA. EVEN BUNTY! THEY'VE GOT IT ALL!
EVEN THIS!
'LAND OF THE RISING KAIJU'? THINK I'LL STICK TO SPORTING LIFE.
RECOGNIZE ANYTHING ON THE COVER, JACK?
RISING KAIJU!
THAT'S THE TURTLE THING THAT DESTROYED THE CASTLE!

THE VERY SAME. AND ON PAGE 10...

THE MIGHTY *FUNINJO* -- LAST SEEN DEMOLISHING POOR OLD ISAMBARD'S BRIDGE BEFORE VANISHING IN A PUFF OF SMOKE.

"ALSO TO BE FOUND ON *JOSH'S T-SHIRT.*"

"FUNINJO *DIDN'T* DISAPPEAR BECAUSE HARRY BLASTED IT WITH HIS PSIONIC CANNON."

IT VANISHED BECAUSE JOSH WAS *UNCONSCIOUS.*

I-I DON'T UNDERSTAND.

I THINK YOU *DO.* THE BRIGADIER'S RIGHT.

"YOUR HUSBAND GAVE HIMSELF POWERS...

"... BUT THEY WERE *PARLOR TRICKS,* NOTHING MORE...

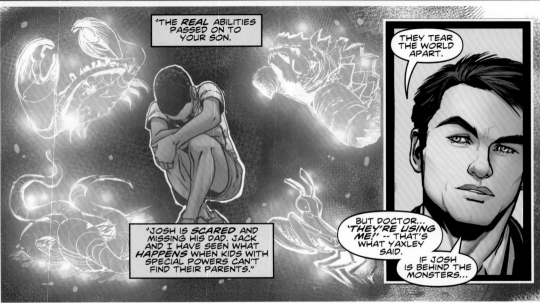

"THE *REAL* ABILITIES PASSED ON TO YOUR SON.

"JOSH IS *SCARED* AND MISSING HIS DAD. JACK AND I HAVE SEEN WHAT *HAPPENS* WHEN KIDS WITH SPECIAL POWERS CAN'T FIND THEIR PARENTS."

THEY TEAR THE WORLD APART.

BUT DOCTOR... *'THEY'RE USING ME!'* -- THAT'S WHAT YAXLEY SAID.

IF JOSH IS BEHIND THE MONSTERS...

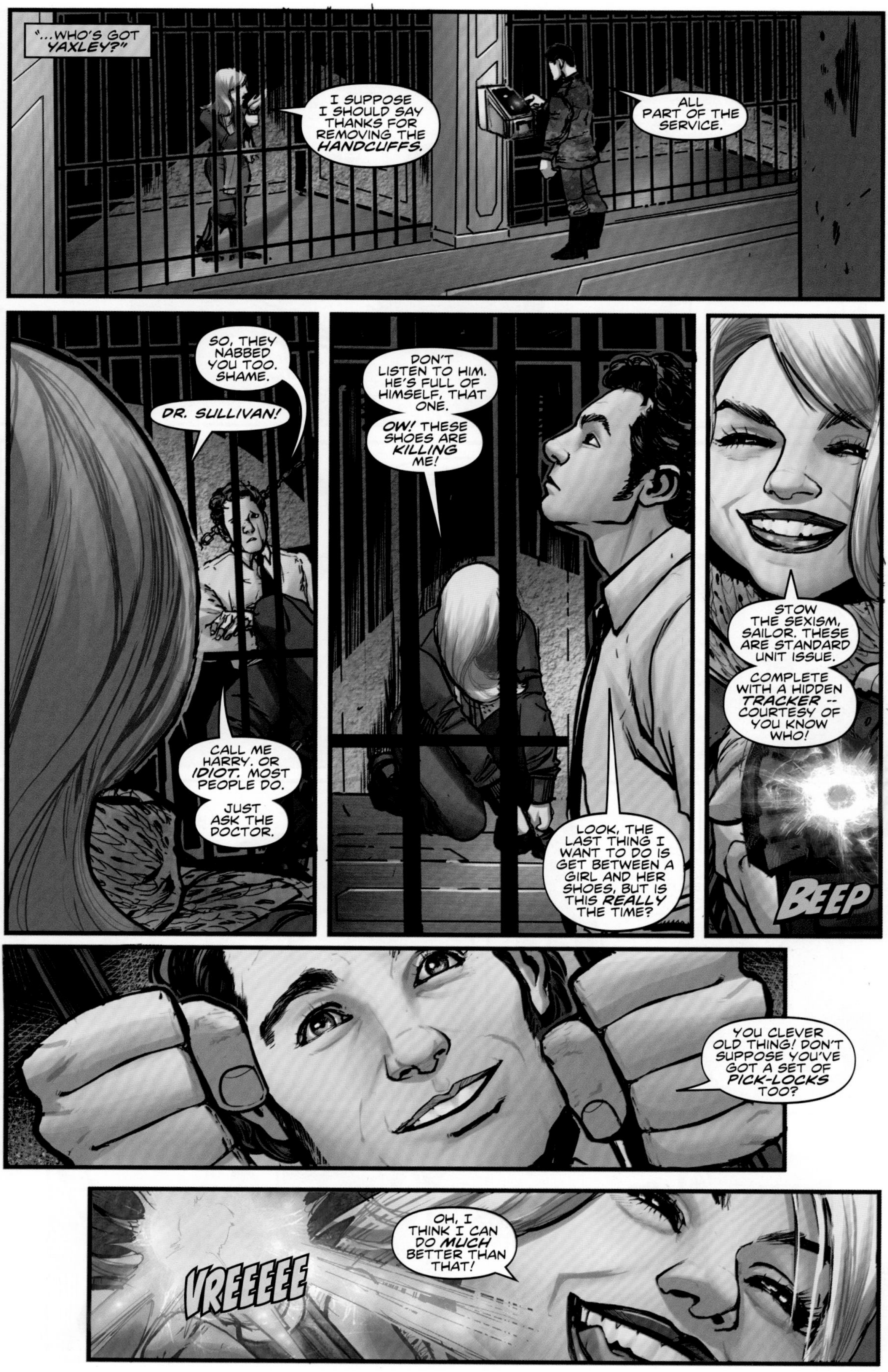
"...WHO'S GOT YAXLEY?"
I SUPPOSE I SHOULD SAY THANKS FOR REMOVING THE HANDCUFFS.
ALL PART OF THE SERVICE.
SO, THEY NABBED YOU TOO. SHAME.
DR. SULLIVAN!
CALL ME HARRY. OR IDIOT. MOST PEOPLE DO.
JUST ASK THE DOCTOR.
DON'T LISTEN TO HIM. HE'S FULL OF HIMSELF, THAT ONE.
OW! THESE SHOES ARE KILLING ME!
LOOK, THE LAST THING I WANT TO DO IS GET BETWEEN A GIRL AND HER SHOES, BUT IS THIS REALLY THE TIME?
STOW THE SEXISM, SAILOR. THESE ARE STANDARD UNIT ISSUE.
COMPLETE WITH A HIDDEN TRACKER -- COURTESY OF YOU KNOW WHO!
BEEP
YOU CLEVER OLD THING! DON'T SUPPOSE YOU'VE GOT A SET OF PICK-LOCKS TOO?
VREEEEE
OH, I THINK I CAN DO MUCH BETTER THAN THAT!

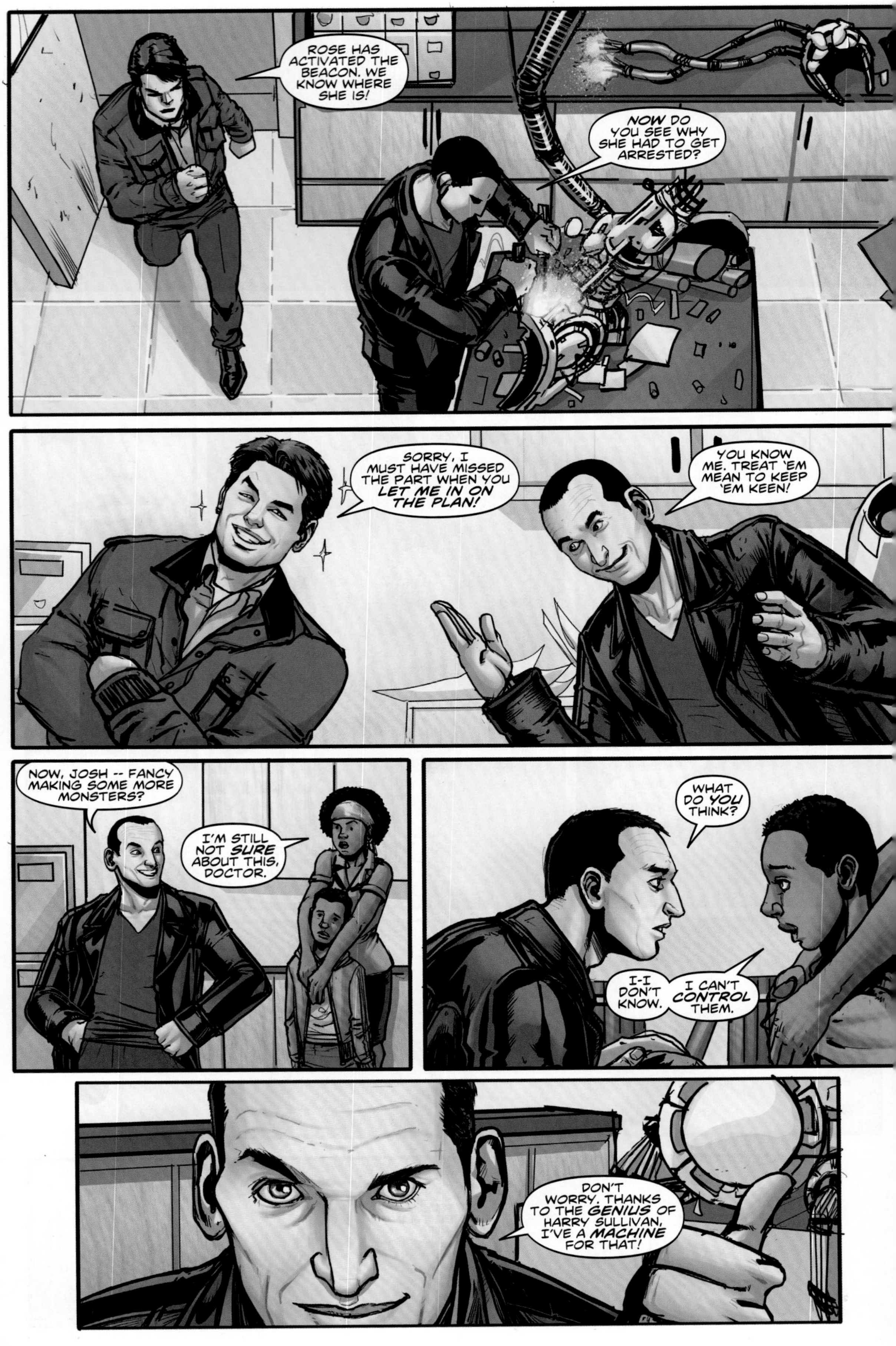

ROSE HAS ACTIVATED THE BEACON. WE KNOW WHERE SHE IS!
NOW DO YOU SEE WHY SHE HAD TO GET ARRESTED?
SORRY, I MUST HAVE MISSED THE PART WHEN YOU LET ME IN ON THE PLAN!
YOU KNOW ME. TREAT 'EM MEAN TO KEEP 'EM KEEN!
NOW, JOSH -- FANCY MAKING SOME MORE MONSTERS?
I'M STILL NOT SURE ABOUT THIS, DOCTOR.
WHAT DO YOU THINK?
I-I DON'T KNOW.
I CAN'T CONTROL THEM.
DON'T WORRY. THANKS TO THE GENIUS OF HARRY SULLIVAN, I'VE A MACHINE FOR THAT!

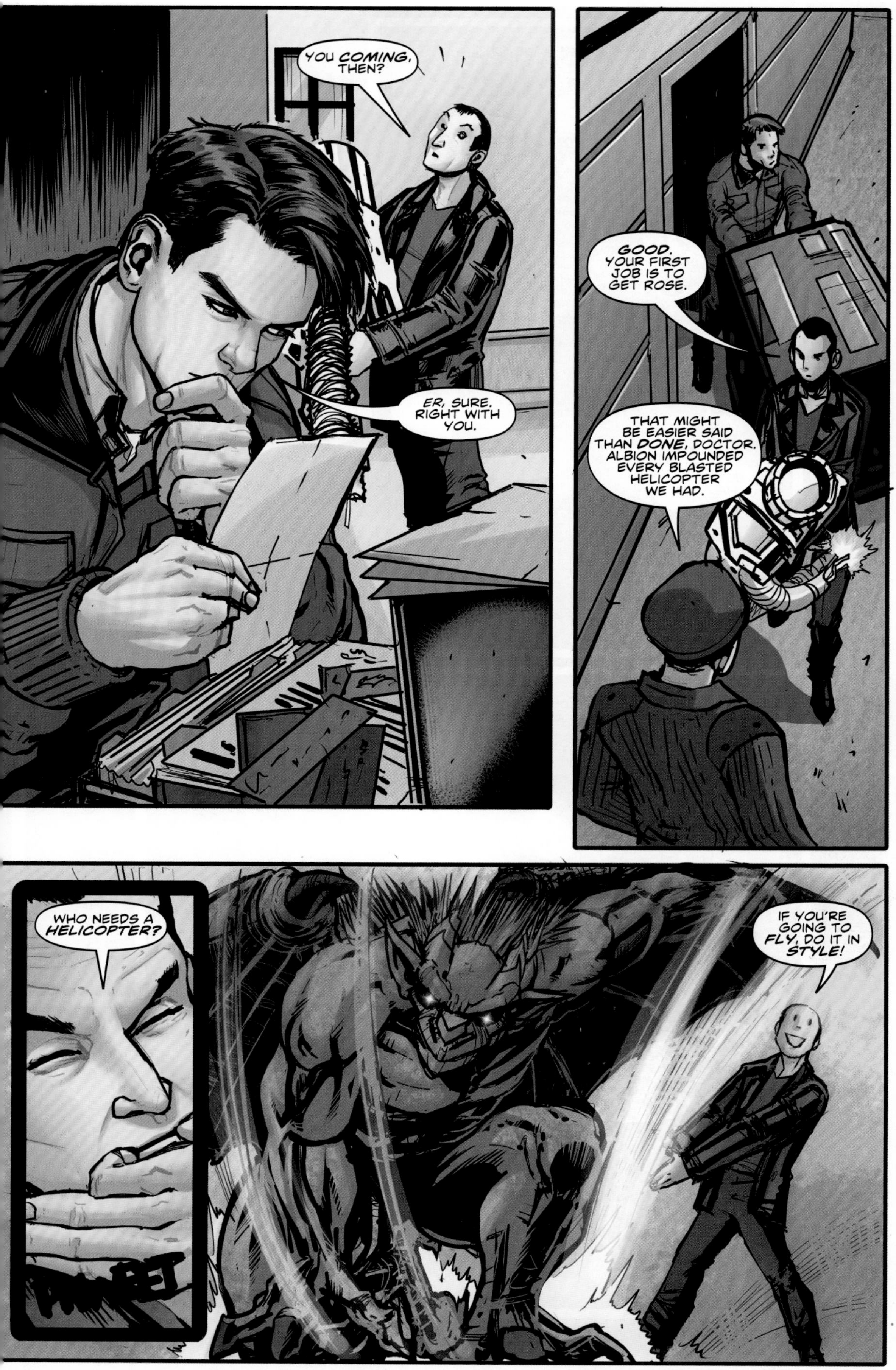
YOU COMING, THEN?
ER, SURE. RIGHT WITH YOU.
GOOD. YOUR FIRST JOB IS TO GET ROSE.
THAT MIGHT BE EASIER SAID THAN DONE, DOCTOR. ALBION IMPOUNDED EVERY BLASTED HELICOPTER WE HAD.
WHO NEEDS A HELICOPTER?
IF YOU'RE GOING TO FLY, DO IT IN STYLE!

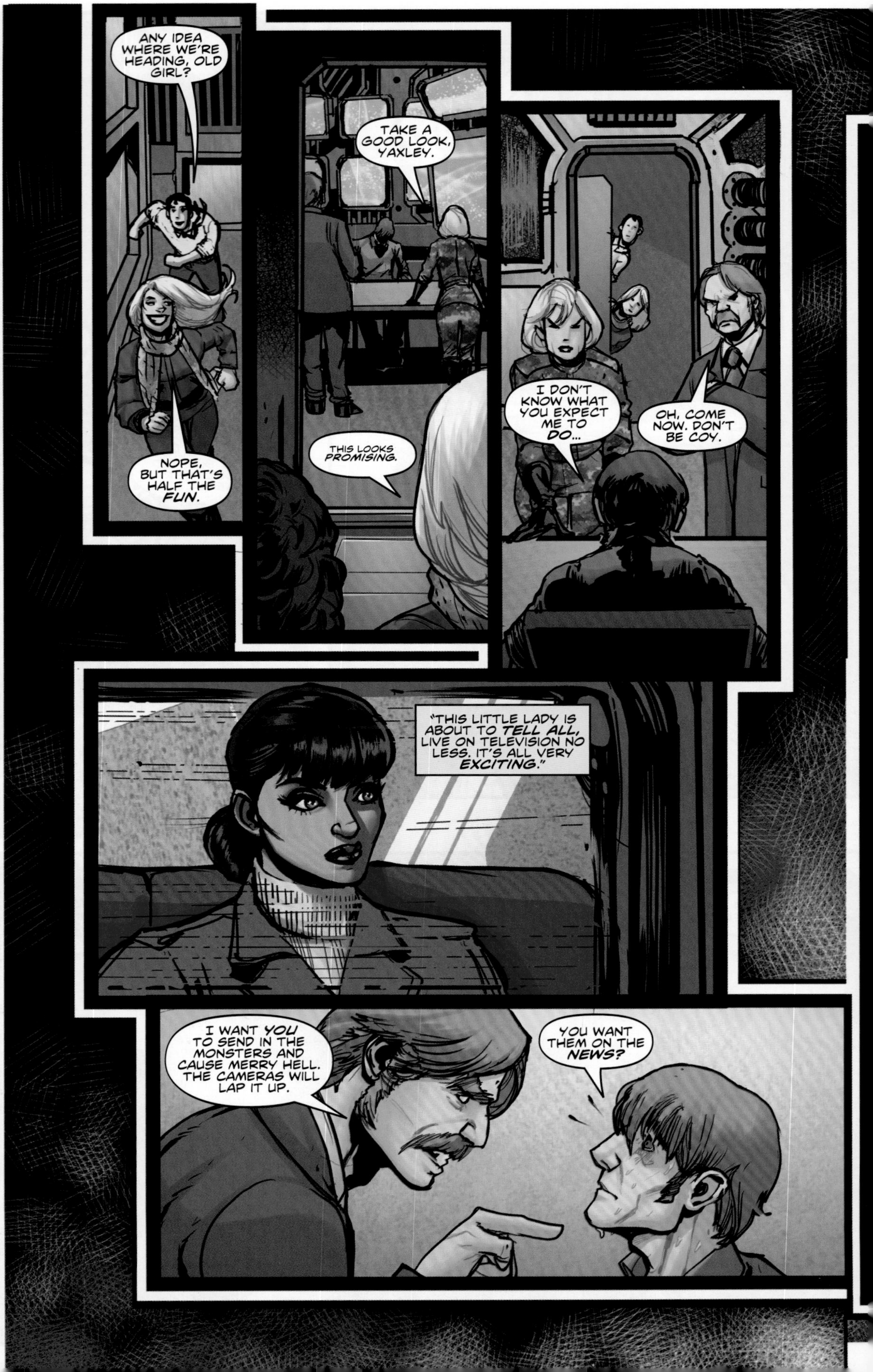
ANY IDEA WHERE WE'RE HEADING, OLD GIRL?
NOPE, BUT THAT'S HALF THE FUN.
TAKE A GOOD LOOK, YAXLEY.
THIS LOOKS PROMISING.
I DON'T KNOW WHAT YOU EXPECT ME TO DO...
OH, COME NOW. DON'T BE COY.
"THIS LITTLE LADY IS ABOUT TO TELL ALL, LIVE ON TELEVISION NO LESS. IT'S ALL VERY EXCITING."
I WANT YOU TO SEND IN THE MONSTERS AND CAUSE MERRY HELL. THE CAMERAS WILL LAP IT UP.
YOU WANT THEM ON THE NEWS?

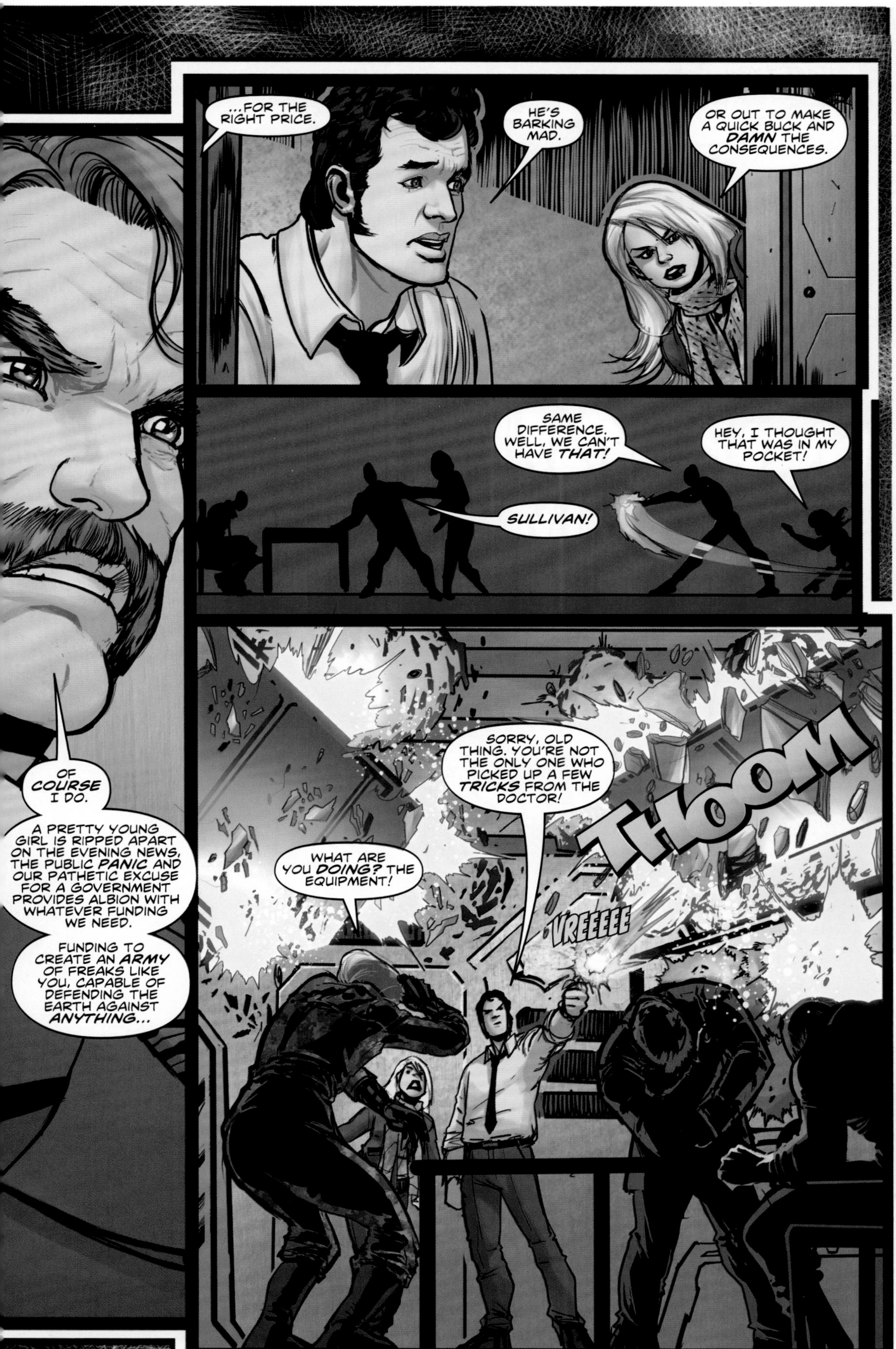
...FOR THE RIGHT PRICE.
HE'S BARKING MAD.
OR OUT TO MAKE A QUICK BUCK AND DAMN THE CONSEQUENCES.
SAME DIFFERENCE. WELL, WE CAN'T HAVE THAT!
HEY, I THOUGHT THAT WAS IN MY POCKET!
SULLIVAN!
OF COURSE I DO.
A PRETTY YOUNG GIRL IS RIPPED APART ON THE EVENING NEWS, THE PUBLIC PANIC AND OUR PATHETIC EXCUSE FOR A GOVERNMENT PROVIDES ALBION WITH WHATEVER FUNDING WE NEED.
FUNDING TO CREATE AN ARMY OF FREAKS LIKE YOU, CAPABLE OF DEFENDING THE EARTH AGAINST ANYTHING...
SORRY, OLD THING. YOU'RE NOT THE ONLY ONE WHO PICKED UP A FEW TRICKS FROM THE DOCTOR!
THOOM
WHAT ARE YOU DOING? THE EQUIPMENT!
VREEEEE

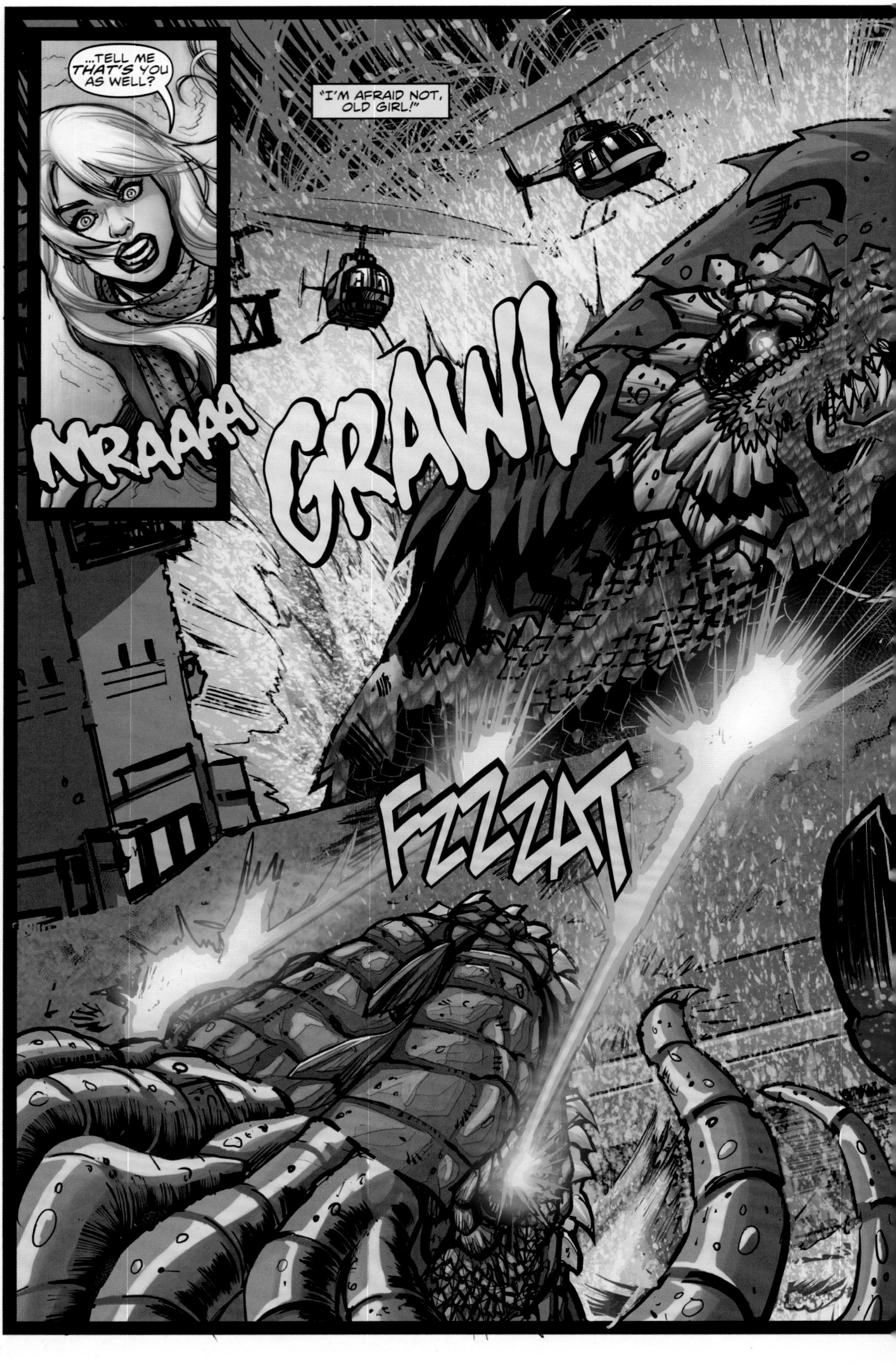

...TELL ME THAT'S YOU AS WELL?
"I'M AFRAID NOT, OLD GIRL!"
MRAAAA
GRAWL
FZZZAT

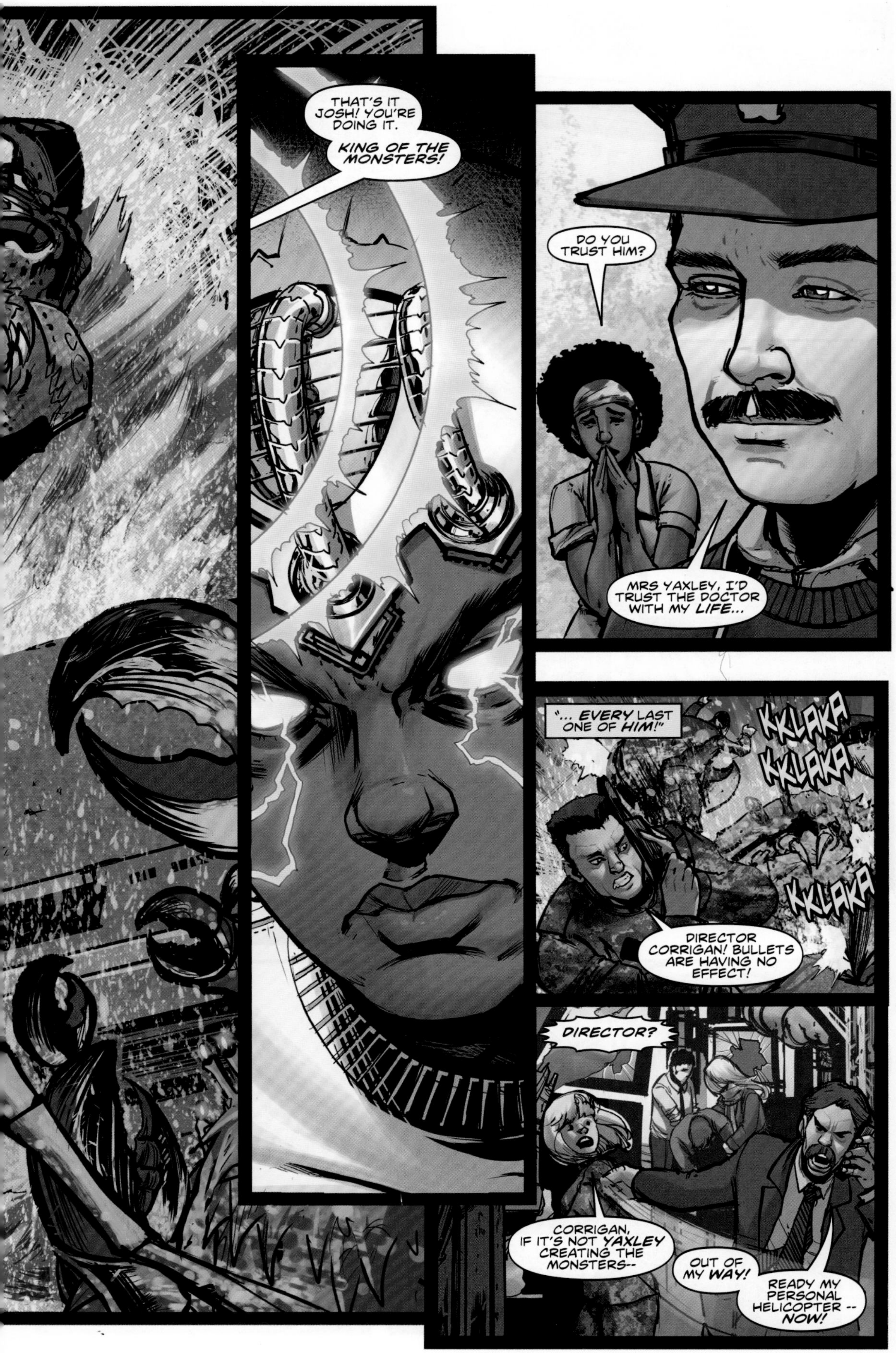
THAT'S IT JOSH! YOU'RE DOING IT.
KING OF THE MONSTERS!
DO YOU TRUST HIM?
MRS YAXLEY, I'D TRUST THE DOCTOR WITH MY LIFE...
"... EVERY LAST ONE OF HIM!"
KKLAKA
KKLAKA
KKLAKA
DIRECTOR CORRIGAN! BULLETS ARE HAVING NO EFFECT!
DIRECTOR?
CORRIGAN, IF IT'S NOT YAXLEY CREATING THE MONSTERS--
OUT OF MY WAY!
READY MY PERSONAL HELICOPTER -- NOW!

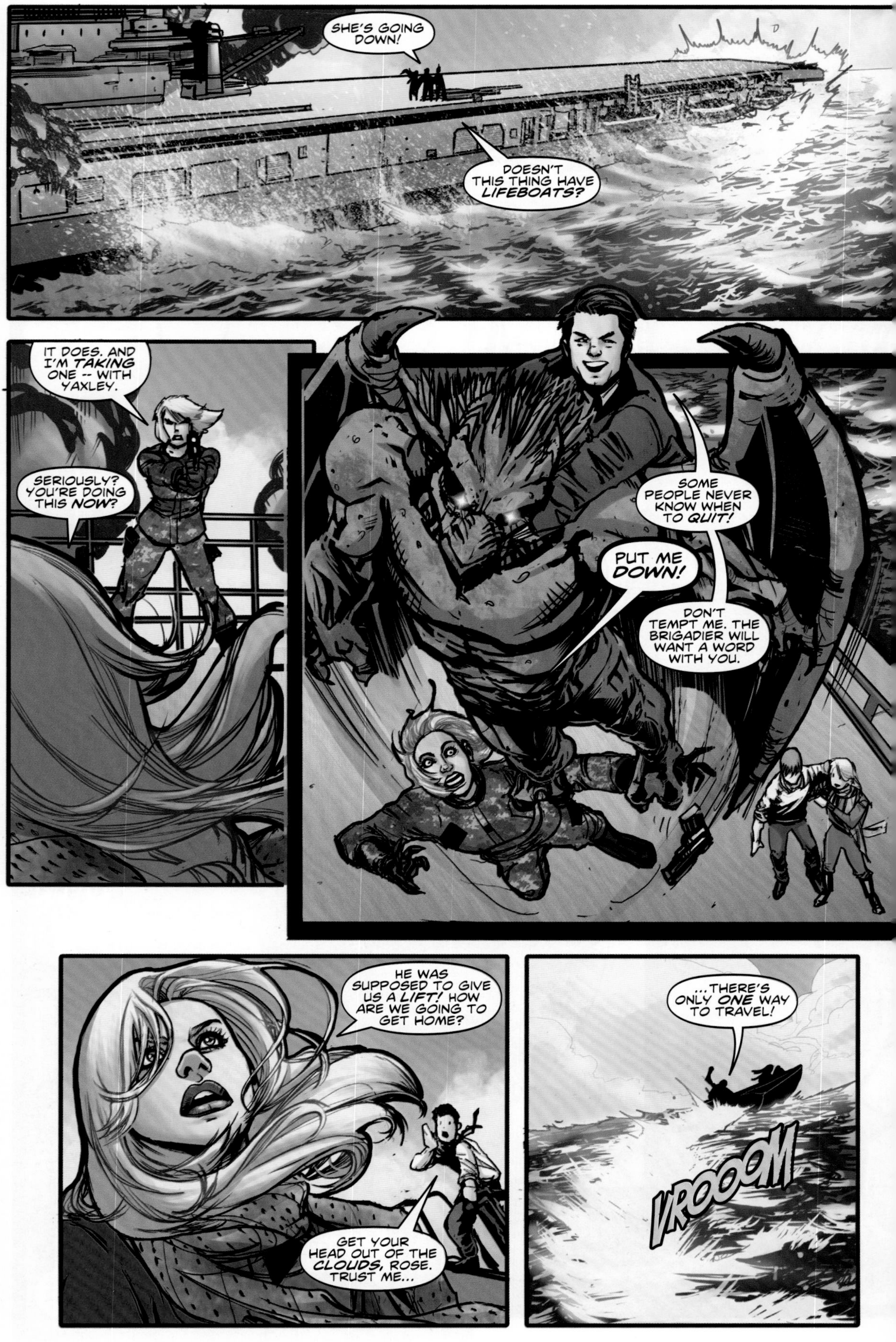
SHE'S GOING DOWN!
DOESN'T THIS THING HAVE *LIFEBOATS?*
IT DOES. AND I'M *TAKING* ONE -- WITH YAXLEY.
SERIOUSLY? YOU'RE DOING THIS *NOW?*
SOME PEOPLE NEVER KNOW WHEN TO *QUIT!*
PUT ME *DOWN!*
DON'T TEMPT ME. THE BRIGADIER WILL WANT A WORD WITH YOU.
HE WAS SUPPOSED TO GIVE US A *LIFT!* HOW ARE WE GOING TO GET HOME?
GET YOUR HEAD OUT OF THE *CLOUDS,* ROSE. TRUST ME...
...THERE'S ONLY *ONE* WAY TO TRAVEL!
VROOOM

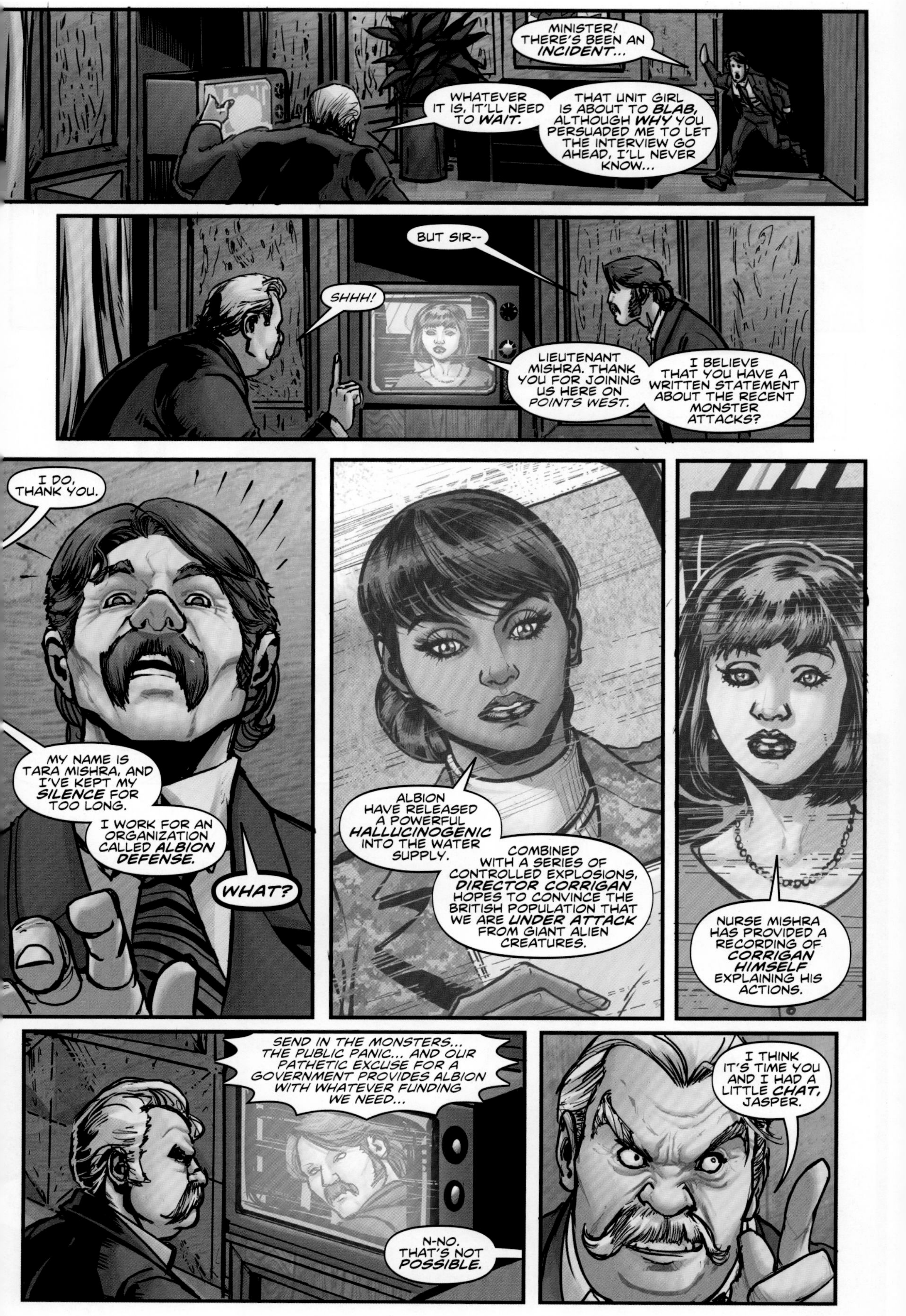
MINISTER! THERE'S BEEN AN INCIDENT...
WHATEVER IT IS, IT'LL NEED TO WAIT.
THAT UNIT GIRL IS ABOUT TO BLAB, ALTHOUGH WHY YOU PERSUADED ME TO LET THE INTERVIEW GO AHEAD, I'LL NEVER KNOW...
BUT SIR--
SHHH!
LIEUTENANT MISHRA. THANK YOU FOR JOINING US HERE ON POINTS WEST.
I BELIEVE THAT YOU HAVE A WRITTEN STATEMENT ABOUT THE RECENT MONSTER ATTACKS?
I DO, THANK YOU.
MY NAME IS TARA MISHRA, AND I'VE KEPT MY SILENCE FOR TOO LONG.
I WORK FOR AN ORGANIZATION CALLED ALBION DEFENSE.
WHAT?
ALBION HAVE RELEASED A POWERFUL HALLUCINOGENIC INTO THE WATER SUPPLY.
COMBINED WITH A SERIES OF CONTROLLED EXPLOSIONS, DIRECTOR CORRIGAN HOPES TO CONVINCE THE BRITISH POPULATION THAT WE ARE UNDER ATTACK FROM GIANT ALIEN CREATURES.
NURSE MISHRA HAS PROVIDED A RECORDING OF CORRIGAN HIMSELF EXPLAINING HIS ACTIONS.
SEND IN THE MONSTERS... THE PUBLIC PANIC... AND OUR PATHETIC EXCUSE FOR A GOVERNMENT PROVIDES ALBION WITH WHATEVER FUNDING WE NEED...
N-NO. THAT'S NOT POSSIBLE.
I THINK IT'S TIME YOU AND I HAD A LITTLE CHAT, JASPER.

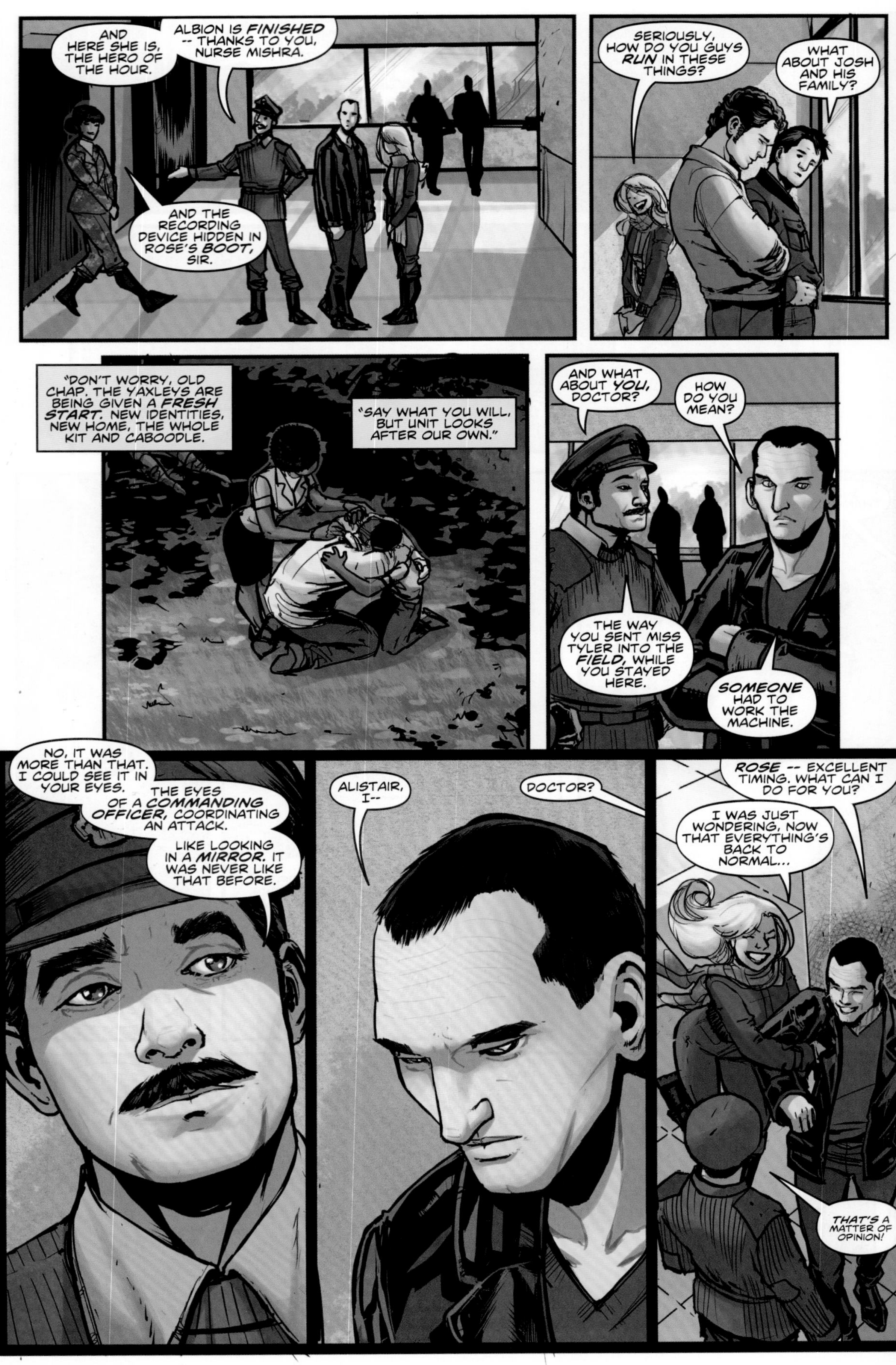
AND HERE SHE IS, THE HERO OF THE HOUR.
ALBION IS FINISHED -- THANKS TO YOU, NURSE MISHRA.
AND THE RECORDING DEVICE HIDDEN IN ROSE'S BOOT, SIR.
SERIOUSLY, HOW DO YOU GUYS RUN IN THESE THINGS?
WHAT ABOUT JOSH AND HIS FAMILY?
"DON'T WORRY, OLD CHAP. THE YAXLEYS ARE BEING GIVEN A FRESH START. NEW IDENTITIES, NEW HOME, THE WHOLE KIT AND CABOODLE.
"SAY WHAT YOU WILL, BUT UNIT LOOKS AFTER OUR OWN."
AND WHAT ABOUT YOU, DOCTOR?
HOW DO YOU MEAN?
THE WAY YOU SENT MISS TYLER INTO THE FIELD, WHILE YOU STAYED HERE.
SOMEONE HAD TO WORK THE MACHINE.
NO, IT WAS MORE THAN THAT. I COULD SEE IT IN YOUR EYES.
THE EYES OF A COMMANDING OFFICER, COORDINATING AN ATTACK.
LIKE LOOKING IN A MIRROR. IT WAS NEVER LIKE THAT BEFORE.
ALISTAIR, I--
DOCTOR?
ROSE -- EXCELLENT TIMING. WHAT CAN I DO FOR YOU?
I WAS JUST WONDERING, NOW THAT EVERYTHING'S BACK TO NORMAL...
THAT'S A MATTER OF OPINION!

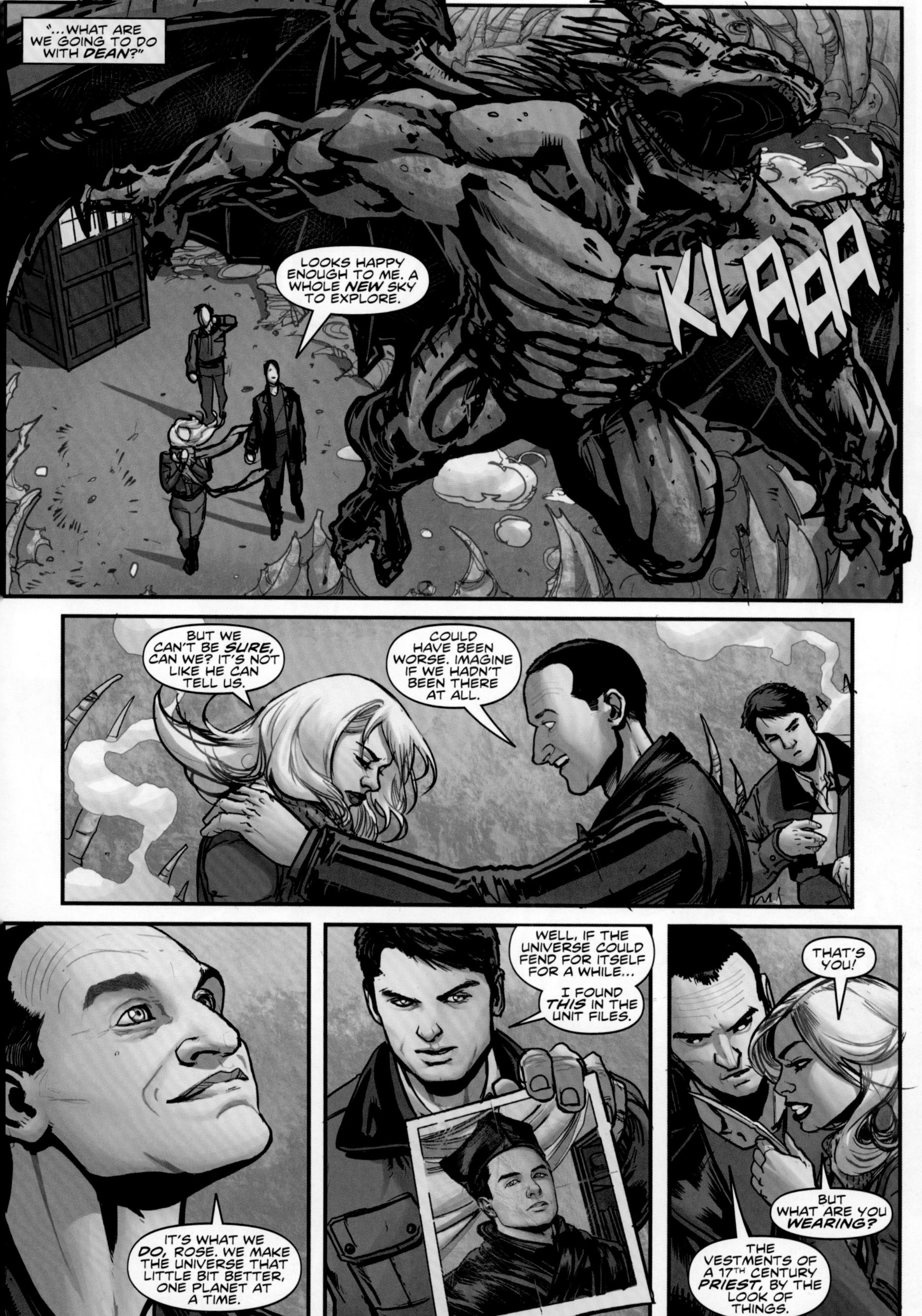
"...WHAT ARE WE GOING TO DO WITH DEAN?"
LOOKS HAPPY ENOUGH TO ME. A WHOLE NEW SKY TO EXPLORE.
KLAAA
BUT WE CAN'T BE SURE, CAN WE? IT'S NOT LIKE HE CAN TELL US.
COULD HAVE BEEN WORSE. IMAGINE IF WE HADN'T BEEN THERE AT ALL.
IT'S WHAT WE DO, ROSE. WE MAKE THE UNIVERSE THAT LITTLE BIT BETTER, ONE PLANET AT A TIME.
WELL, IF THE UNIVERSE COULD FEND FOR ITSELF FOR A WHILE...
I FOUND THIS IN THE UNIT FILES.
THAT'S YOU!
BUT WHAT ARE YOU WEARING?
THE VESTMENTS OF A 17TH CENTURY PRIEST, BY THE LOOK OF THINGS.

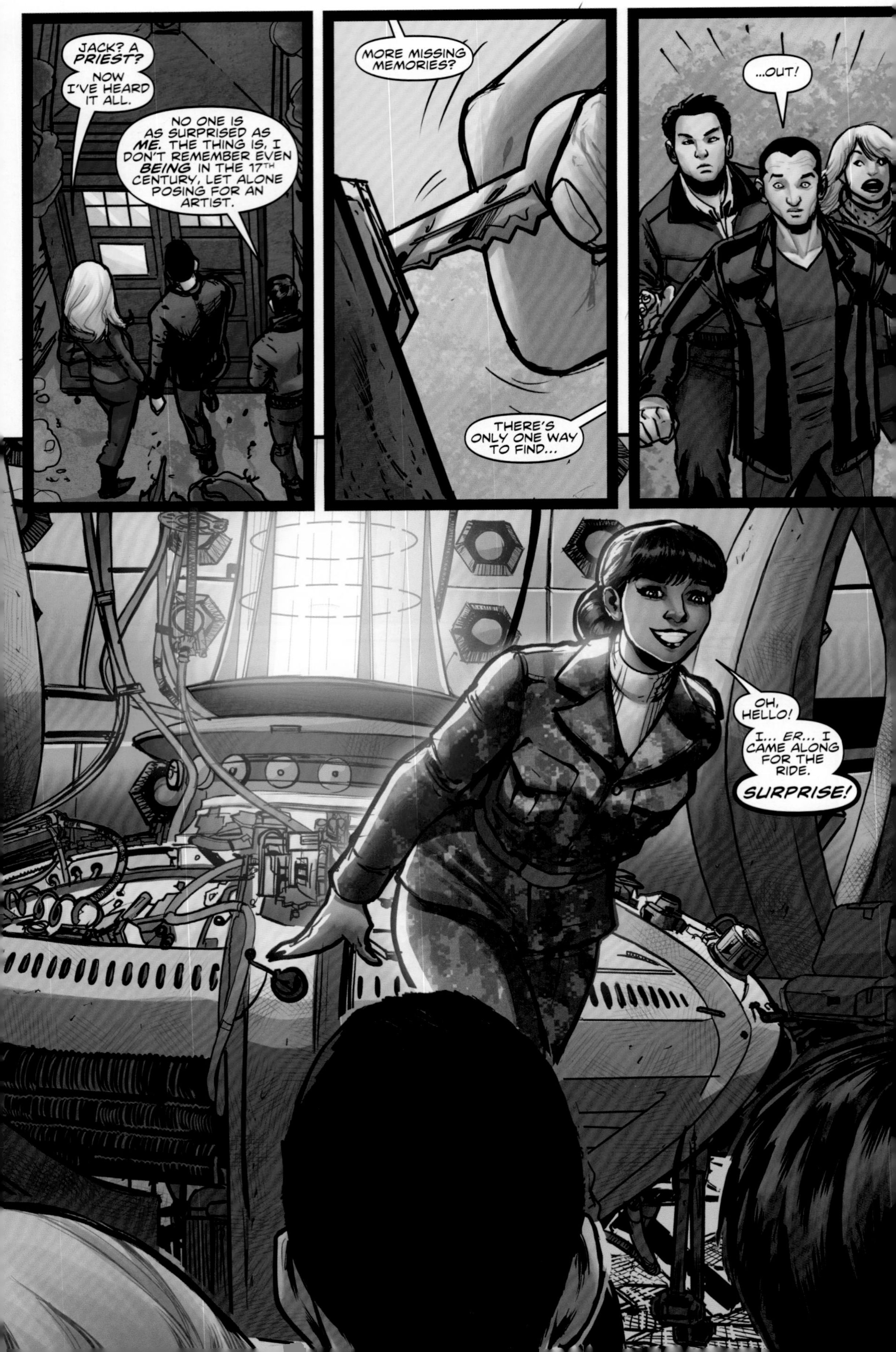
JACK? A PRIEST? NOW I'VE HEARD IT ALL.
NO ONE IS AS SURPRISED AS ME. THE THING IS, I DON'T REMEMBER EVEN BEING IN THE 17TH CENTURY, LET ALONE POSING FOR AN ARTIST.
MORE MISSING MEMORIES?
THERE'S ONLY ONE WAY TO FIND...
...OUT!
OH, HELLO!
I... ER... I CAME ALONG FOR THE RIDE.
SURPRISE!

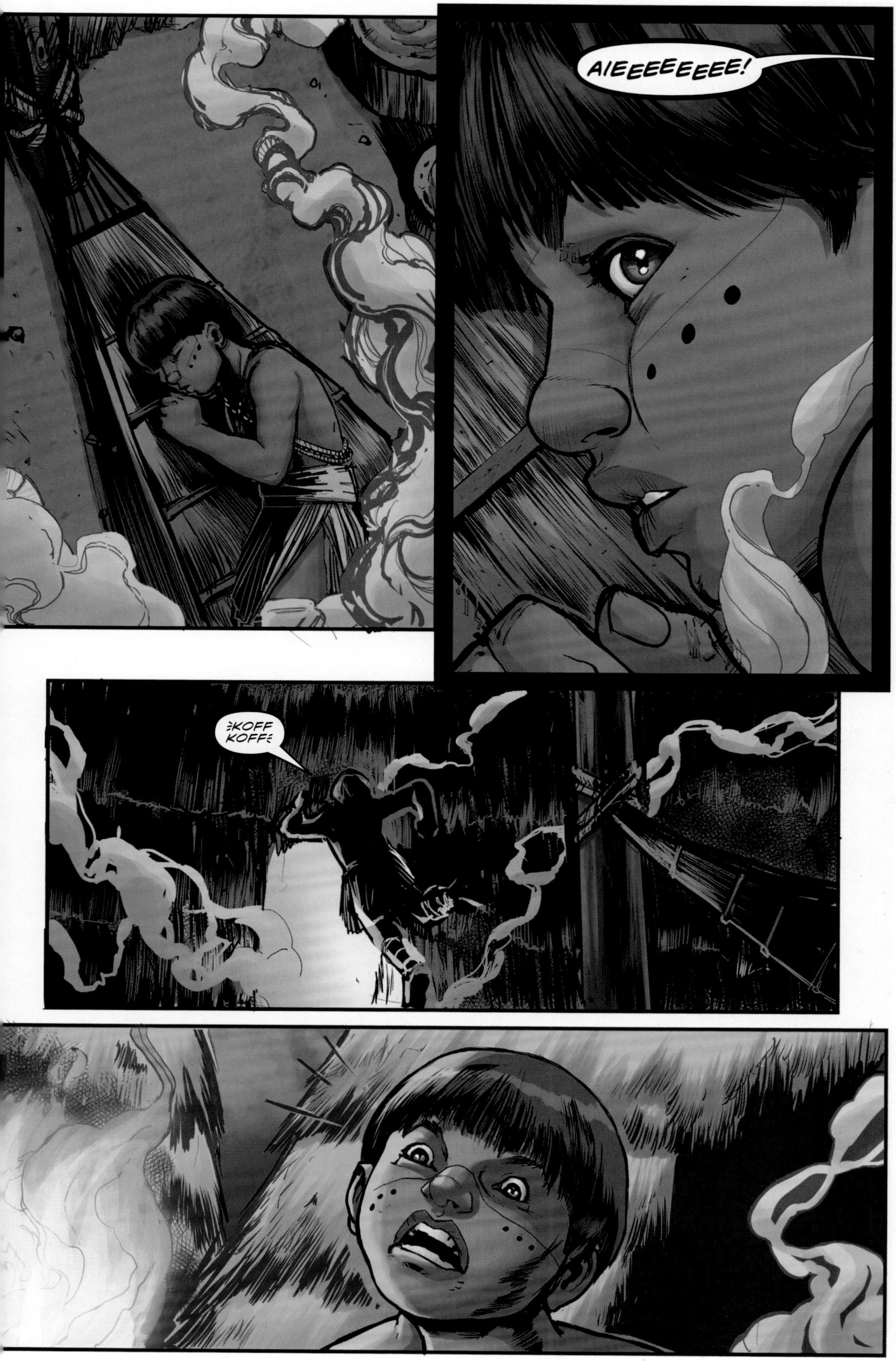
AIEEEEEEEE!
KOFF KOFF

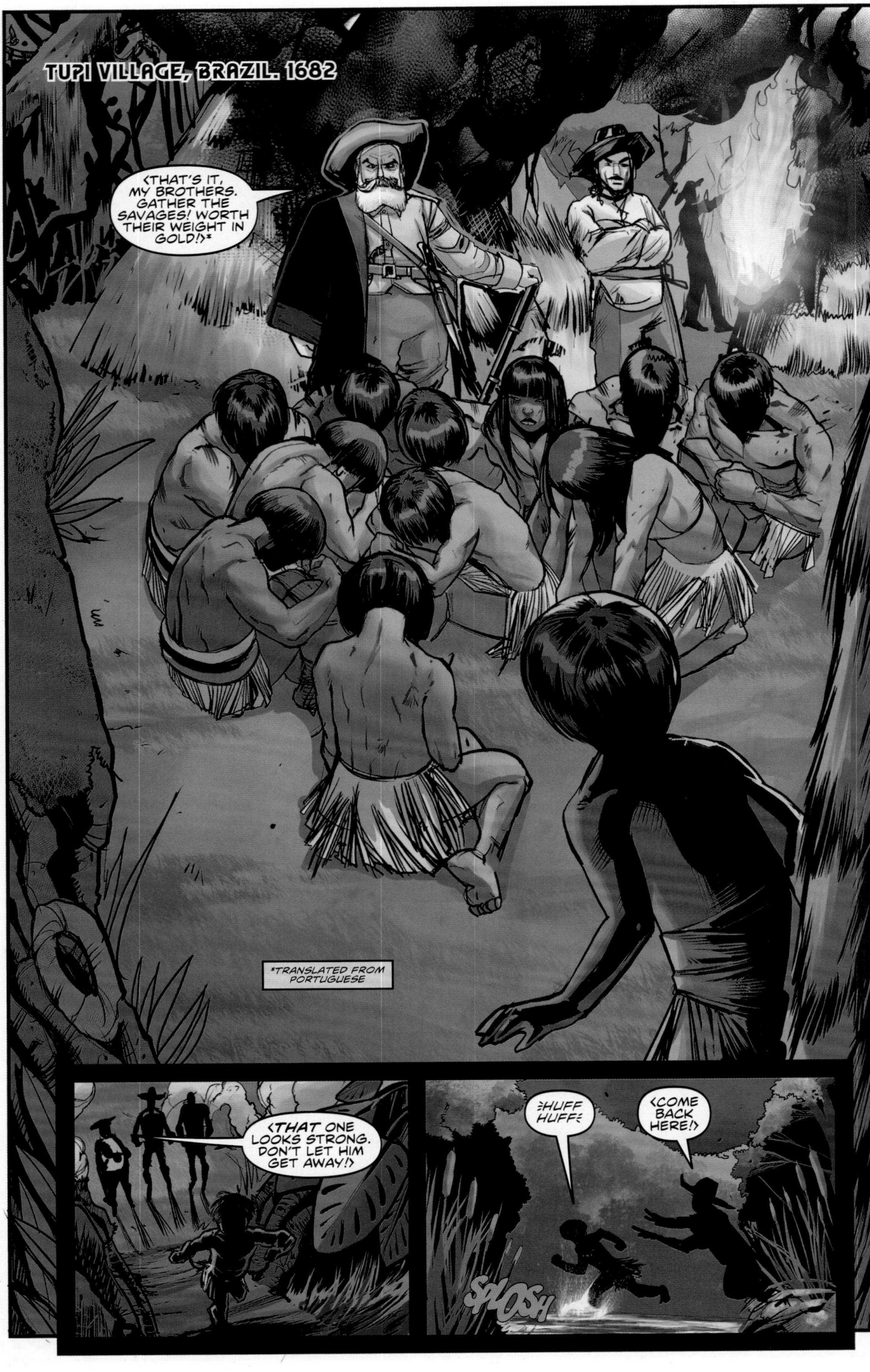
TUPI VILLAGE, BRAZIL. 1682
<THAT'S IT, MY BROTHERS. GATHER THE SAVAGES! WORTH THEIR WEIGHT IN GOLD!>*
*TRANSLATED FROM PORTUGUESE
<THAT ONE LOOKS STRONG. DON'T LET HIM GET AWAY!>
HUFF HUFF
<COME BACK HERE!>
SPLOSH

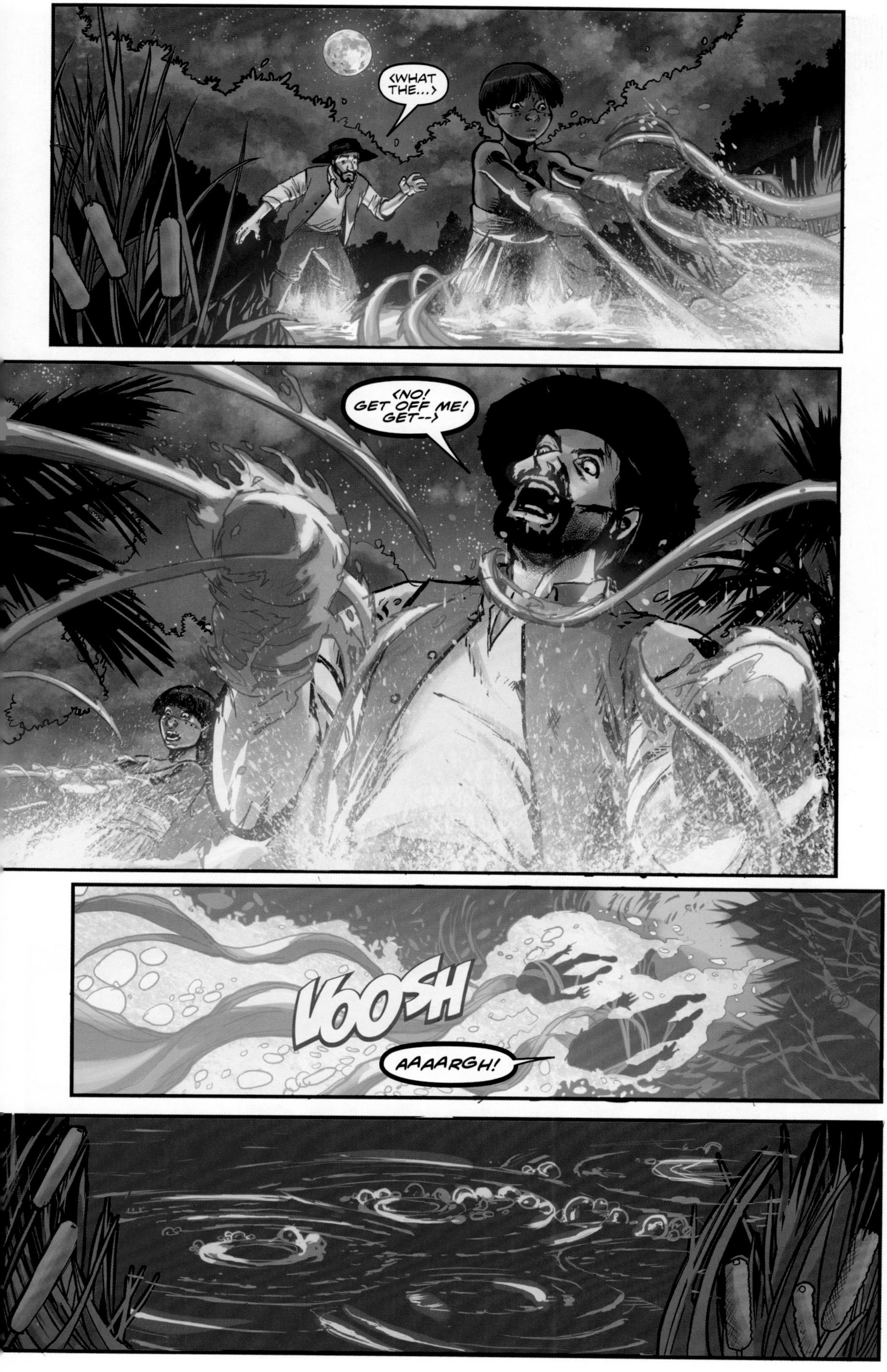
<WHAT THE...>
<NO! GET OFF ME! GET-->
VOOSH
AAAARGH!

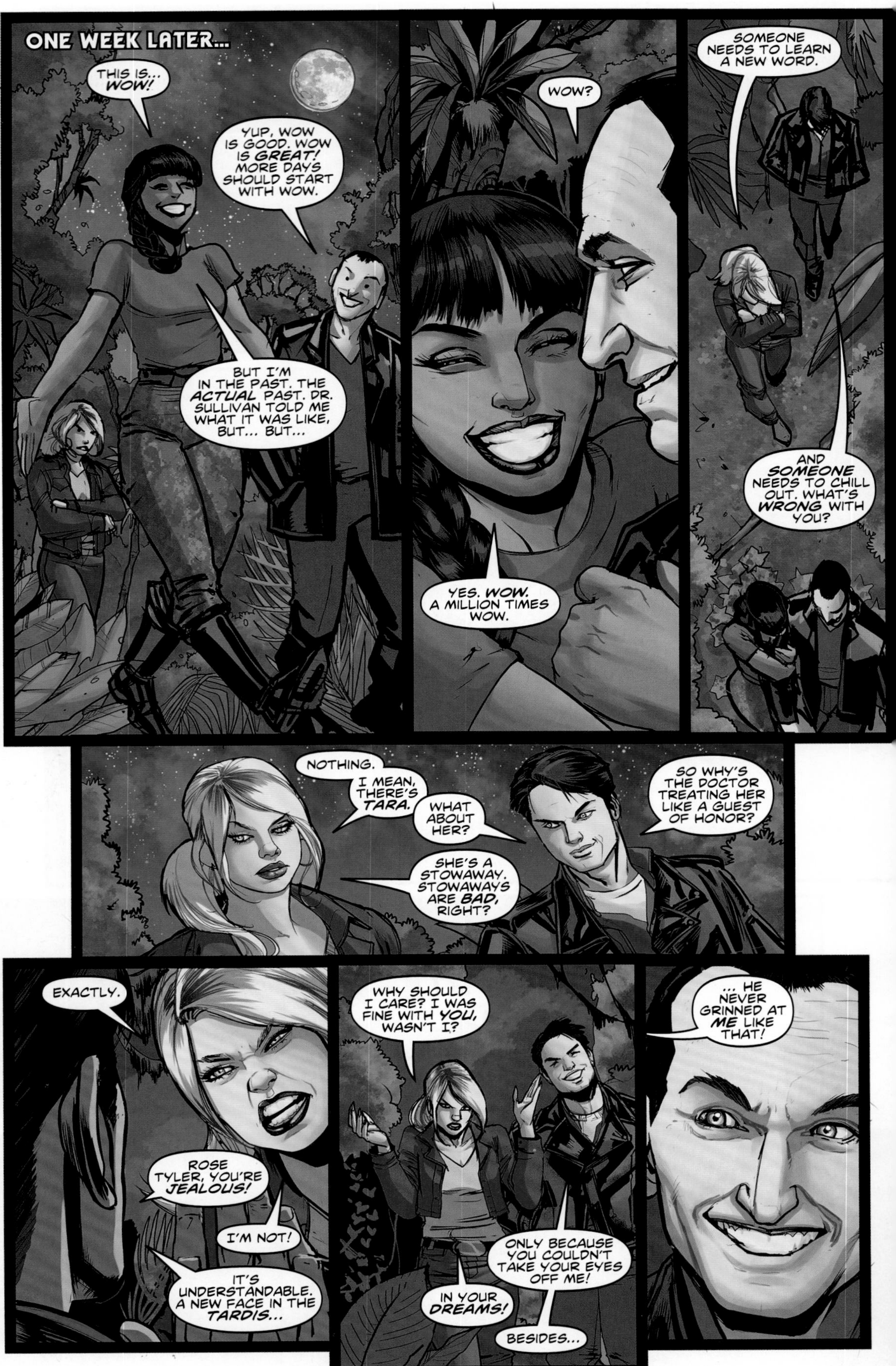
ONE WEEK LATER...
THIS IS... WOW!
YUP, WOW IS GOOD. WOW IS GREAT! MORE DAYS SHOULD START WITH WOW.
BUT I'M IN THE PAST. THE ACTUAL PAST. DR. SULLIVAN TOLD ME WHAT IT WAS LIKE, BUT... BUT...
WOW?
YES. WOW. A MILLION TIMES WOW.
SOMEONE NEEDS TO LEARN A NEW WORD.
AND SOMEONE NEEDS TO CHILL OUT. WHAT'S WRONG WITH YOU?
NOTHING. I MEAN, THERE'S TARA.
WHAT ABOUT HER?
SHE'S A STOWAWAY. STOWAWAYS ARE BAD, RIGHT?
SO WHY'S THE DOCTOR TREATING HER LIKE A GUEST OF HONOR?
EXACTLY.
ROSE TYLER, YOU'RE JEALOUS!
I'M NOT!
IT'S UNDERSTANDABLE. A NEW FACE IN THE TARDIS...
WHY SHOULD I CARE? I WAS FINE WITH YOU, WASN'T I?
ONLY BECAUSE YOU COULDN'T TAKE YOUR EYES OFF ME!
IN YOUR DREAMS!
BESIDES...
... HE NEVER GRINNED AT ME LIKE THAT!

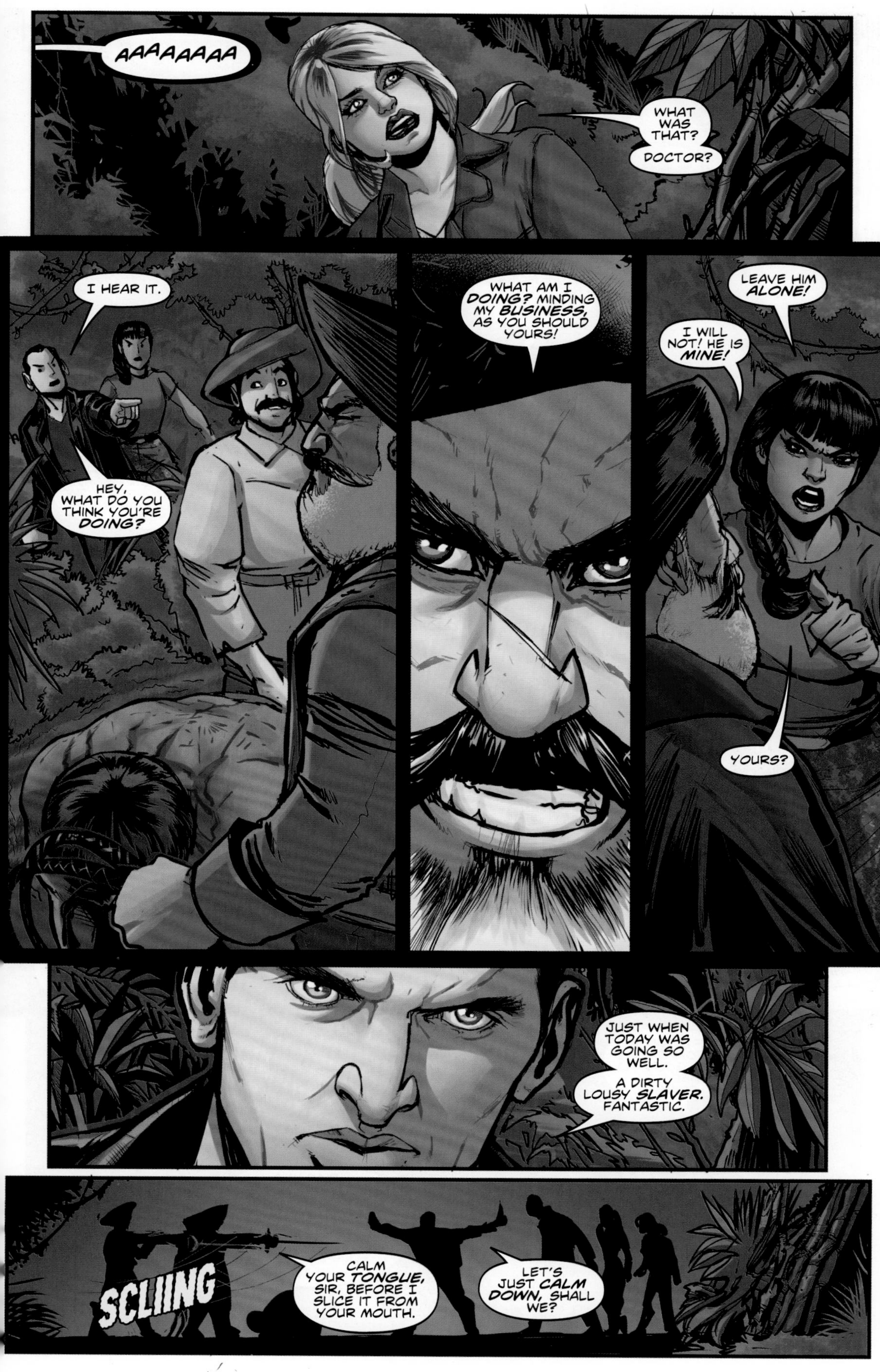
AAAAAAAA
WHAT WAS THAT?
DOCTOR?
I HEAR IT.
HEY, WHAT DO YOU THINK YOU'RE DOING?
WHAT AM I DOING? MINDING MY BUSINESS, AS YOU SHOULD YOURS!
LEAVE HIM ALONE!
I WILL NOT! HE IS MINE!
YOURS?
JUST WHEN TODAY WAS GOING SO WELL.
A DIRTY LOUSY SLAVER. FANTASTIC.
SCLIING
CALM YOUR TONGUE, SIR, BEFORE I SLICE IT FROM YOUR MOUTH.
LET'S JUST CALM DOWN, SHALL WE?

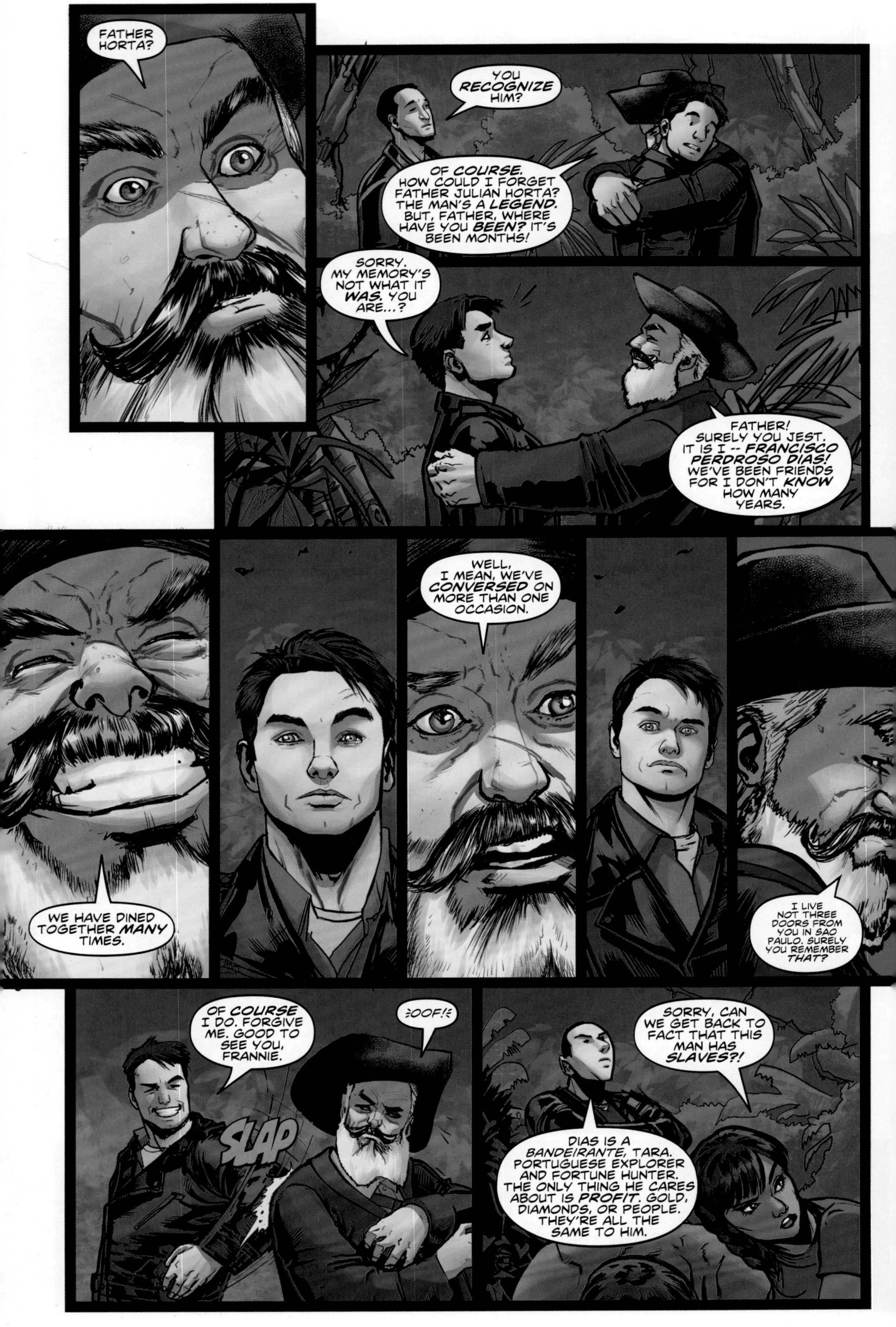
FATHER HORTA?
YOU RECOGNIZE HIM?
OF COURSE. HOW COULD I FORGET FATHER JULIAN HORTA? THE MAN'S A LEGEND. BUT, FATHER, WHERE HAVE YOU BEEN? IT'S BEEN MONTHS!
SORRY. MY MEMORY'S NOT WHAT IT WAS. YOU ARE...?
FATHER! SURELY YOU JEST. IT IS I -- FRANCISCO PERDROSO DIAS! WE'VE BEEN FRIENDS FOR I DON'T KNOW HOW MANY YEARS.
WE HAVE DINED TOGETHER MANY TIMES.
WELL, I MEAN, WE'VE CONVERSED ON MORE THAN ONE OCCASION.
I LIVE NOT THREE DOORS FROM YOU IN SAO PAULO. SURELY YOU REMEMBER THAT?
OF COURSE I DO. FORGIVE ME. GOOD TO SEE YOU, FRANNIE.
OOF!
SLAP
SORRY, CAN WE GET BACK TO FACT THAT THIS MAN HAS SLAVES?!
DIAS IS A BANDEIRANTE, TARA. PORTUGUESE EXPLORER AND FORTUNE HUNTER. THE ONLY THING HE CARES ABOUT IS PROFIT. GOLD, DIAMONDS, OR PEOPLE. THEY'RE ALL THE SAME TO HIM.

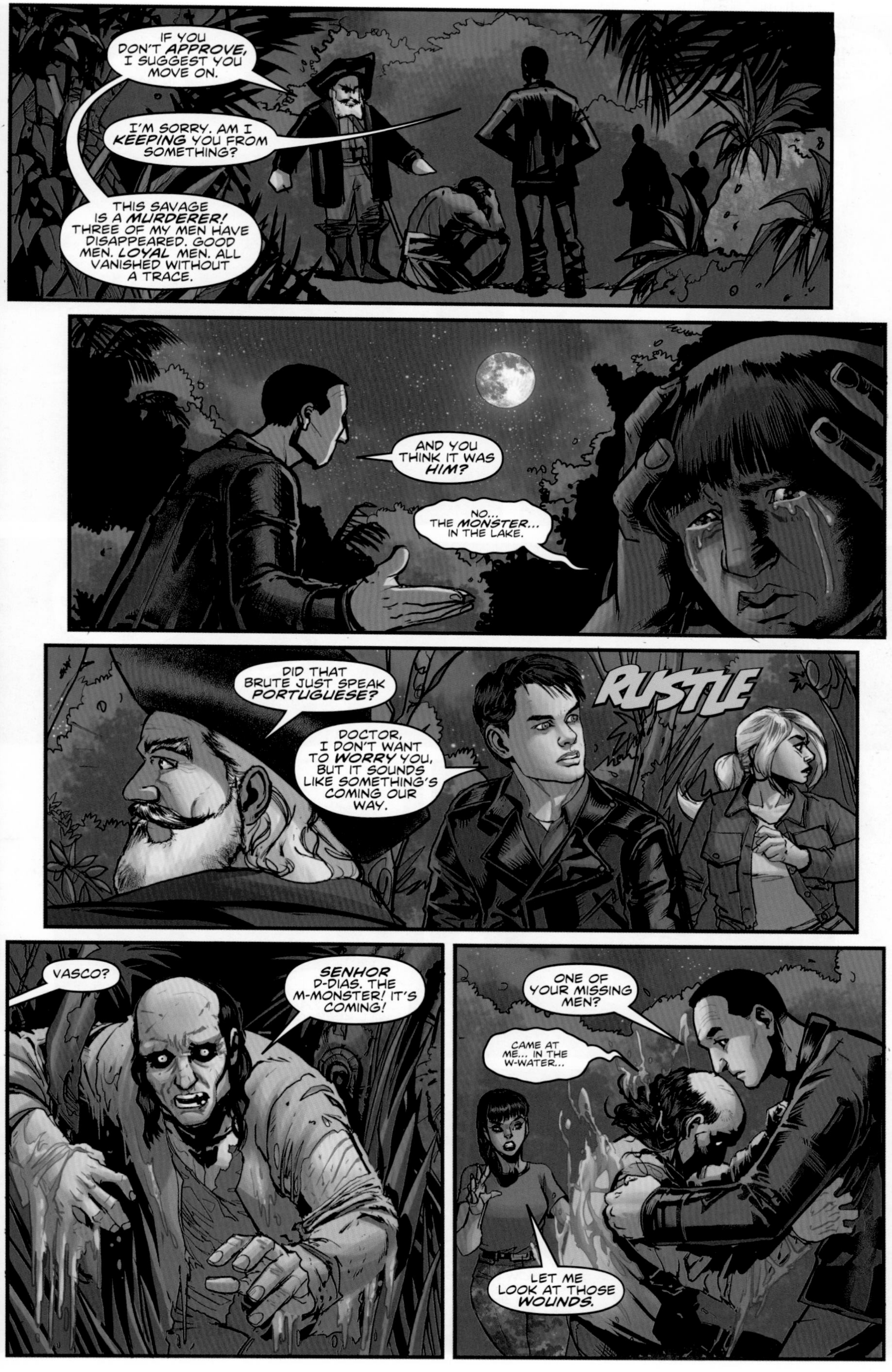
IF YOU DON'T APPROVE, I SUGGEST YOU MOVE ON.
I'M SORRY. AM I KEEPING YOU FROM SOMETHING?
THIS SAVAGE IS A MURDERER! THREE OF MY MEN HAVE DISAPPEARED. GOOD MEN. LOYAL MEN. ALL VANISHED WITHOUT A TRACE.
AND YOU THINK IT WAS HIM?
NO... THE MONSTER... IN THE LAKE.
DID THAT BRUTE JUST SPEAK PORTUGUESE?
RUSTLE
DOCTOR, I DON'T WANT TO WORRY YOU, BUT IT SOUNDS LIKE SOMETHING'S COMING OUR WAY.
VASCO?
SENHOR D-DIAS. THE M-MONSTER! IT'S COMING!
ONE OF YOUR MISSING MEN?
CAME AT ME... IN THE W-WATER...
LET ME LOOK AT THOSE WOUNDS.

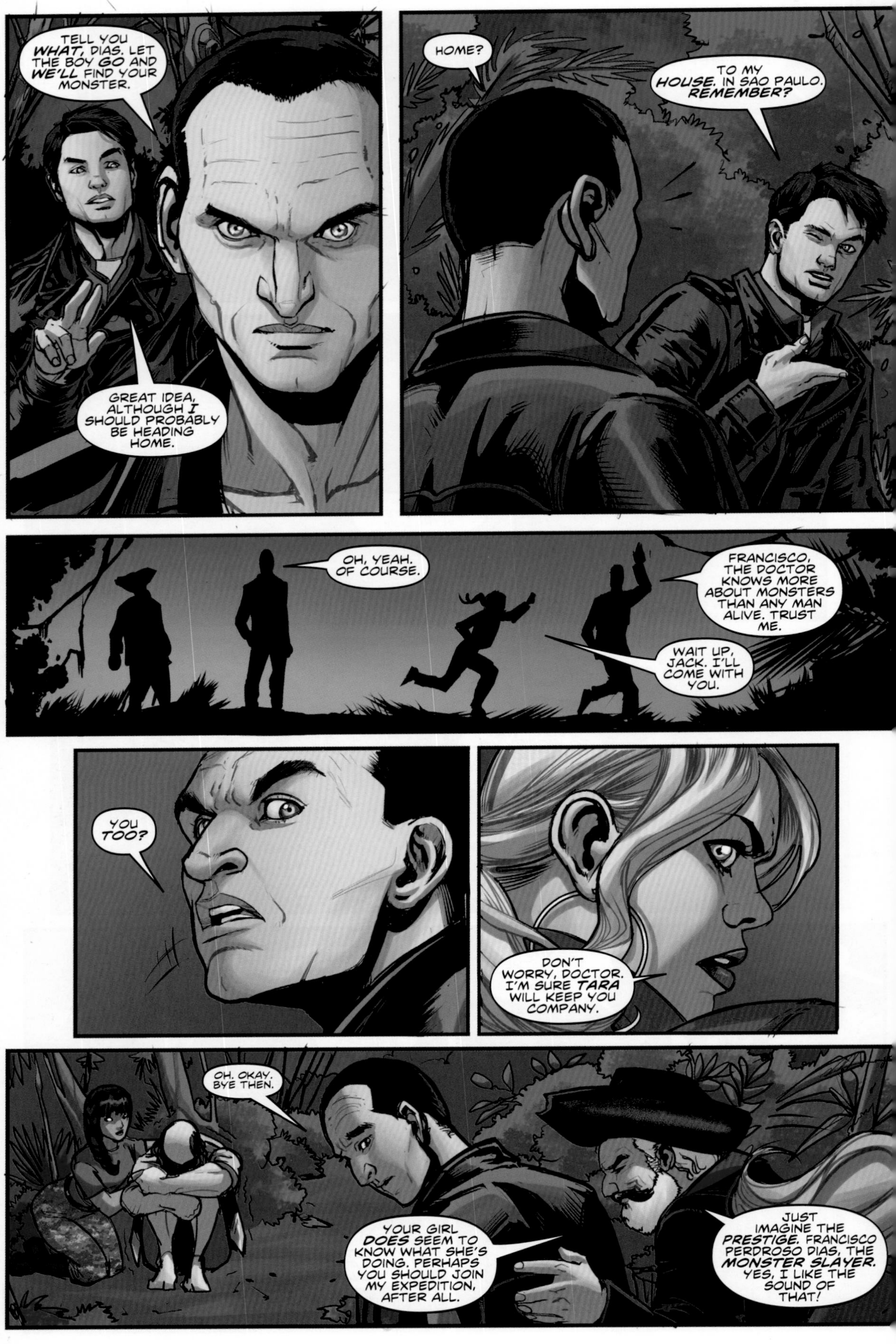
TELL YOU WHAT, DIAS. LET THE BOY GO AND WE'LL FIND YOUR MONSTER.
GREAT IDEA, ALTHOUGH I SHOULD PROBABLY BE HEADING HOME.
HOME?
TO MY HOUSE. IN SAO PAULO. REMEMBER?
OH, YEAH. OF COURSE.
FRANCISCO, THE DOCTOR KNOWS MORE ABOUT MONSTERS THAN ANY MAN ALIVE. TRUST ME.
WAIT UP, JACK. I'LL COME WITH YOU.
YOU TOO?
DON'T WORRY, DOCTOR. I'M SURE TARA WILL KEEP YOU COMPANY.
OH. OKAY. BYE THEN.
YOUR GIRL DOES SEEM TO KNOW WHAT SHE'S DOING. PERHAPS YOU SHOULD JOIN MY EXPEDITION, AFTER ALL.
JUST IMAGINE THE PRESTIGE. FRANCISCO PERDROSO DIAS, THE MONSTER SLAYER. YES, I LIKE THE SOUND OF THAT!

AND YOU DON'T REMEMBER *ANY* OF THIS?

MY LIFE AS A JESUIT PRIEST? NOT A THING.

BUT THAT'S WHAT HAPPENS WHEN THE *TIME AGENCY* WIPES YOUR MEMORIES.

BAM

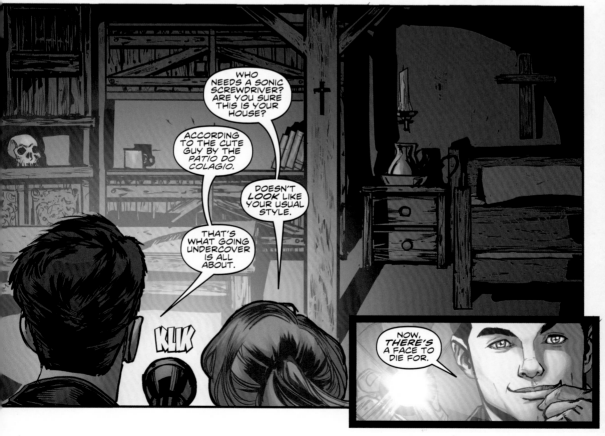

WHO NEEDS A SONIC SCREWDRIVER? ARE YOU SURE THIS IS YOUR HOUSE?

ACCORDING TO THE CUTE GUY BY THE PATIO DO COLAGIO.

DOESN'T *LOOK* LIKE YOUR USUAL STYLE.

THAT'S WHAT GOING UNDERCOVER IS ALL ABOUT.

KLIK

NOW, *THERE'S* A FACE TO DIE FOR.

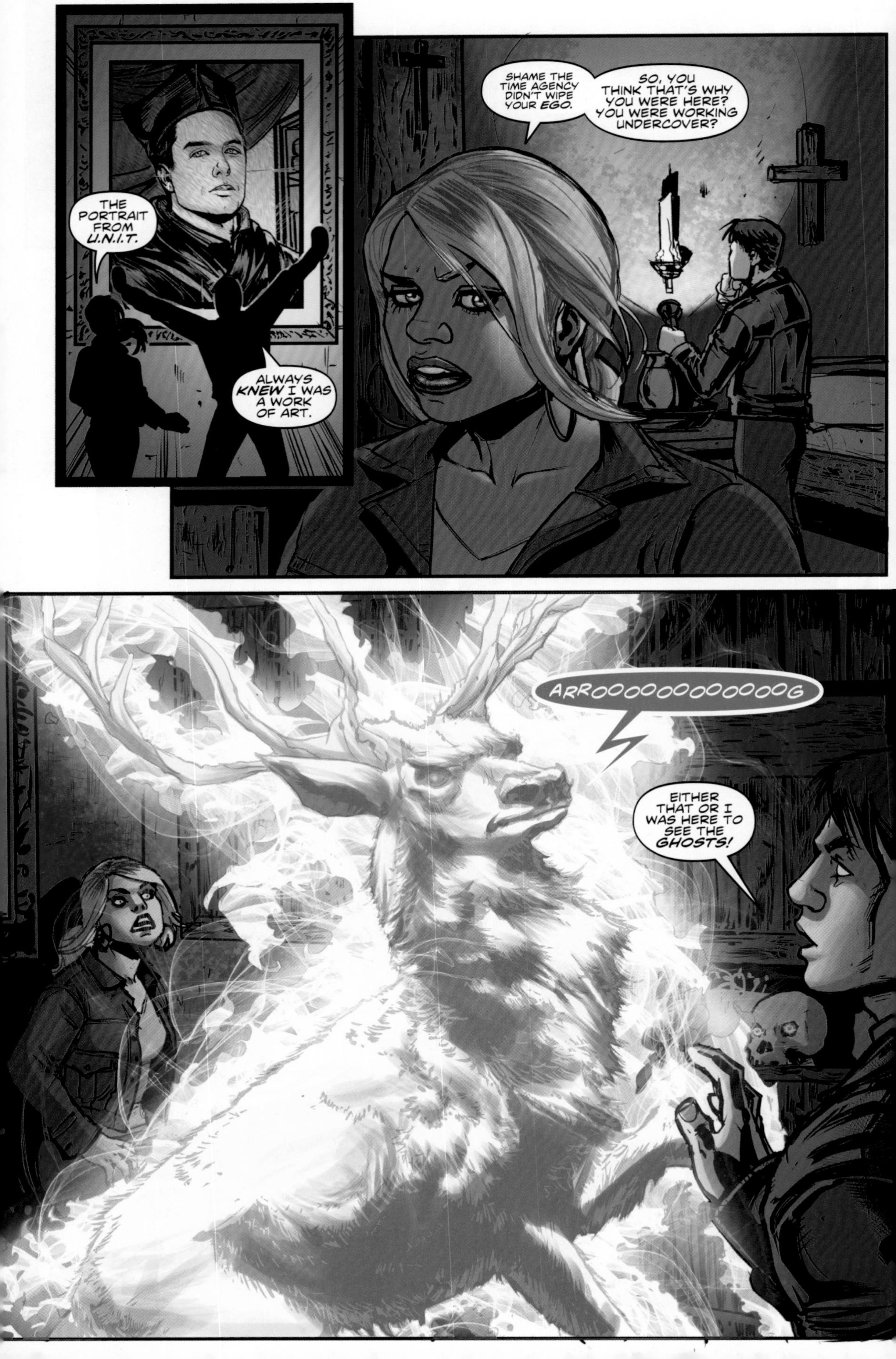
THE PORTRAIT FROM U.N.I.T.
ALWAYS KNEW I WAS A WORK OF ART.
SHAME THE TIME AGENCY DIDN'T WIPE YOUR EGO.
SO, YOU THINK THAT'S WHY YOU WERE HERE? YOU WERE WORKING UNDERCOVER?
ARROOOOOOOOOOOOOG
EITHER THAT OR I WAS HERE TO SEE THE GHOSTS!

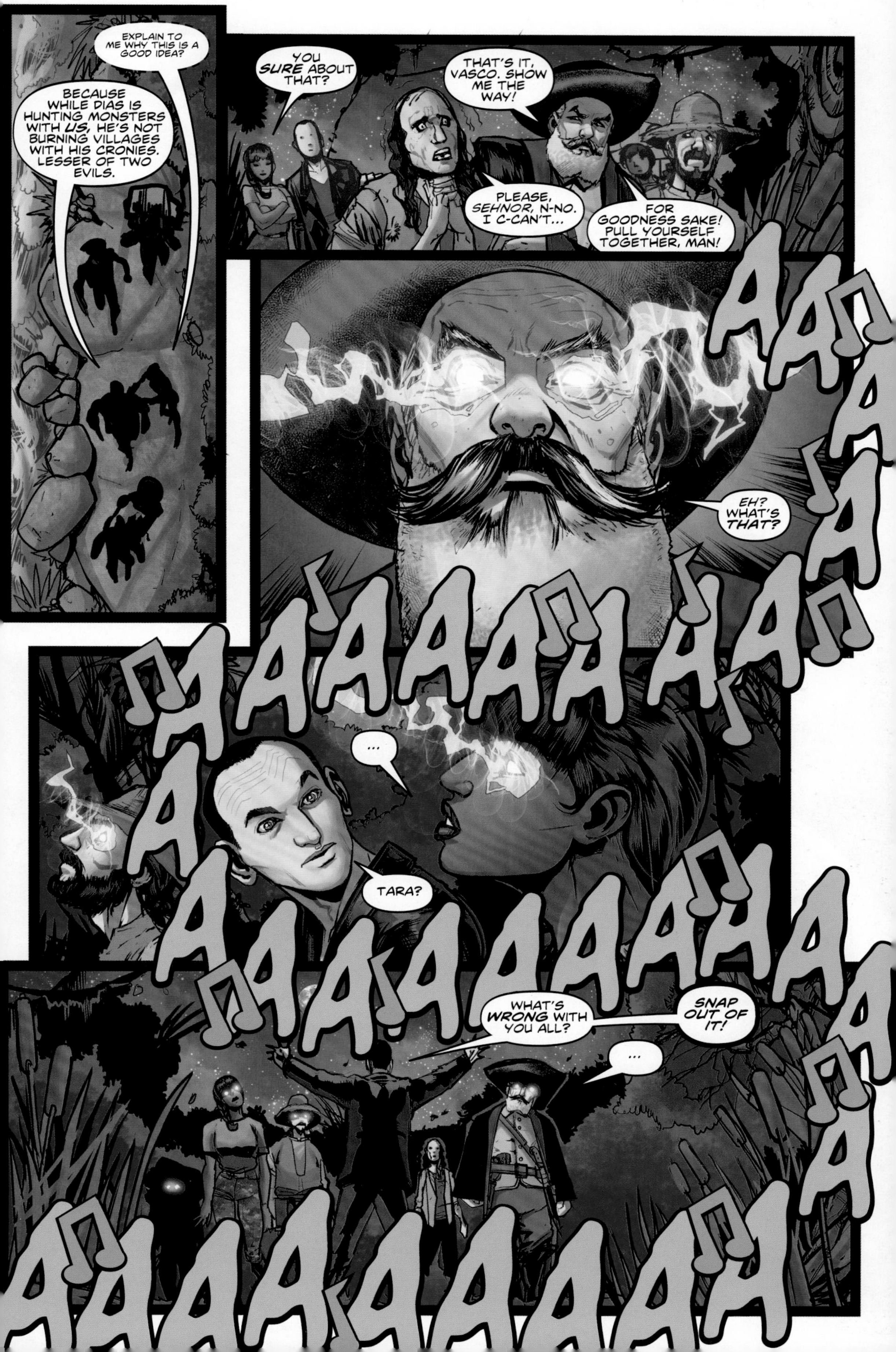
EXPLAIN TO ME WHY THIS IS A GOOD IDEA?
BECAUSE WHILE DIAS IS HUNTING MONSTERS WITH US, HE'S NOT BURNING VILLAGES WITH HIS CRONIES. LESSER OF TWO EVILS.
YOU SURE ABOUT THAT?
THAT'S IT, VASCO. SHOW ME THE WAY!
PLEASE, SEHNOR, N-NO. I C-CAN'T...
FOR GOODNESS SAKE! PULL YOURSELF TOGETHER, MAN!
AAAAAAAAAAAA
EH? WHAT'S THAT?
...
TARA?
AAAAAAAAAAAAAA
WHAT'S WRONG WITH YOU ALL?
SNAP OUT OF IT!
...
AAAAAAAAAAAA

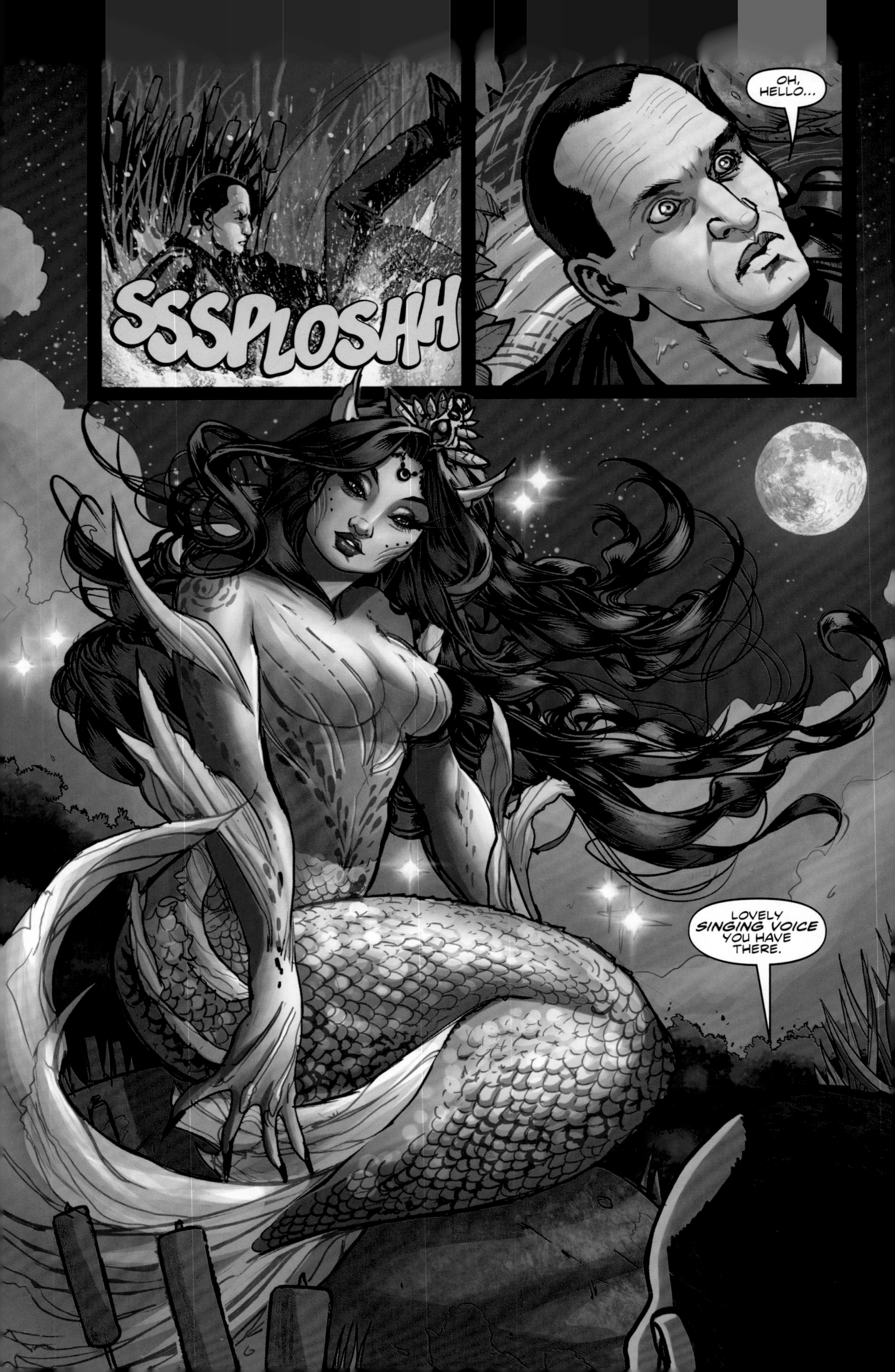
SSSPLOSHH
OH, HELLO...
LOVELY SINGING VOICE YOU HAVE THERE.

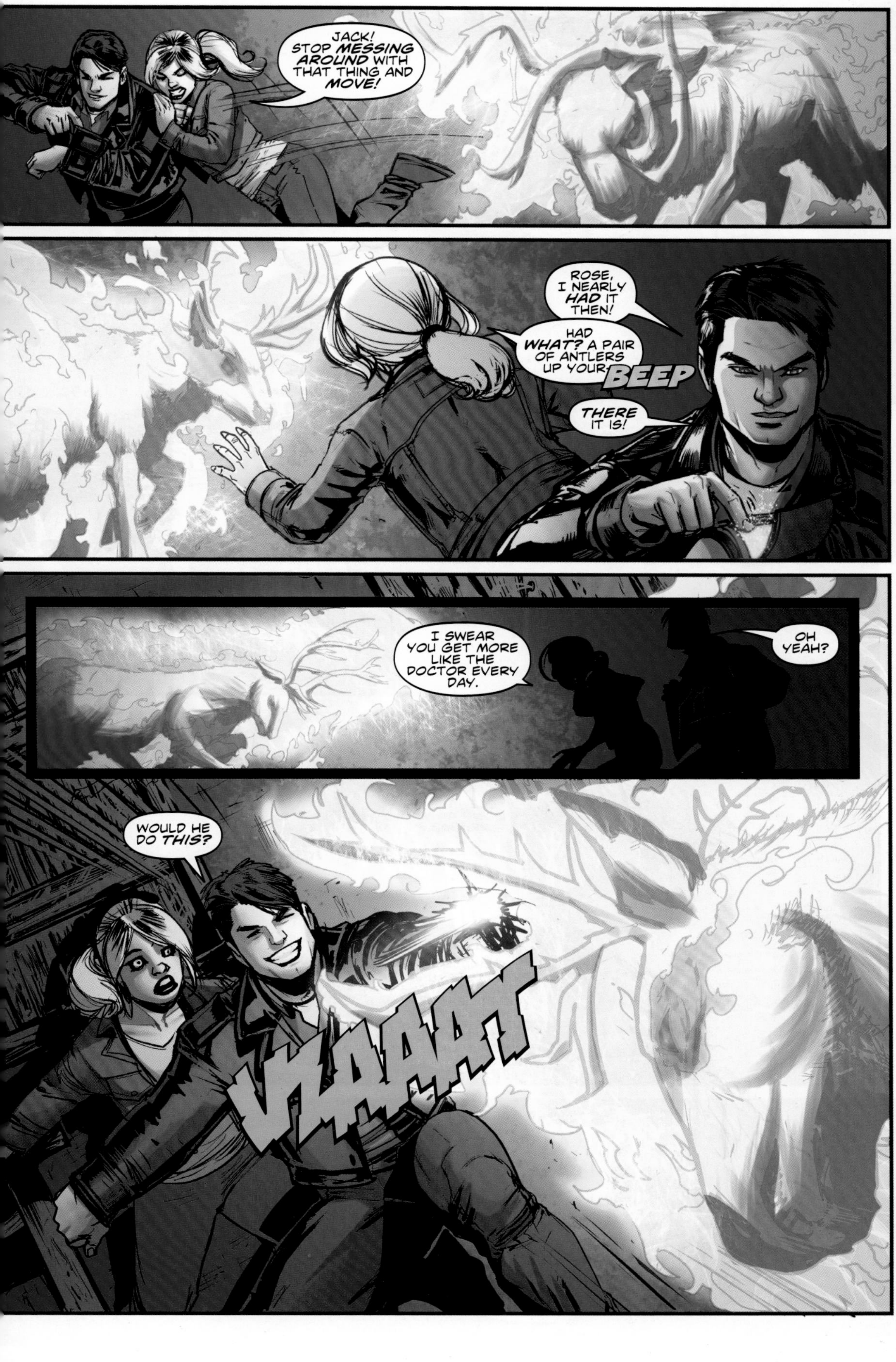

JACK! STOP MESSING AROUND WITH THAT THING AND MOVE!
ROSE, I NEARLY HAD IT THEN!
HAD WHAT? A PAIR OF ANTLERS UP YOUR BEEP
THERE IT IS!
I SWEAR YOU GET MORE LIKE THE DOCTOR EVERY DAY.
OH YEAH?
WOULD HE DO THIS?
VZAAAT

KRAKK

VRMMMMM

SEE YOU ON THE OTHER SIDE!

WHAT DID YOU DO? CROSS THE STREAMS?

IT WASN'T REAL. JUST A HOLOGRAM TO SCARE AWAY THE NATIVES. NO HOLO-PROJECTOR, NO GHOST!

BUT WHY A STAG?

YOUR GUESS IS AS GOOD AS MINE. PROBABLY A LOCAL LEGEND.

STANDARD PROCEDURE. USE INDIGENOUS CUSTOMS AND BELIEFS TO REINFORCE YOUR COVER, ESPECIALLY ON A PRIMITIVE WORLD LIKE THIS.

OI! THAT'S MY PLANET YOU'RE TALKING ABOUT!

NO OFFENSE!

A-HA!

CLIK

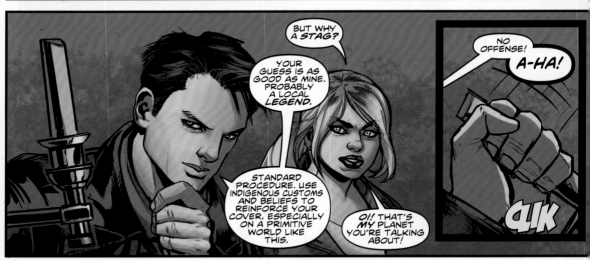

FSSSSSSSSH

REALLY? A FAKE WALL? WHAT IS THIS -- SCOOBY DOO?

HEY, A CLICHÉ ONLY BECOMES A CLICHÉ BECAUSE IT WORKS!

ESPECIALLY ON PRIMITIVE WORLDS.

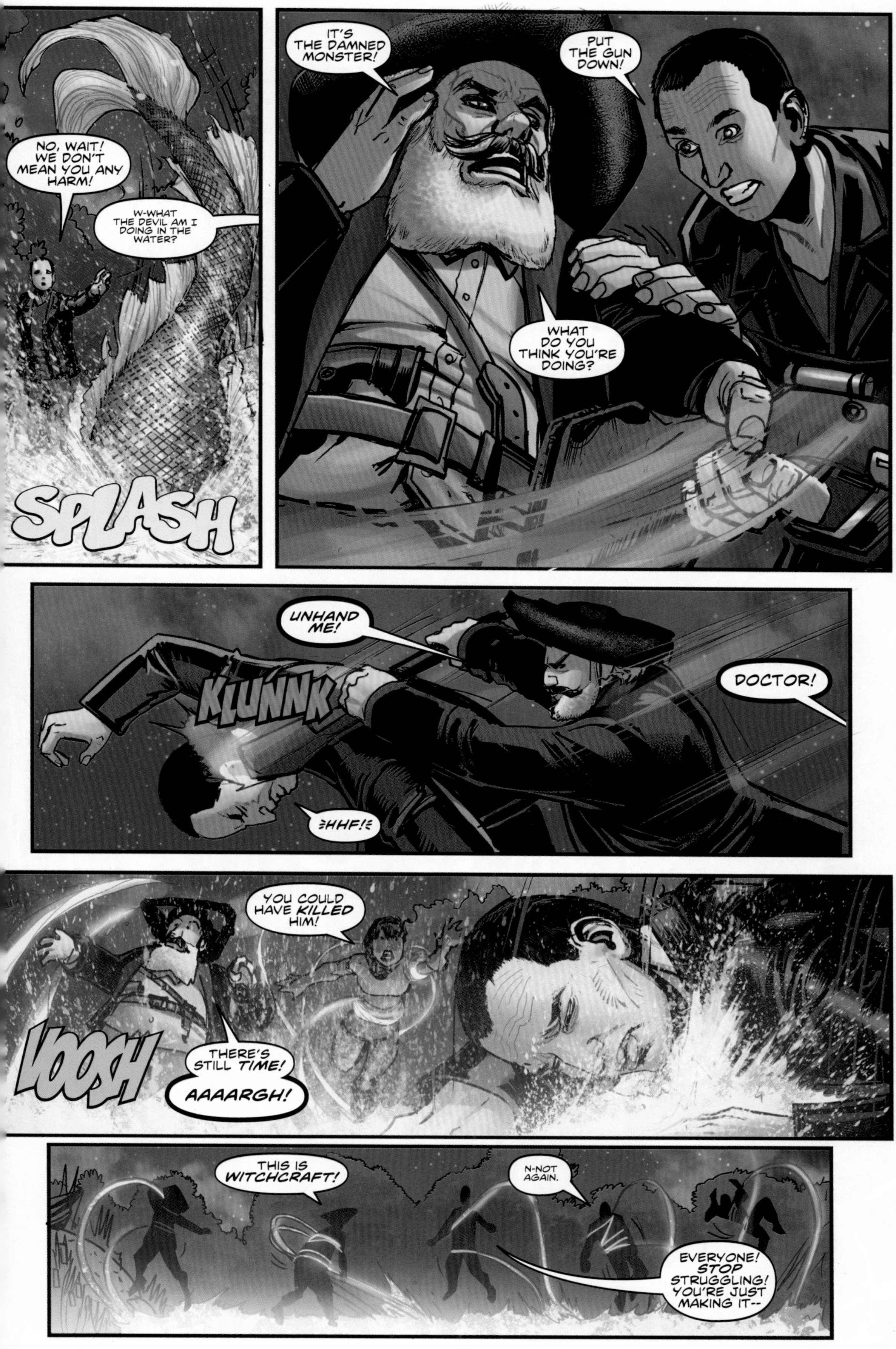
NO, WAIT! WE DON'T MEAN YOU ANY HARM!
W-WHAT THE DEVIL AM I DOING IN THE WATER?
SPLASH
IT'S THE DAMNED MONSTER!
PUT THE GUN DOWN!
WHAT DO YOU THINK YOU'RE DOING?
UNHAND ME!
KLUNNK
DOCTOR!
HHF!
YOU COULD HAVE KILLED HIM!
VOOSH
THERE'S STILL TIME!
AAAARGH!
THIS IS WITCHCRAFT!
N-NOT AGAIN.
EVERYONE! STOP STRUGGLING! YOU'RE JUST MAKING IT--

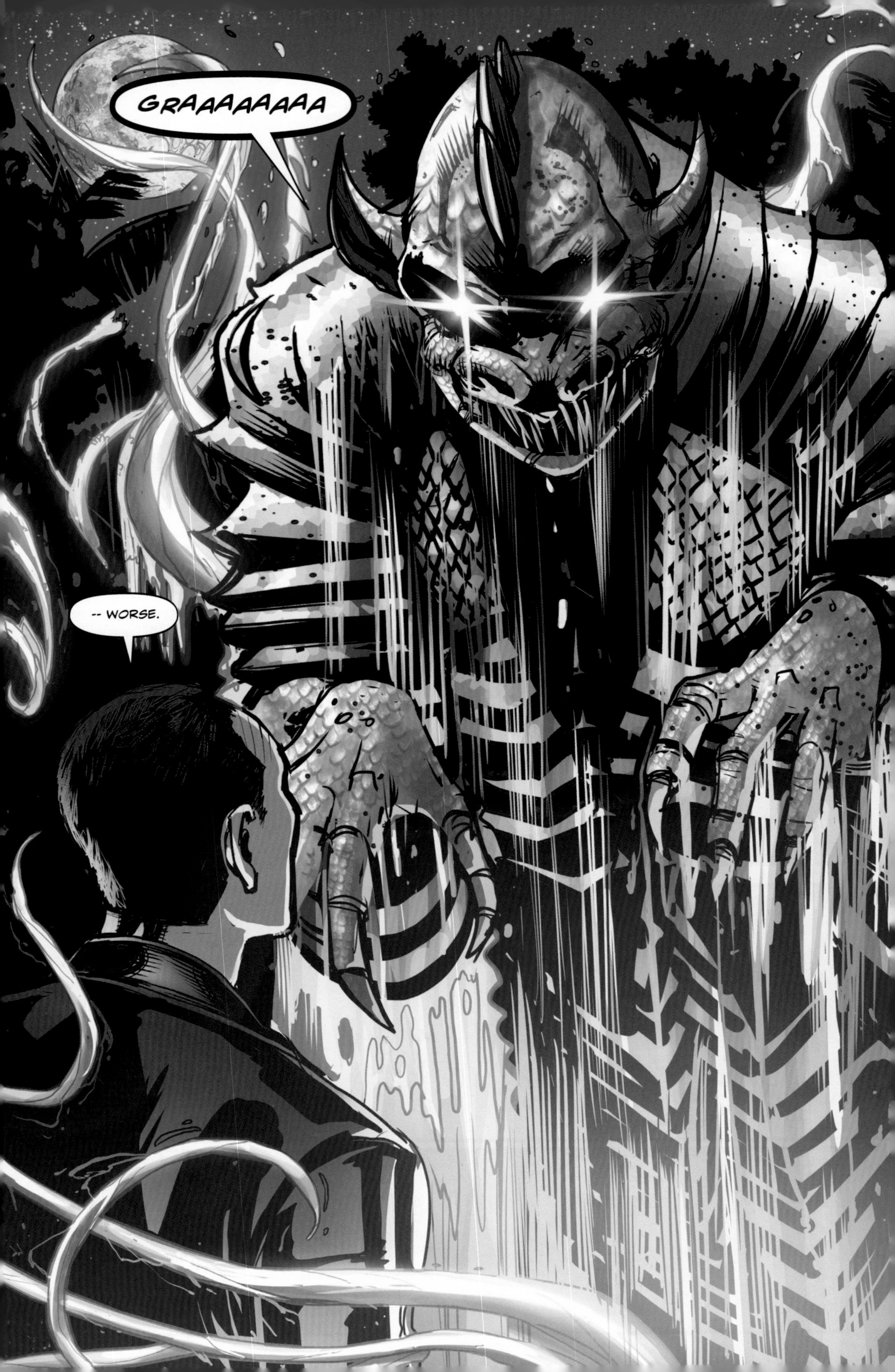
GRAAAAAAAA
-- WORSE.

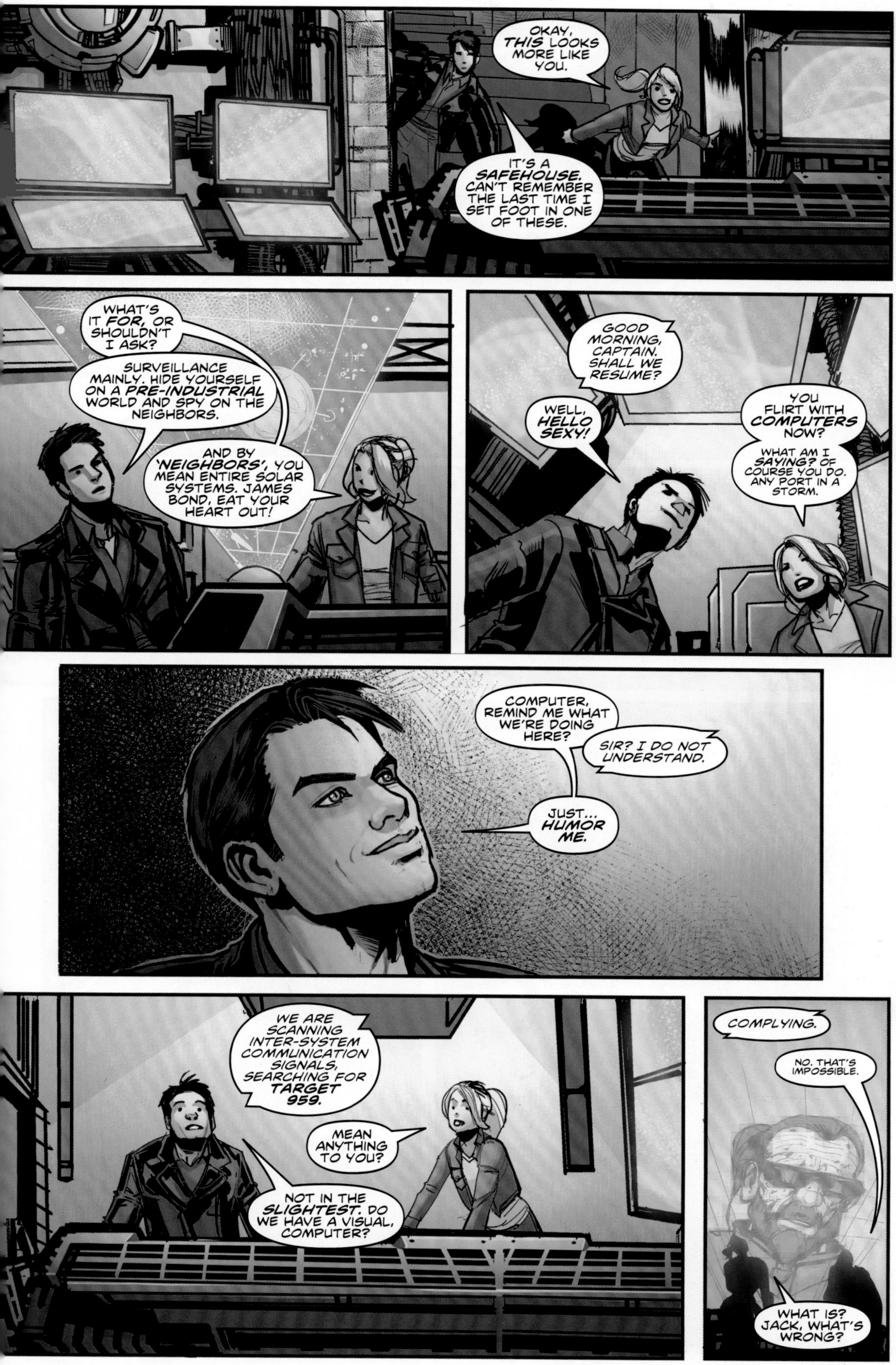
OKAY, THIS LOOKS MORE LIKE YOU.
IT'S A SAFEHOUSE. CAN'T REMEMBER THE LAST TIME I SET FOOT IN ONE OF THESE.
WHAT'S IT FOR, OR SHOULDN'T I ASK?
SURVEILLANCE MAINLY. HIDE YOURSELF ON A PRE-INDUSTRIAL WORLD AND SPY ON THE NEIGHBORS.
AND BY 'NEIGHBORS', YOU MEAN ENTIRE SOLAR SYSTEMS. JAMES BOND, EAT YOUR HEART OUT!
GOOD MORNING, CAPTAIN. SHALL WE RESUME?
WELL, HELLO SEXY!
YOU FLIRT WITH COMPUTERS NOW?
WHAT AM I SAYING? OF COURSE YOU DO. ANY PORT IN A STORM.
COMPUTER, REMIND ME WHAT WE'RE DOING HERE?
SIR? I DO NOT UNDERSTAND.
JUST... HUMOR ME.
WE ARE SCANNING INTER-SYSTEM COMMUNICATION SIGNALS, SEARCHING FOR TARGET 959.
MEAN ANYTHING TO YOU?
NOT IN THE SLIGHTEST. DO WE HAVE A VISUAL, COMPUTER?
COMPLYING.
NO. THAT'S IMPOSSIBLE.
WHAT IS? JACK, WHAT'S WRONG?

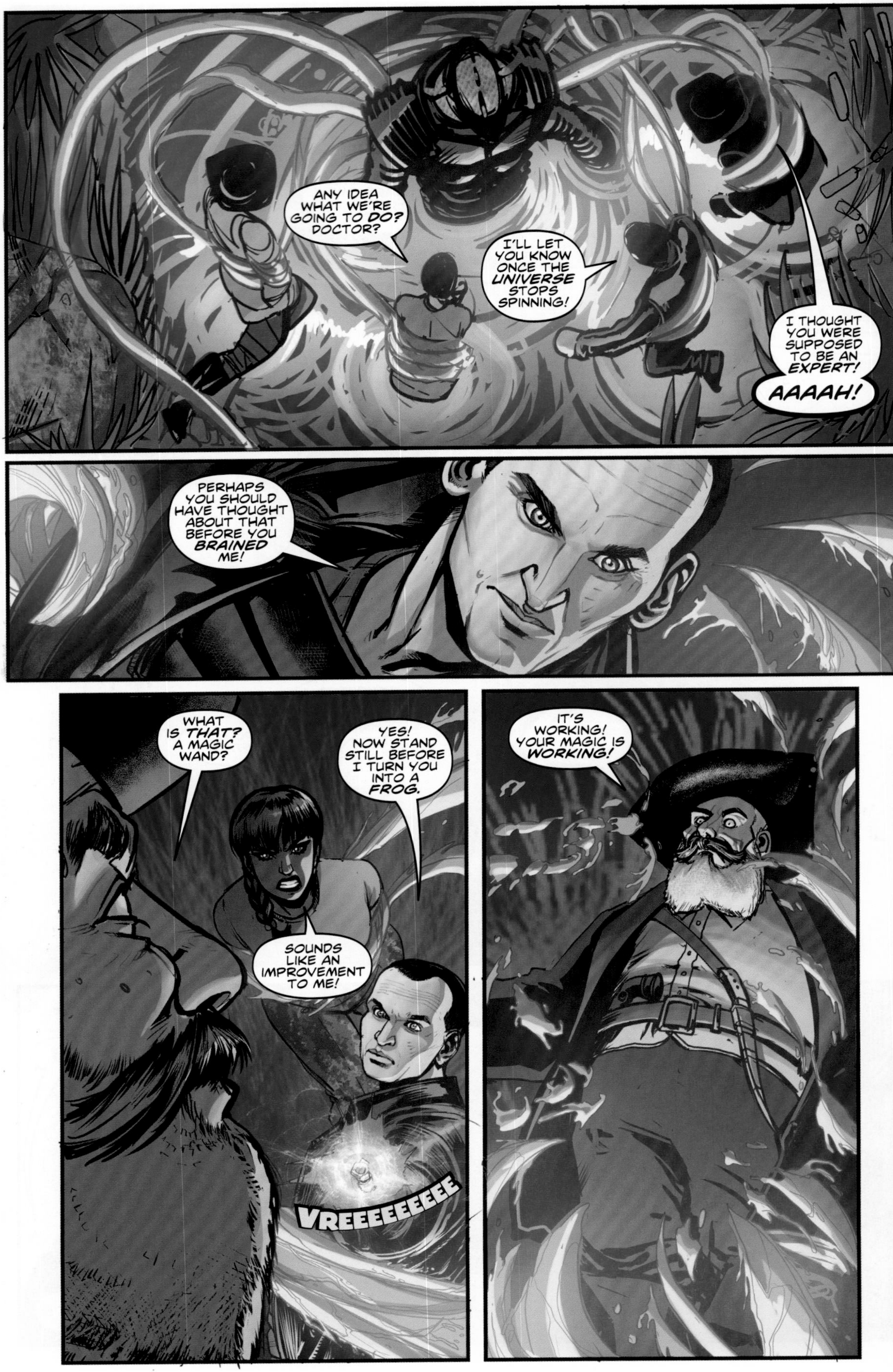
ANY IDEA WHAT WE'RE GOING TO DO? DOCTOR?
I'LL LET YOU KNOW ONCE THE UNIVERSE STOPS SPINNING!
I THOUGHT YOU WERE SUPPOSED TO BE AN EXPERT!
AAAAH!
PERHAPS YOU SHOULD HAVE THOUGHT ABOUT THAT BEFORE YOU BRAINED ME!
WHAT IS THAT? A MAGIC WAND?
YES! NOW STAND STILL BEFORE I TURN YOU INTO A FROG.
SOUNDS LIKE AN IMPROVEMENT TO ME!
VREEEEEEEEE
IT'S WORKING! YOUR MAGIC IS WORKING!

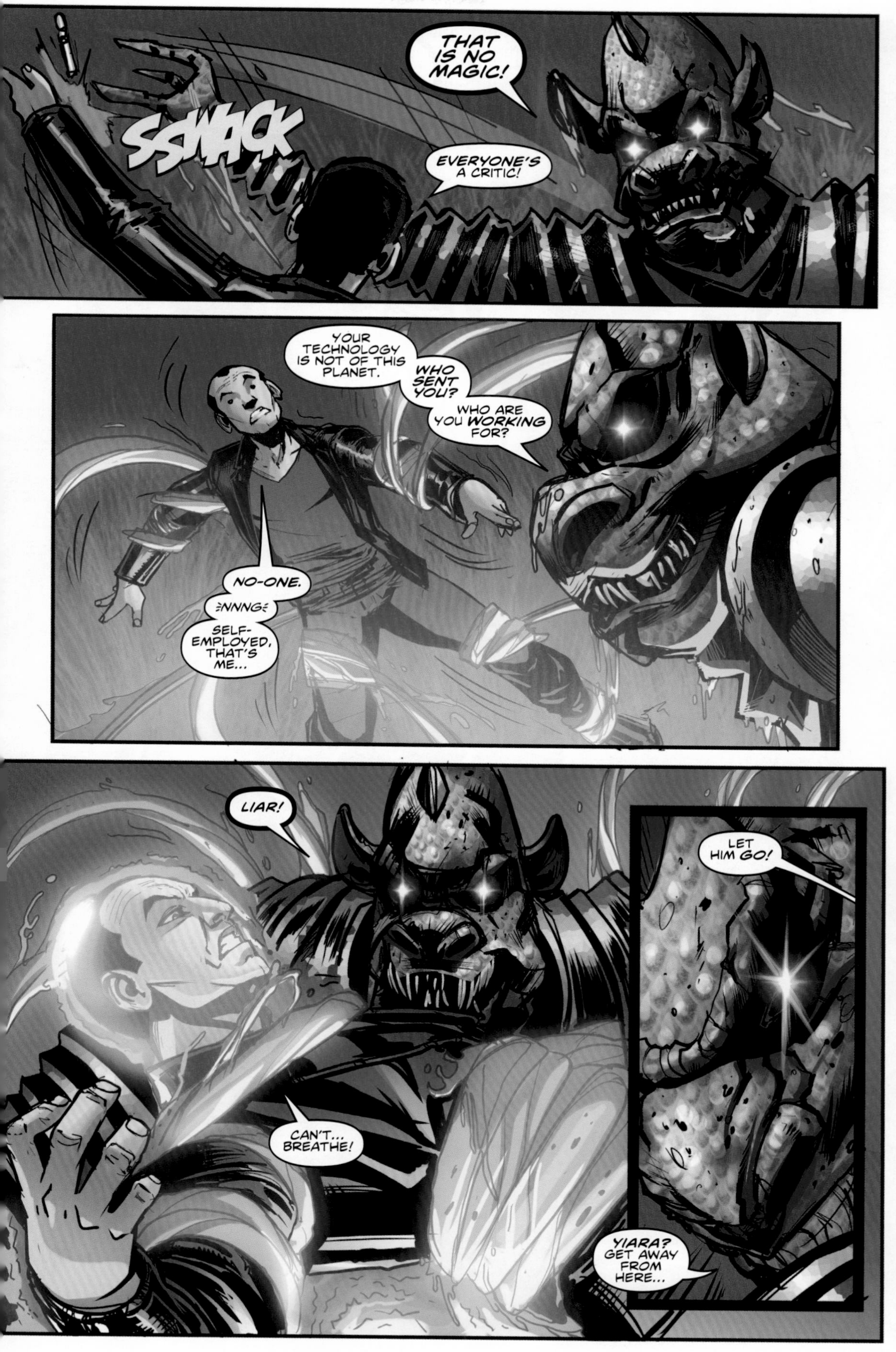

THAT IS NO MAGIC!
SSWACK
EVERYONE'S A CRITIC!
YOUR TECHNOLOGY IS NOT OF THIS PLANET.
WHO SENT YOU?
WHO ARE YOU WORKING FOR?
NO-ONE.
NNNG
SELF-EMPLOYED, THAT'S ME...
LIAR!
LET HIM GO!
CAN'T... BREATHE!
YIARA? GET AWAY FROM HERE...

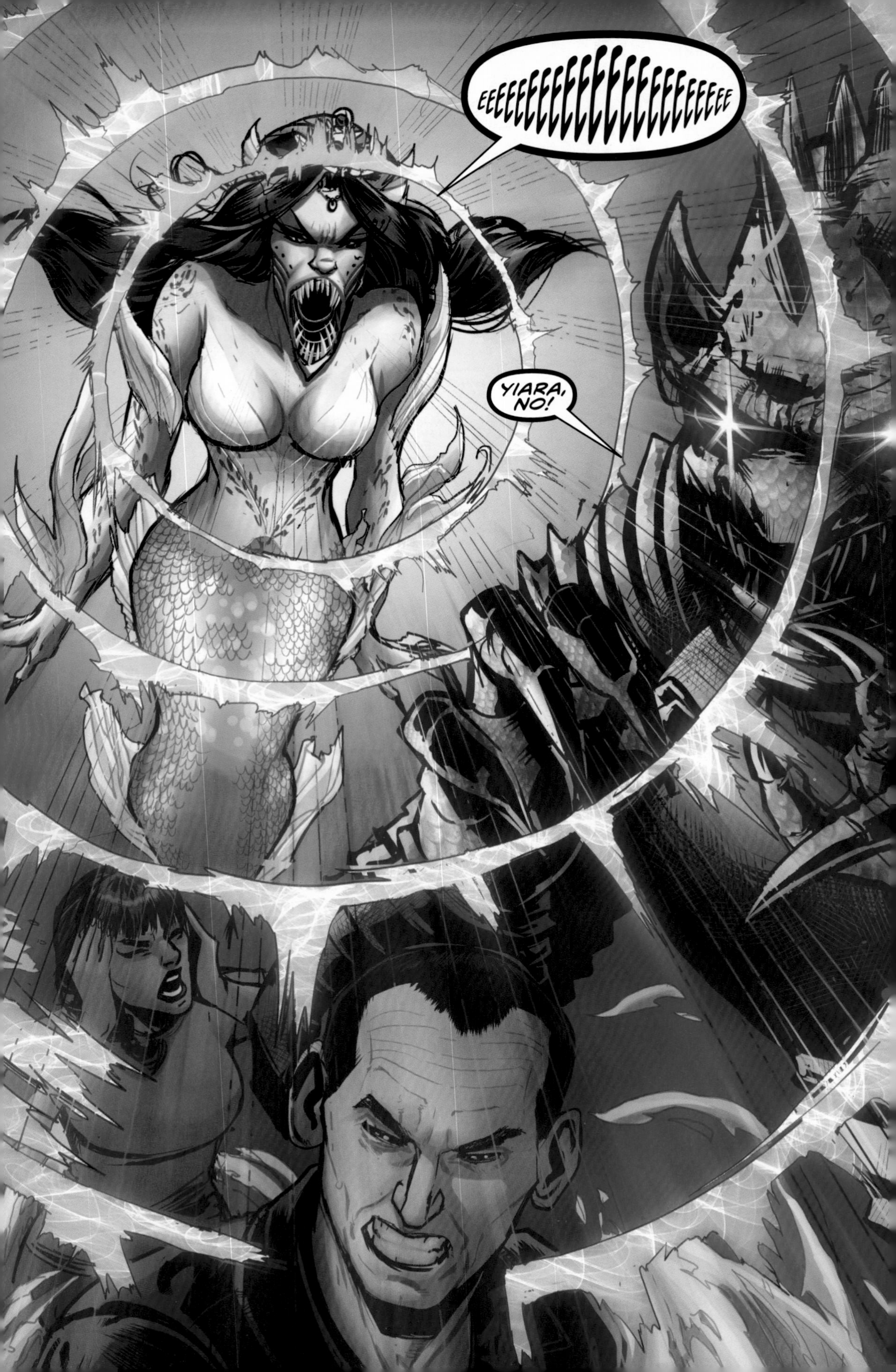
EEEEEEEEEEEEEEEEEEEEE
YIARA, NO!

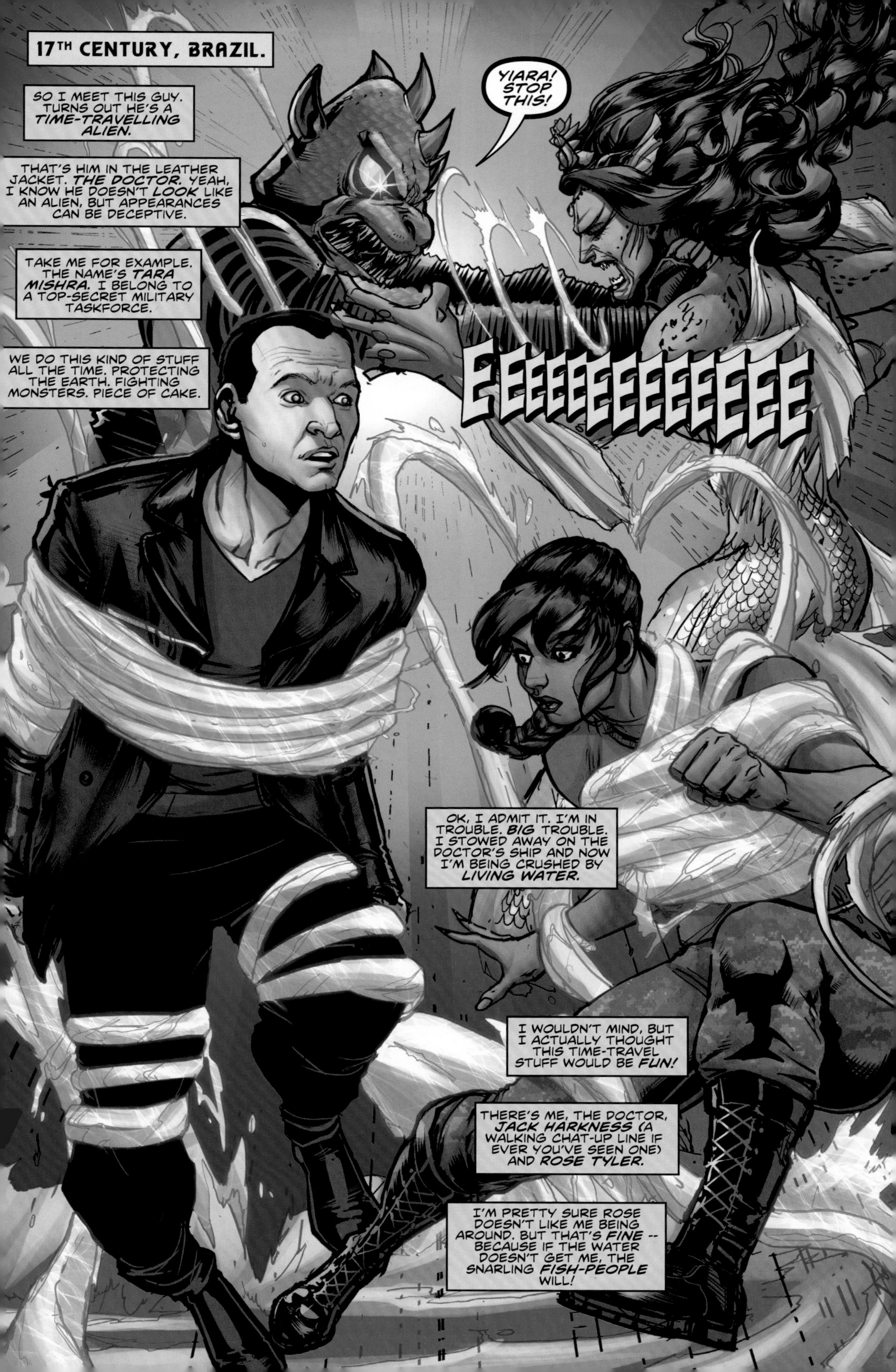
17TH CENTURY, BRAZIL.
SO I MEET THIS GUY. TURNS OUT HE'S A TIME-TRAVELLING ALIEN.
THAT'S HIM IN THE LEATHER JACKET. THE DOCTOR. YEAH, I KNOW HE DOESN'T LOOK LIKE AN ALIEN, BUT APPEARANCES CAN BE DECEPTIVE.
TAKE ME FOR EXAMPLE. THE NAME'S TARA MISHRA. I BELONG TO A TOP-SECRET MILITARY TASKFORCE.
WE DO THIS KIND OF STUFF ALL THE TIME. PROTECTING THE EARTH. FIGHTING MONSTERS. PIECE OF CAKE.
YIARA! STOP THIS!
EEEEEEEEEEEEEE
OK, I ADMIT IT. I'M IN TROUBLE. BIG TROUBLE. I STOWED AWAY ON THE DOCTOR'S SHIP AND NOW I'M BEING CRUSHED BY LIVING WATER.
I WOULDN'T MIND, BUT I ACTUALLY THOUGHT THIS TIME-TRAVEL STUFF WOULD BE FUN!
THERE'S ME, THE DOCTOR, JACK HARKNESS (A WALKING CHAT-UP LINE IF EVER YOU'VE SEEN ONE) AND ROSE TYLER.
I'M PRETTY SURE ROSE DOESN'T LIKE ME BEING AROUND. BUT THAT'S FINE -- BECAUSE IF THE WATER DOESN'T GET ME, THE SNARLING FISH-PEOPLE WILL!

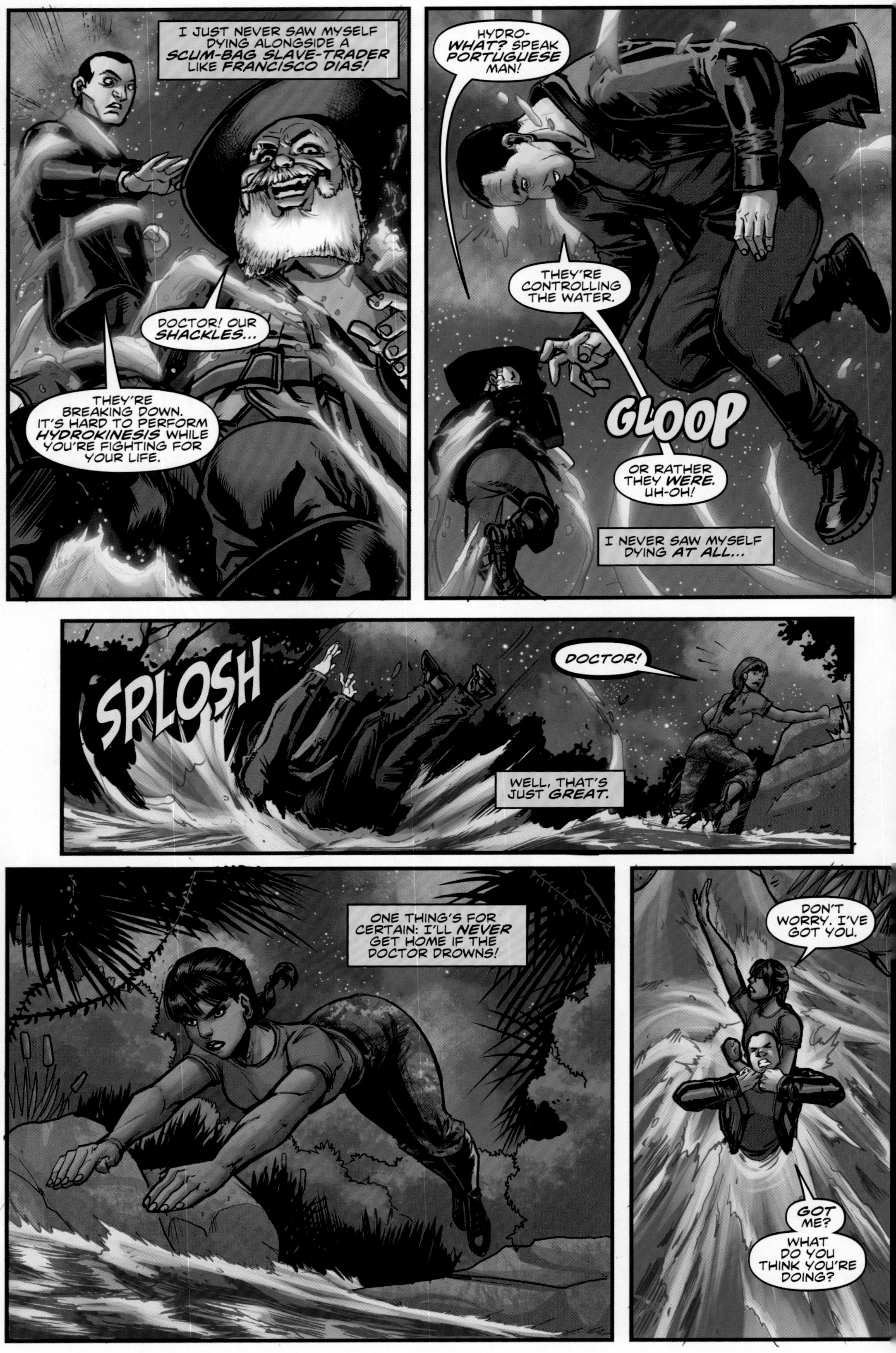
I JUST NEVER SAW MYSELF DYING ALONGSIDE A SCUM-BAG SLAVE-TRADER LIKE FRANCISCO DIAS!
DOCTOR! OUR SHACKLES...
THEY'RE BREAKING DOWN. IT'S HARD TO PERFORM HYDROKINESIS WHILE YOU'RE FIGHTING FOR YOUR LIFE.
HYDRO-WHAT? SPEAK PORTUGUESE MAN!
THEY'RE CONTROLLING THE WATER.
GLOOP
OR RATHER THEY WERE. UH-OH!
I NEVER SAW MYSELF DYING AT ALL...
SPLOSH
DOCTOR!
WELL, THAT'S JUST GREAT.
ONE THING'S FOR CERTAIN: I'LL NEVER GET HOME IF THE DOCTOR DROWNS!
DON'T WORRY. I'VE GOT YOU.
GOT ME? WHAT DO YOU THINK YOU'RE DOING?

ER... SAVING YOU?

DID I LOOK LIKE I NEEDED SAVING?

WELL... YEAH, AS IT HAPPENS.

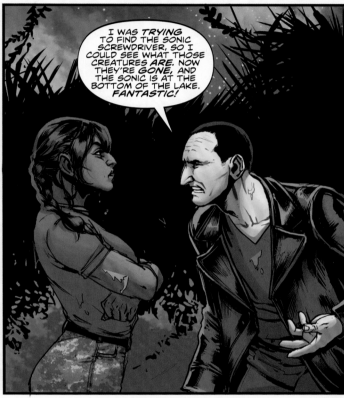

I WAS TRYING TO FIND THE SONIC SCREWDRIVER, SO I COULD SEE WHAT THOSE CREATURES ARE. NOW THEY'RE GONE, AND THE SONIC IS AT THE BOTTOM OF THE LAKE. FANTASTIC!

SONIC SCREWDRIVER?

DO YOU MEAN THIS?

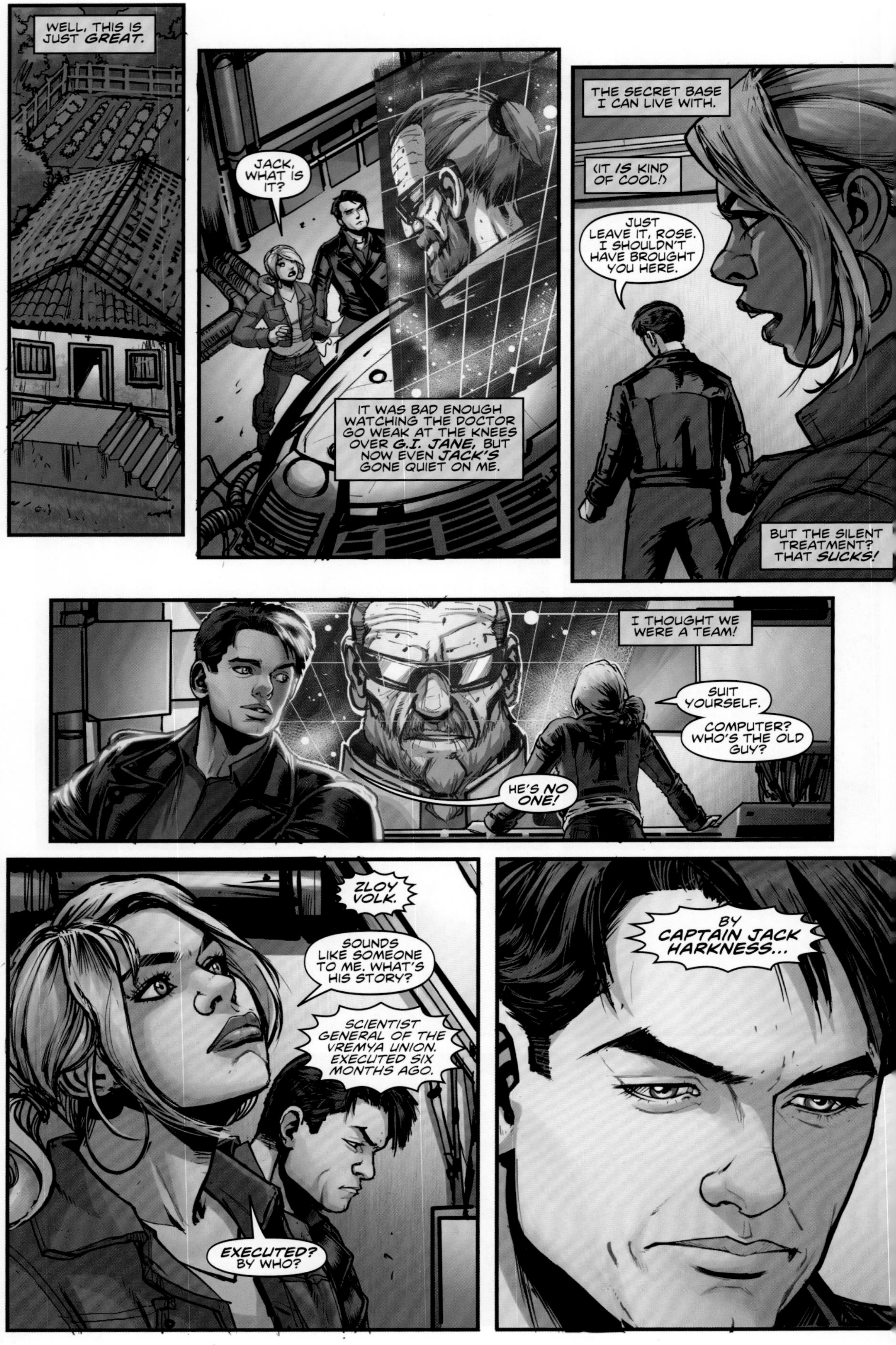
WELL, THIS IS JUST GREAT.
JACK, WHAT IS IT?
IT WAS BAD ENOUGH WATCHING THE DOCTOR GO WEAK AT THE KNEES OVER G.I. JANE, BUT NOW EVEN JACK'S GONE QUIET ON ME.
THE SECRET BASE I CAN LIVE WITH.
(IT IS KIND OF COOL!)
JUST LEAVE IT, ROSE. I SHOULDN'T HAVE BROUGHT YOU HERE.
BUT THE SILENT TREATMENT? THAT SUCKS!
I THOUGHT WE WERE A TEAM!
SUIT YOURSELF.
COMPUTER? WHO'S THE OLD GUY?
HE'S NO ONE!
ZLOY VOLK.
SOUNDS LIKE SOMEONE TO ME. WHAT'S HIS STORY?
SCIENTIST GENERAL OF THE VREMYA UNION. EXECUTED SIX MONTHS AGO.
EXECUTED? BY WHO?
BY CAPTAIN JACK HARKNESS...

ЭNNNGЭ

STAND ASIDE. I CAN'T GET A CLEAR SHOT.

GOOD! CAN'T YOU SEE -- SHE'S *HURT!*

...

AAAAAAAAAAA

OH NO YOU DON'T. IF YOU WANT ME TO LOOK AT THOSE *SCRATCHES,* YOU'LL DROP THE MIND-CONTROL ACT PRONTO.

I'M NO FAN OF DIAS, BUT EVEN *HE* DOESN'T DESERVE THAT.

VERY WELL...

... HE IS FREE.

WHAT THE *DEVIL?*

CALM DOWN, YEAH? LET TARA DO HER JOB.

WHAT'S YOUR NAME?

YIARA.

ЭNNNNЭ

SORRY, I KNOW IT HURTS. THESE CUTS ARE DEEP.

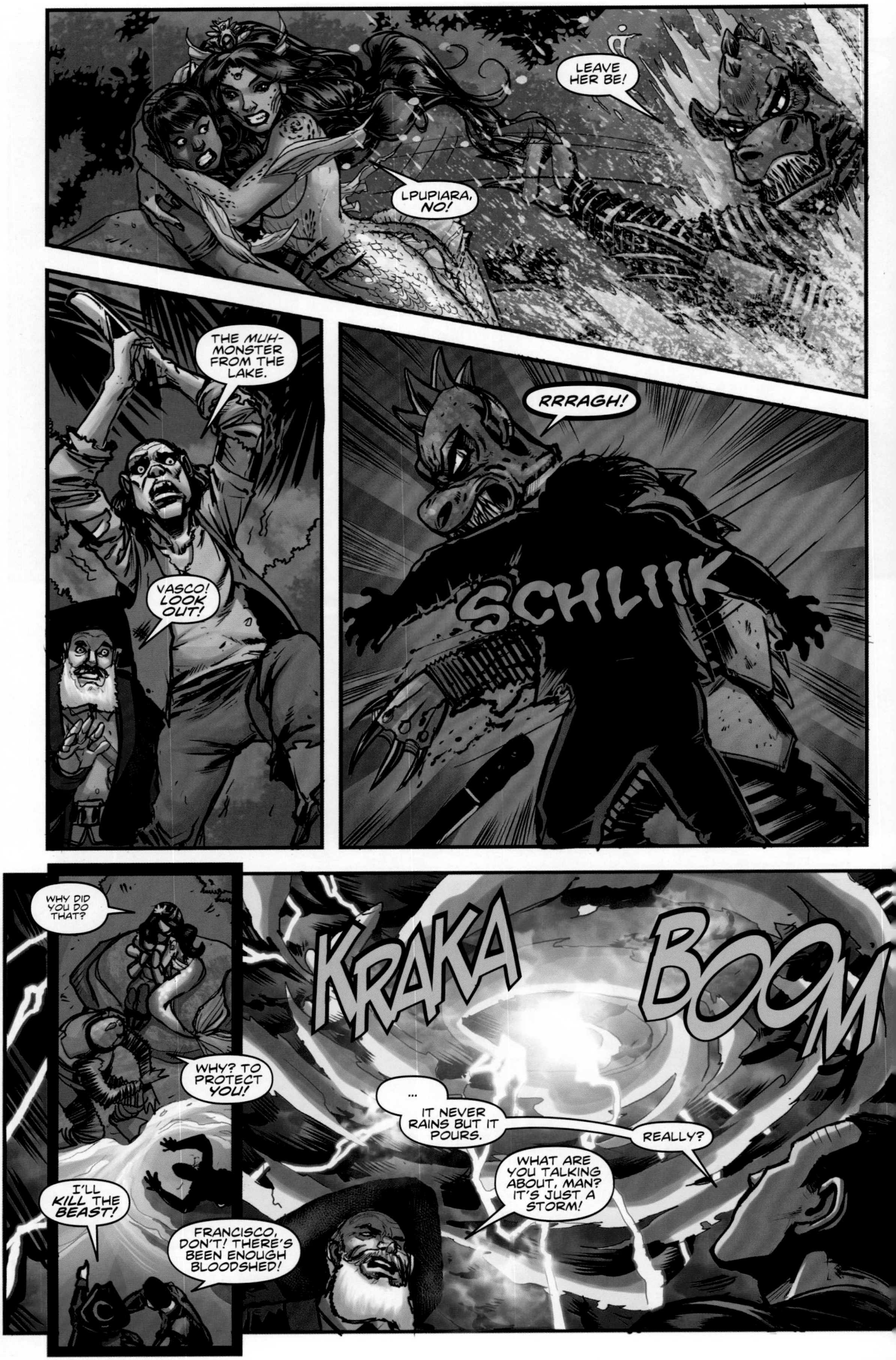
LEAVE HER BE!
LPUPIARA, NO!
THE MUH-MONSTER FROM THE LAKE.
VASCO! LOOK OUT!
RRRAGH!
SCHLIIK
WHY DID YOU DO THAT?
WHY? TO PROTECT YOU!
I'LL KILL THE BEAST!
FRANCISCO, DON'T! THERE'S BEEN ENOUGH BLOODSHED!
KRAKA BOOM
... IT NEVER RAINS BUT IT POURS.
REALLY?
WHAT ARE YOU TALKING ABOUT, MAN? IT'S JUST A STORM!

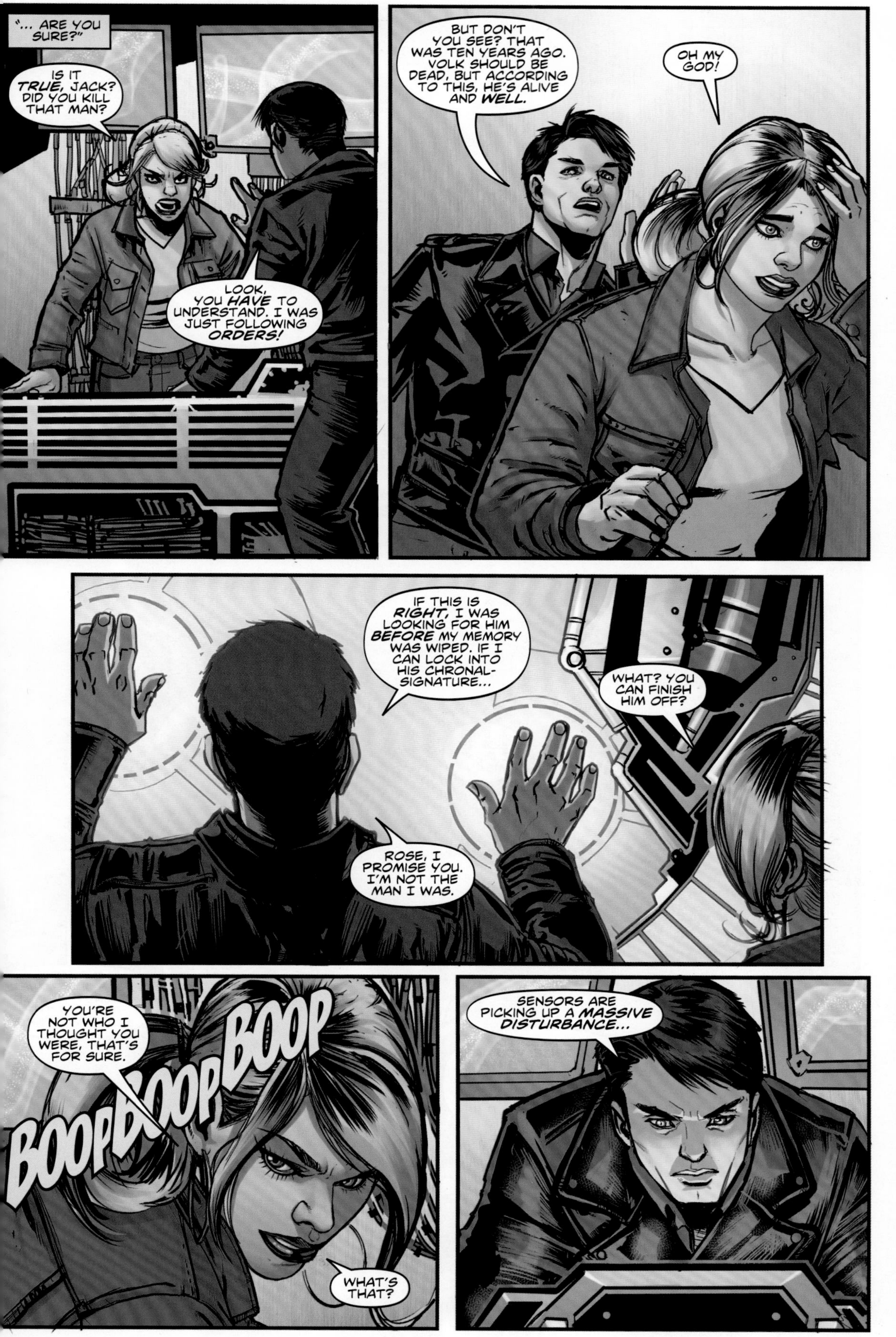
"... ARE YOU SURE?"
IS IT TRUE, JACK? DID YOU KILL THAT MAN?
LOOK, YOU HAVE TO UNDERSTAND. I WAS JUST FOLLOWING ORDERS!
BUT DON'T YOU SEE? THAT WAS TEN YEARS AGO. VOLK SHOULD BE DEAD, BUT ACCORDING TO THIS, HE'S ALIVE AND WELL.
OH MY GOD!
IF THIS IS RIGHT, I WAS LOOKING FOR HIM BEFORE MY MEMORY WAS WIPED. IF I CAN LOCK INTO HIS CHRONAL-SIGNATURE...
WHAT? YOU CAN FINISH HIM OFF?
ROSE, I PROMISE YOU. I'M NOT THE MAN I WAS.
YOU'RE NOT WHO I THOUGHT YOU WERE, THAT'S FOR SURE.
BOOP BOOP BOOP
WHAT'S THAT?
SENSORS ARE PICKING UP A MASSIVE DISTURBANCE...

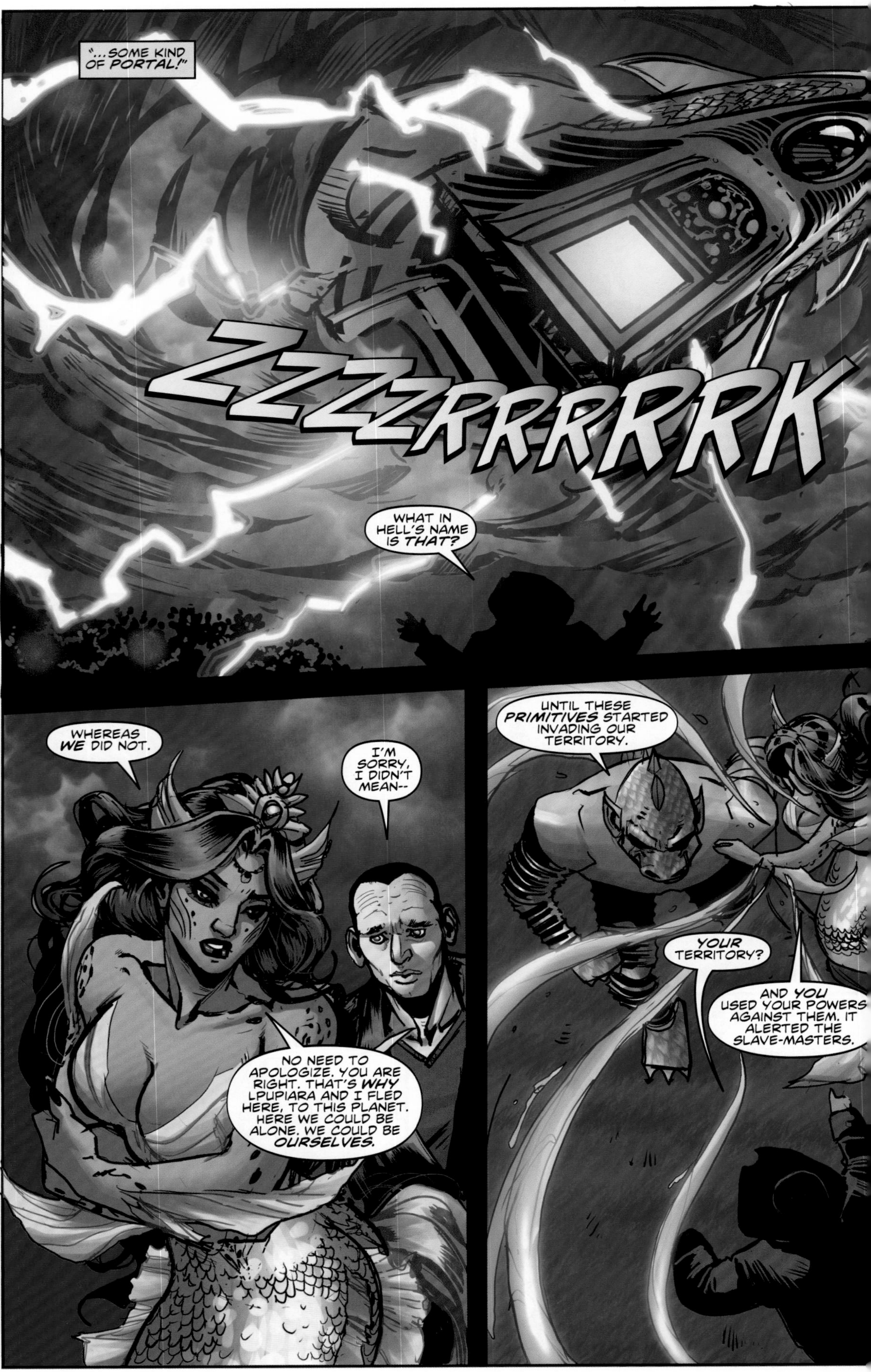
"...SOME KIND OF PORTAL!"
ZZZZRRRRRRK
WHAT IN HELL'S NAME IS *THAT?*
WHEREAS *WE* DID NOT.
I'M SORRY, I DIDN'T MEAN--
NO NEED TO APOLOGIZE. YOU ARE RIGHT. THAT'S *WHY* LPUPIARA AND I FLED HERE, TO THIS PLANET. HERE WE COULD BE ALONE. WE COULD BE *OURSELVES.*
UNTIL THESE *PRIMITIVES* STARTED INVADING OUR TERRITORY.
YOUR TERRITORY?
AND *YOU* USED YOUR POWERS AGAINST THEM. IT ALERTED THE SLAVE-MASTERS.

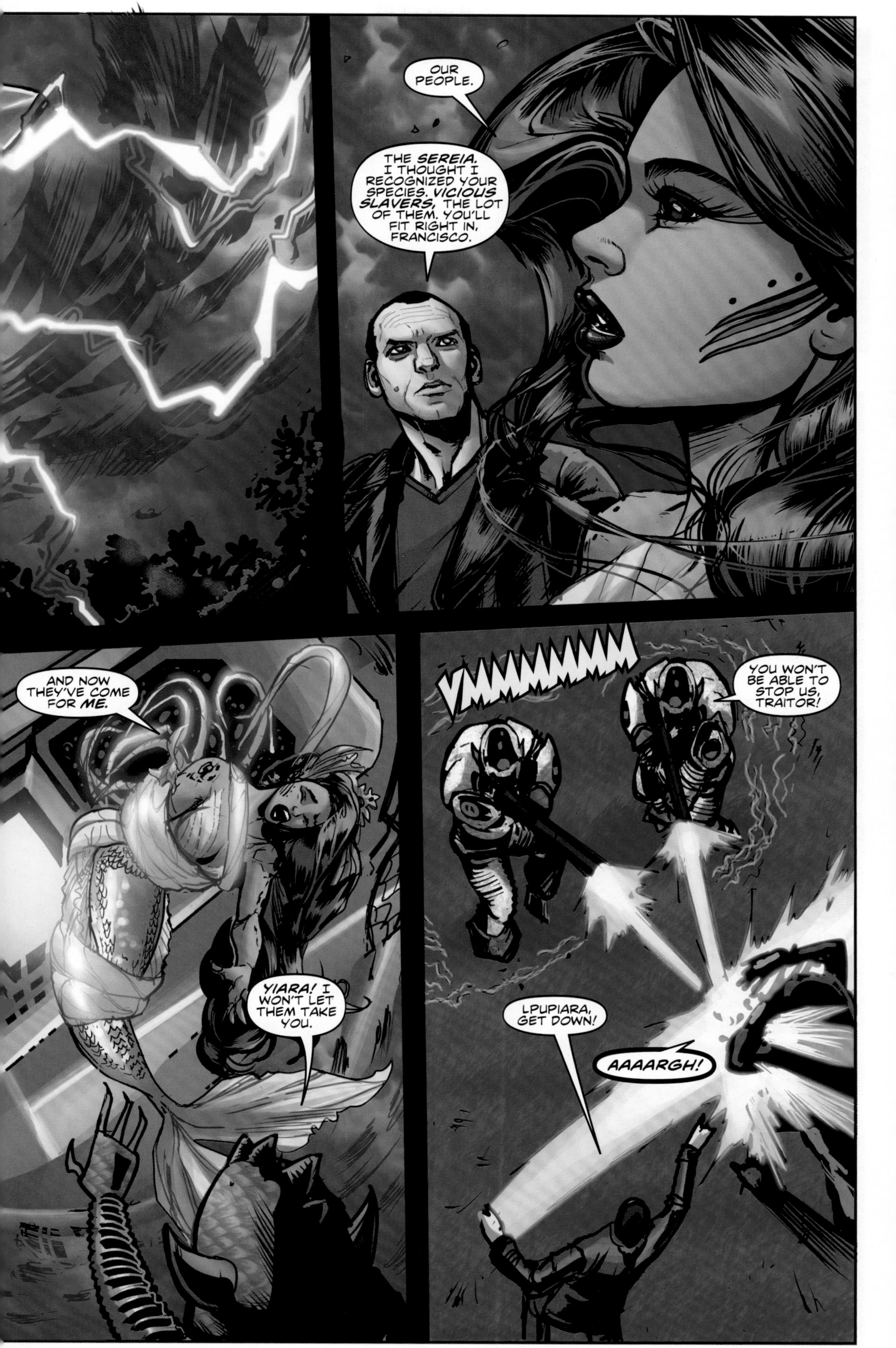
OUR PEOPLE.
THE SEREIA. I THOUGHT I RECOGNIZED YOUR SPECIES. VICIOUS SLAVERS, THE LOT OF THEM. YOU'LL FIT RIGHT IN, FRANCISCO.
AND NOW THEY'VE COME FOR ME.
YIARA! I WON'T LET THEM TAKE YOU.
VMMMMMM
YOU WON'T BE ABLE TO STOP US, TRAITOR!
LPUPIARA, GET DOWN!
AAAARGH!

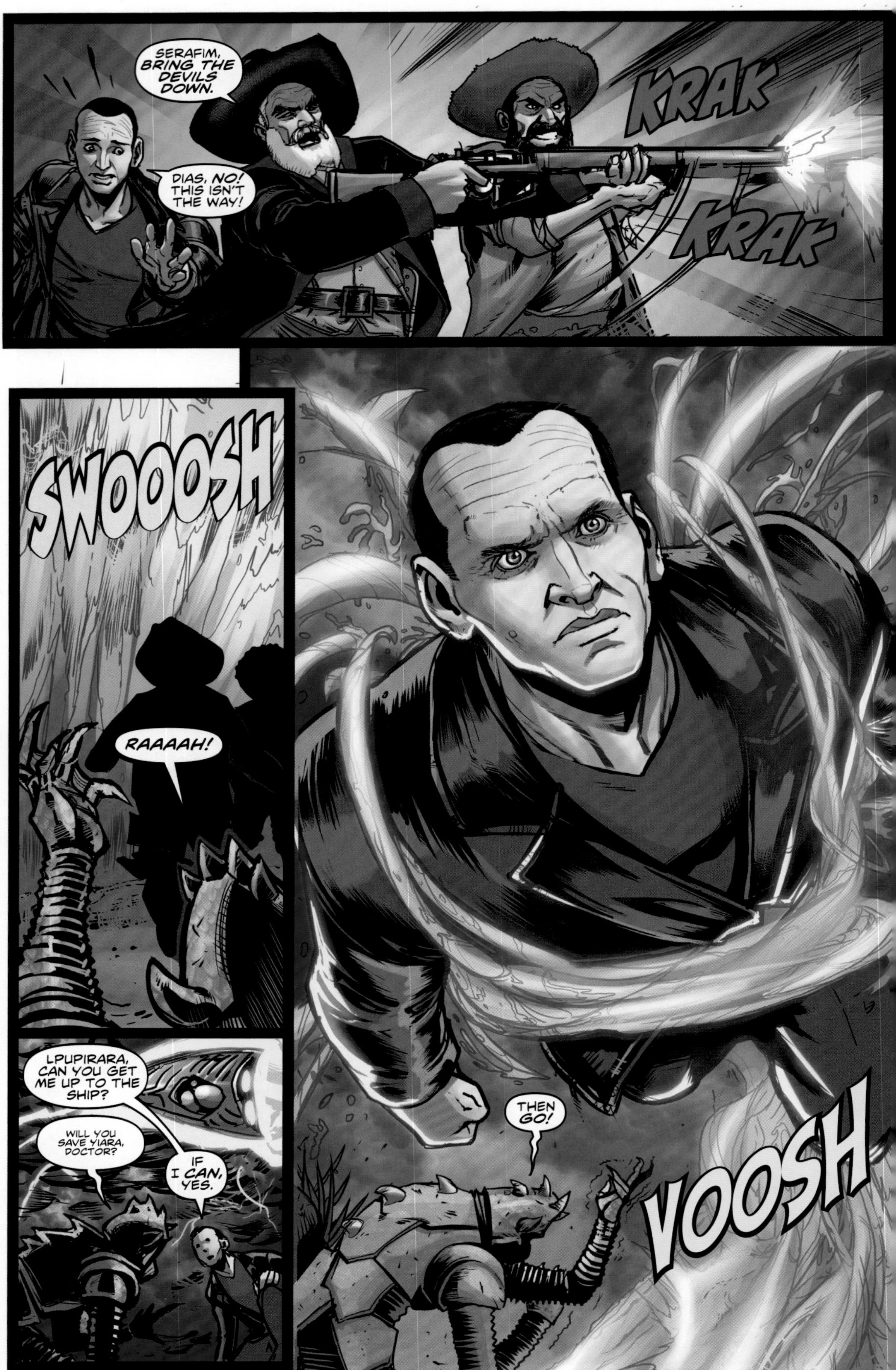
SERAFIM, BRING THE DEVILS DOWN.
DIAS, NO! THIS ISN'T THE WAY!
KRAK
KRAK
SWOOOSH
RAAAAH!
LPUPIRARA, CAN YOU GET ME UP TO THE SHIP?
WILL YOU SAVE YIARA, DOCTOR?
IF I CAN, YES.
THEN GO!
VOOSH

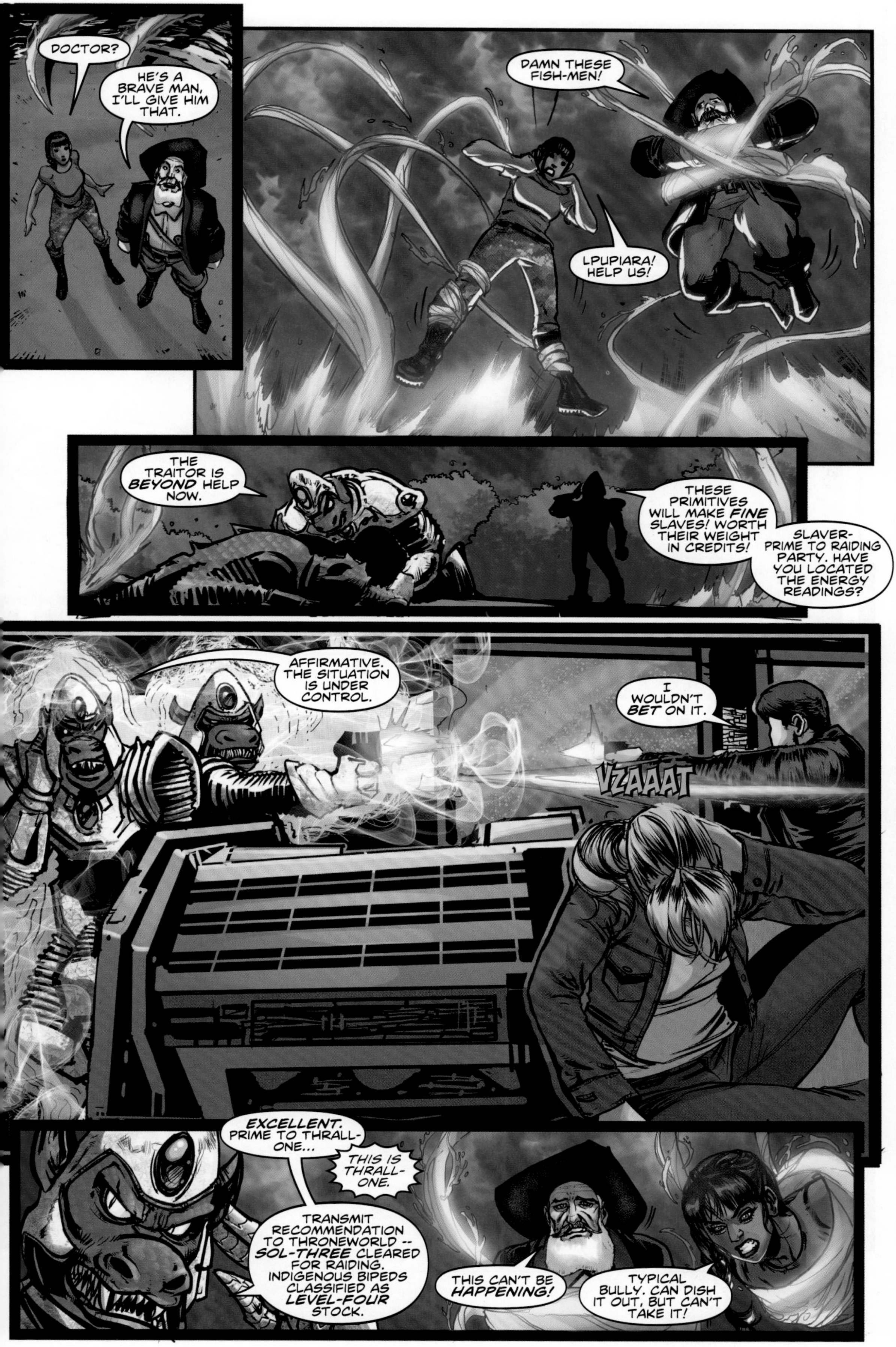
DOCTOR?
HE'S A BRAVE MAN, I'LL GIVE HIM THAT.
DAMN THESE FISH-MEN!
LPUPIARA! HELP US!
THE TRAITOR IS BEYOND HELP NOW.
THESE PRIMITIVES WILL MAKE FINE SLAVES! WORTH THEIR WEIGHT IN CREDITS!
SLAVER-PRIME TO RAIDING PARTY. HAVE YOU LOCATED THE ENERGY READINGS?
AFFIRMATIVE. THE SITUATION IS UNDER CONTROL.
I WOULDN'T BET ON IT.
VZAAAT
EXCELLENT. PRIME TO THRALL-ONE...
THIS IS THRALL-ONE.
TRANSMIT RECOMMENDATION TO THRONEWORLD -- SOL-THREE CLEARED FOR RAIDING. INDIGENOUS BIPEDS CLASSIFIED AS LEVEL-FOUR STOCK.
THIS CAN'T BE HAPPENING!
TYPICAL BULLY. CAN DISH IT OUT, BUT CAN'T TAKE IT!

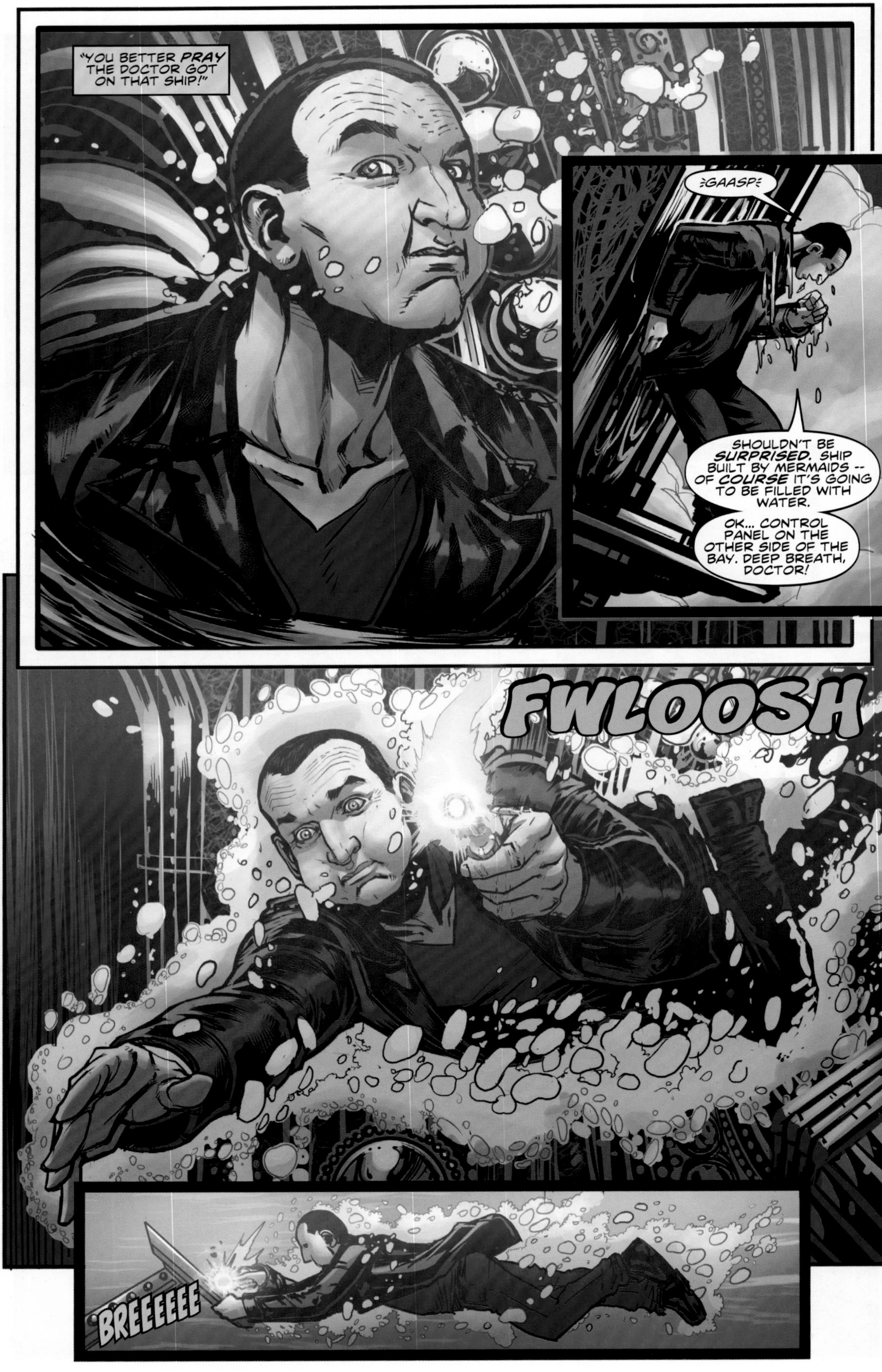
"YOU BETTER PRAY THE DOCTOR GOT ON THAT SHIP!"
GAASP
SHOULDN'T BE SURPRISED. SHIP BUILT BY MERMAIDS -- OF COURSE IT'S GOING TO BE FILLED WITH WATER.
OK... CONTROL PANEL ON THE OTHER SIDE OF THE BAY. DEEP BREATH, DOCTOR!
FWLOOSH
BREEEEEE

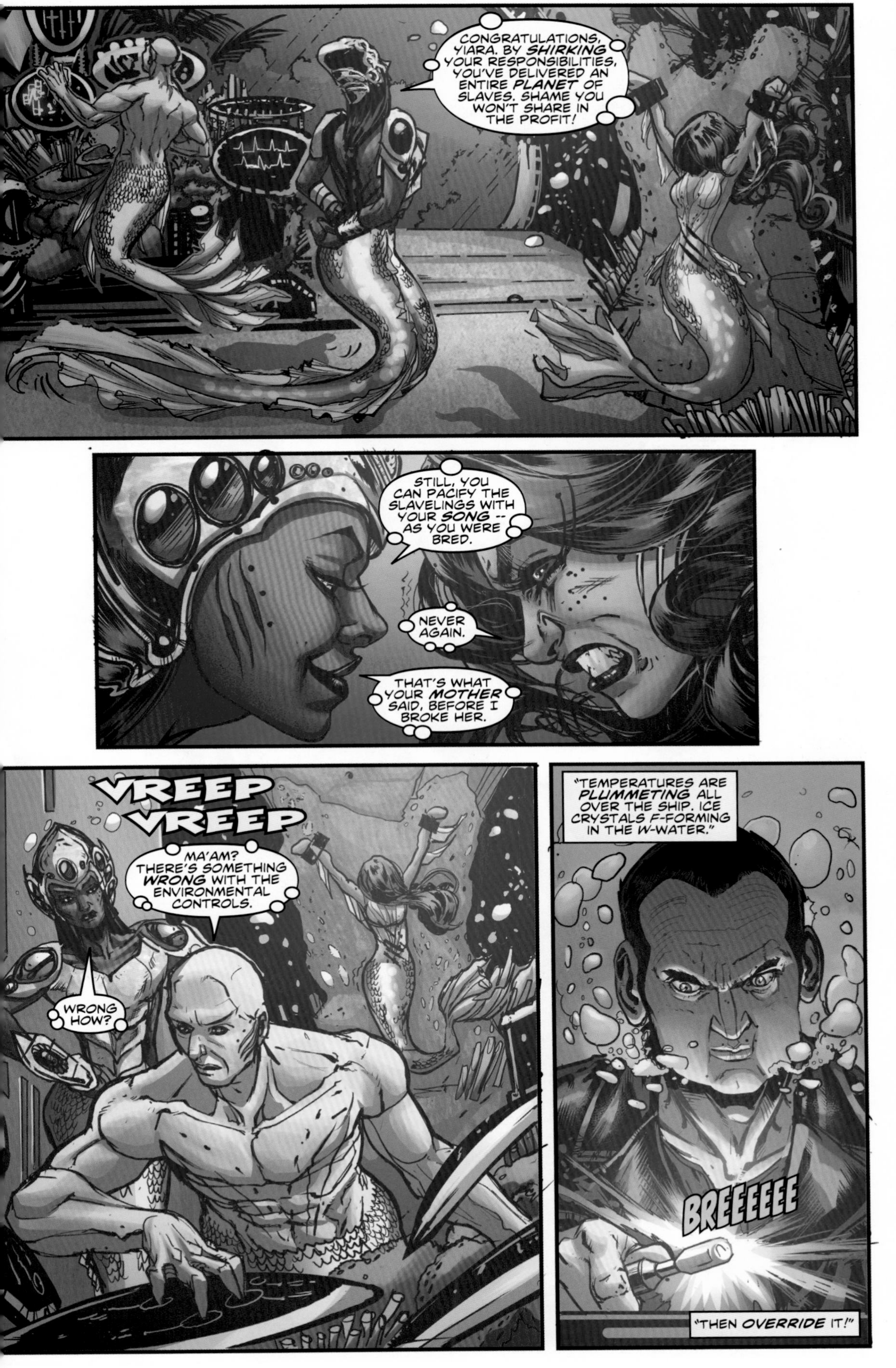
CONGRATULATIONS, YIARA. BY SHIRKING YOUR RESPONSIBILITIES, YOU'VE DELIVERED AN ENTIRE PLANET OF SLAVES. SHAME YOU WON'T SHARE IN THE PROFIT!
STILL, YOU CAN PACIFY THE SLAVELINGS WITH YOUR SONG -- AS YOU WERE BRED.
NEVER AGAIN.
THAT'S WHAT YOUR MOTHER SAID, BEFORE I BROKE HER.
VREEP VREEP
MA'AM? THERE'S SOMETHING WRONG WITH THE ENVIRONMENTAL CONTROLS.
WRONG HOW?
"TEMPERATURES ARE PLUMMETING ALL OVER THE SHIP. ICE CRYSTALS F-FORMING IN THE W-WATER."
BREEEEEE
"THEN OVERRIDE IT!"

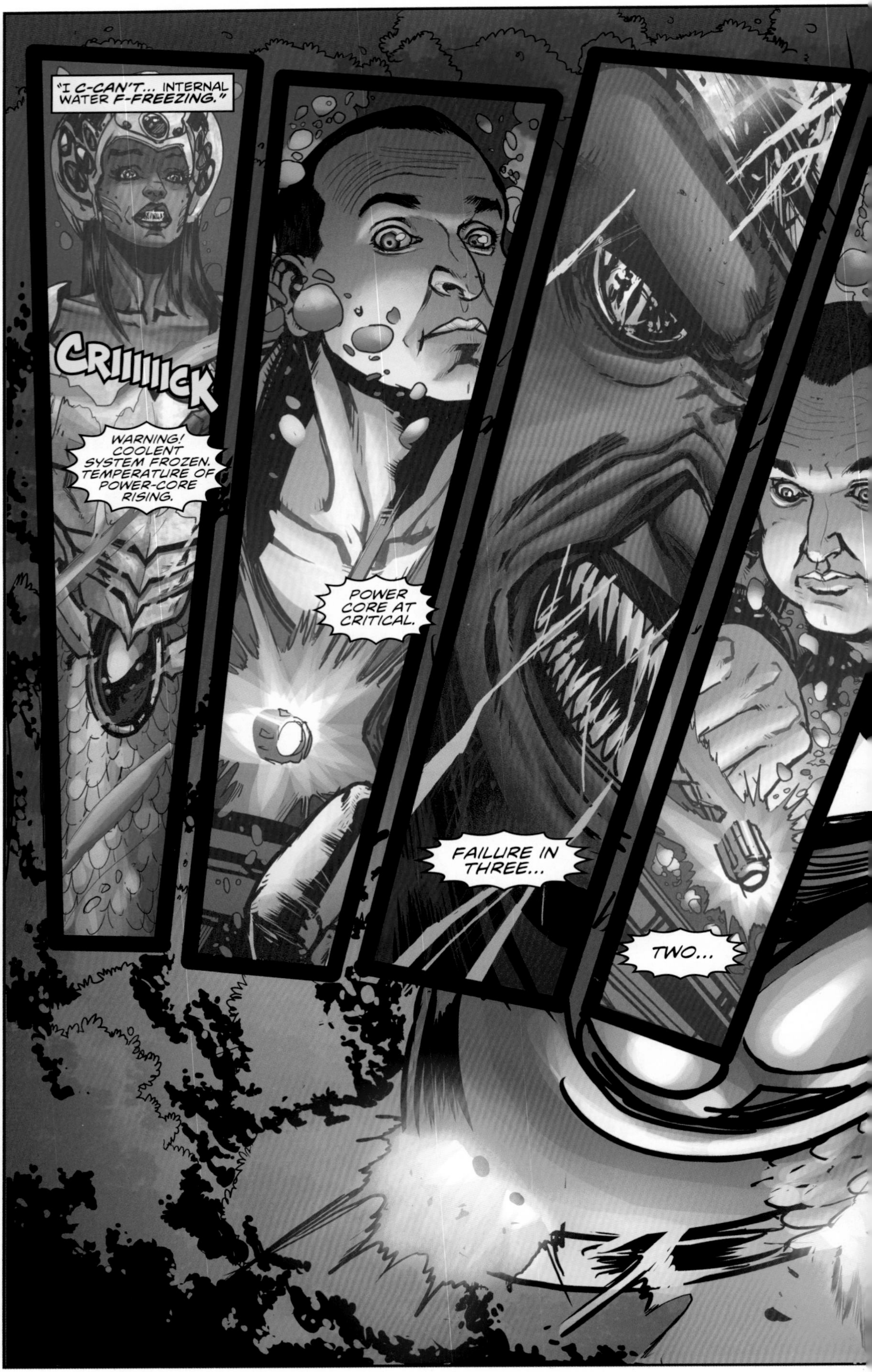
"I C-CAN'T... INTERNAL WATER F-FREEZING."
CRIIIIICK
WARNING! COOLENT SYSTEM FROZEN. TEMPERATURE OF POWER-CORE RISING.
POWER CORE AT CRITICAL.
FAILURE IN THREE...
TWO...

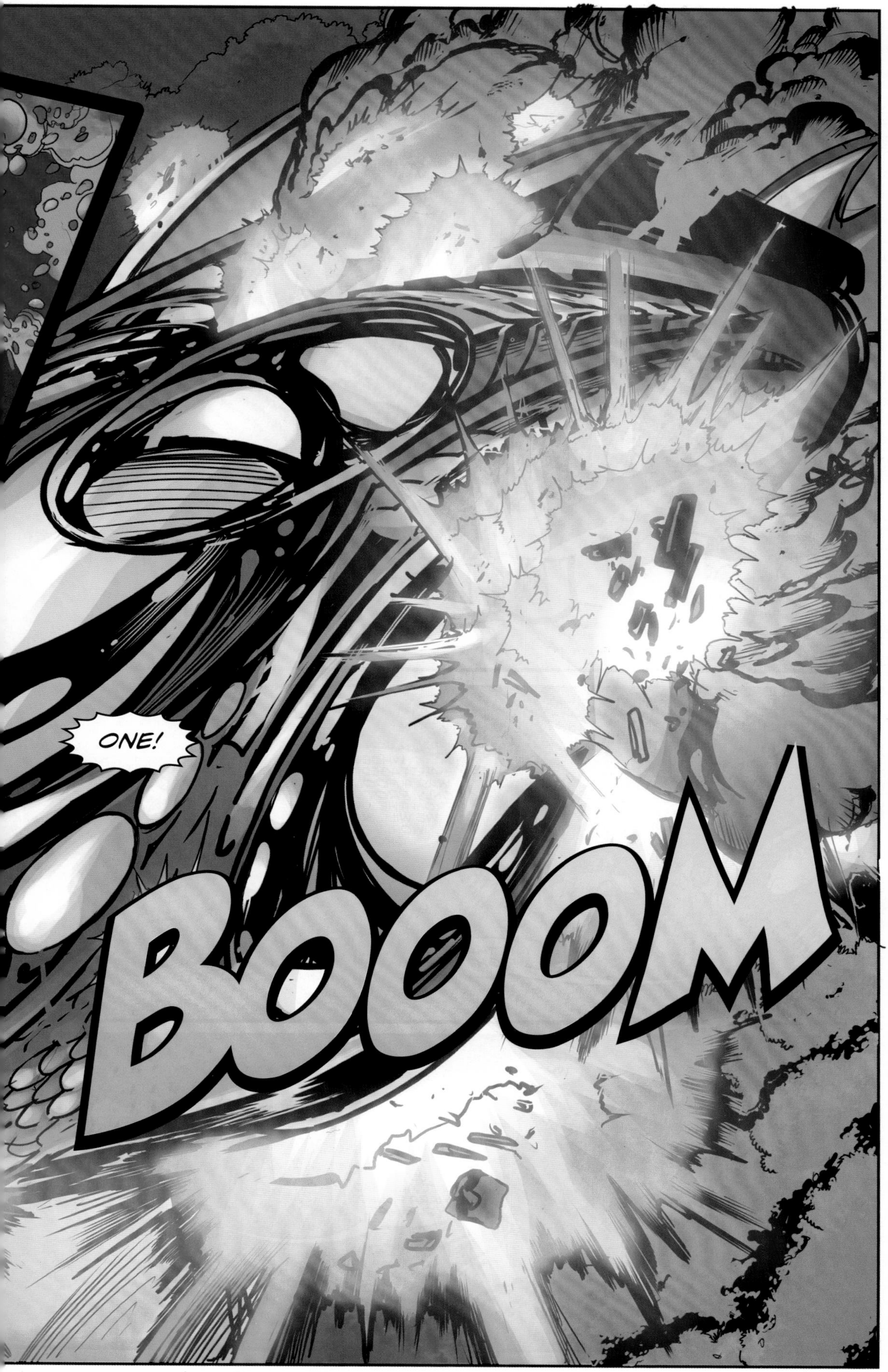
ONE!
BOOOM

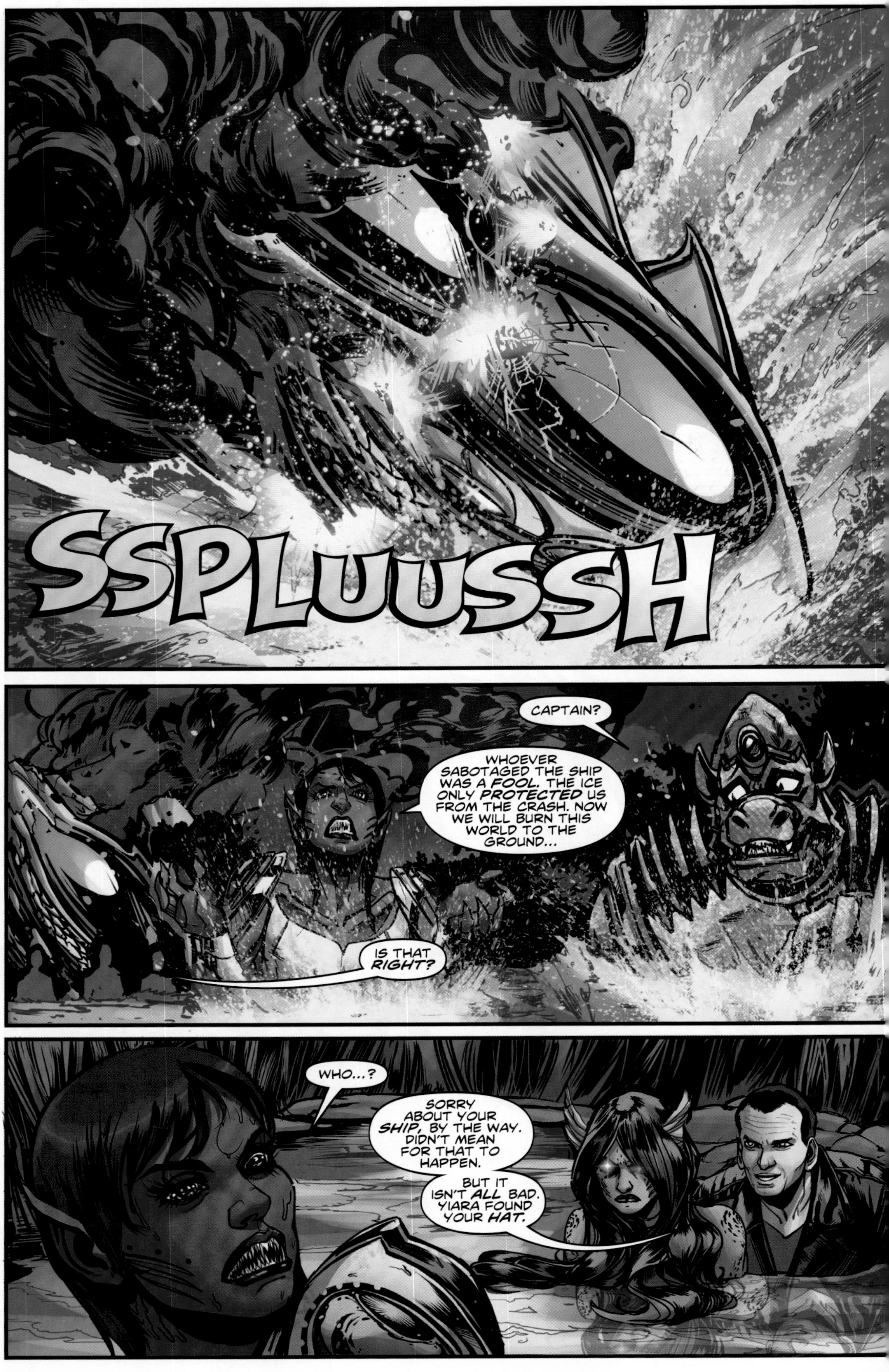
SSPLUUSSH
CAPTAIN?
WHOEVER SABOTAGED THE SHIP WAS A FOOL. THE ICE ONLY PROTECTED US FROM THE CRASH. NOW WE WILL BURN THIS WORLD TO THE GROUND...
IS THAT RIGHT?
WHO...?
SORRY ABOUT YOUR SHIP, BY THE WAY. DIDN'T MEAN FOR THAT TO HAPPEN.
BUT IT ISN'T ALL BAD. YIARA FOUND YOUR HAT.

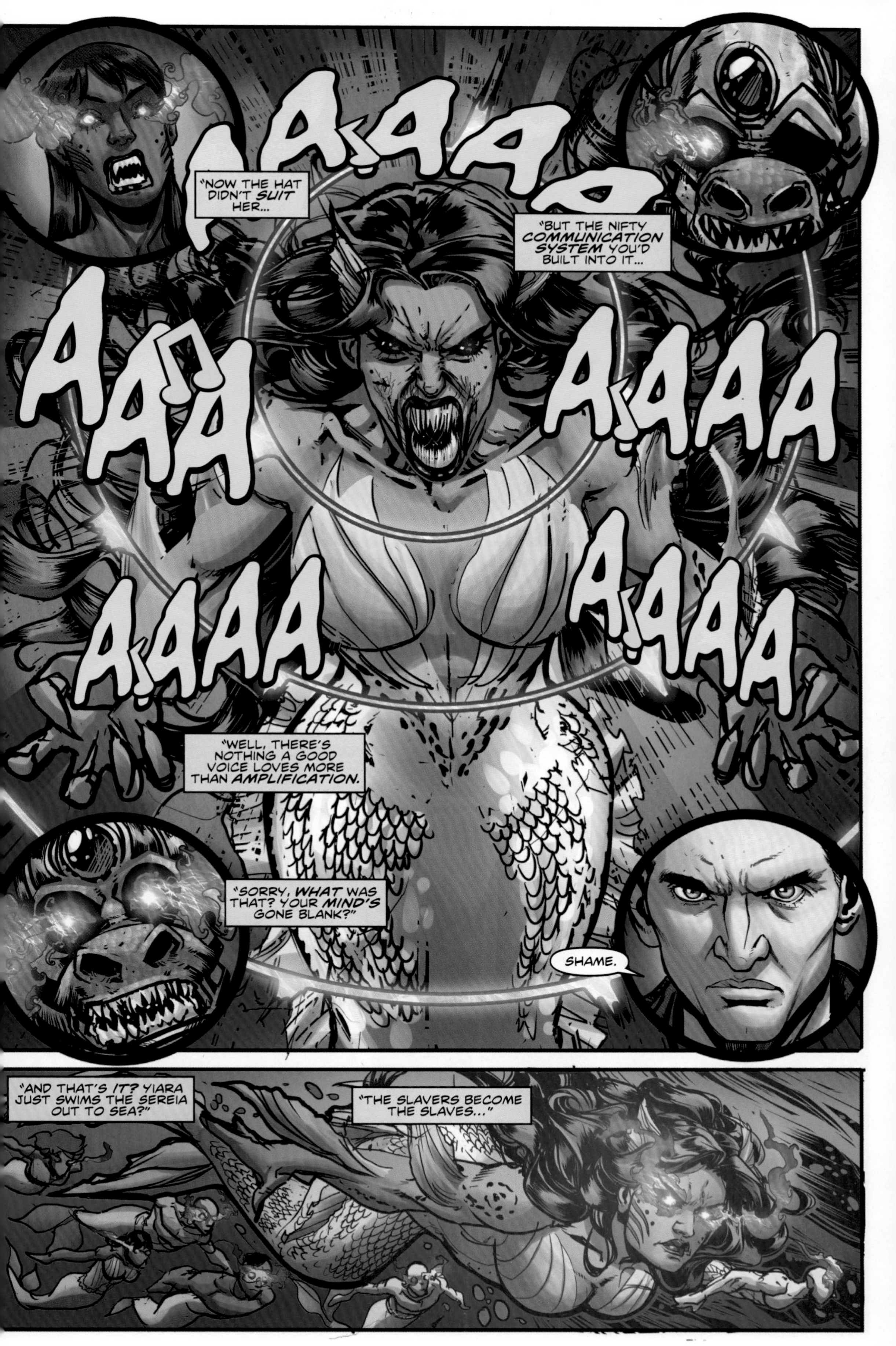
AAAAA
"NOW THE HAT DIDN'T SUIT HER...
"BUT THE NIFTY COMMUNICATION SYSTEM YOU'D BUILT INTO IT...
AAA
AAAAA
AAAA
AAAA
"WELL, THERE'S NOTHING A GOOD VOICE LOVES MORE THAN AMPLIFICATION.
"SORRY, WHAT WAS THAT? YOUR MIND'S GONE BLANK?"
SHAME.
"AND THAT'S IT? YIARA JUST SWIMS THE SEREIA OUT TO SEA?"
"THE SLAVERS BECOME THE SLAVES..."

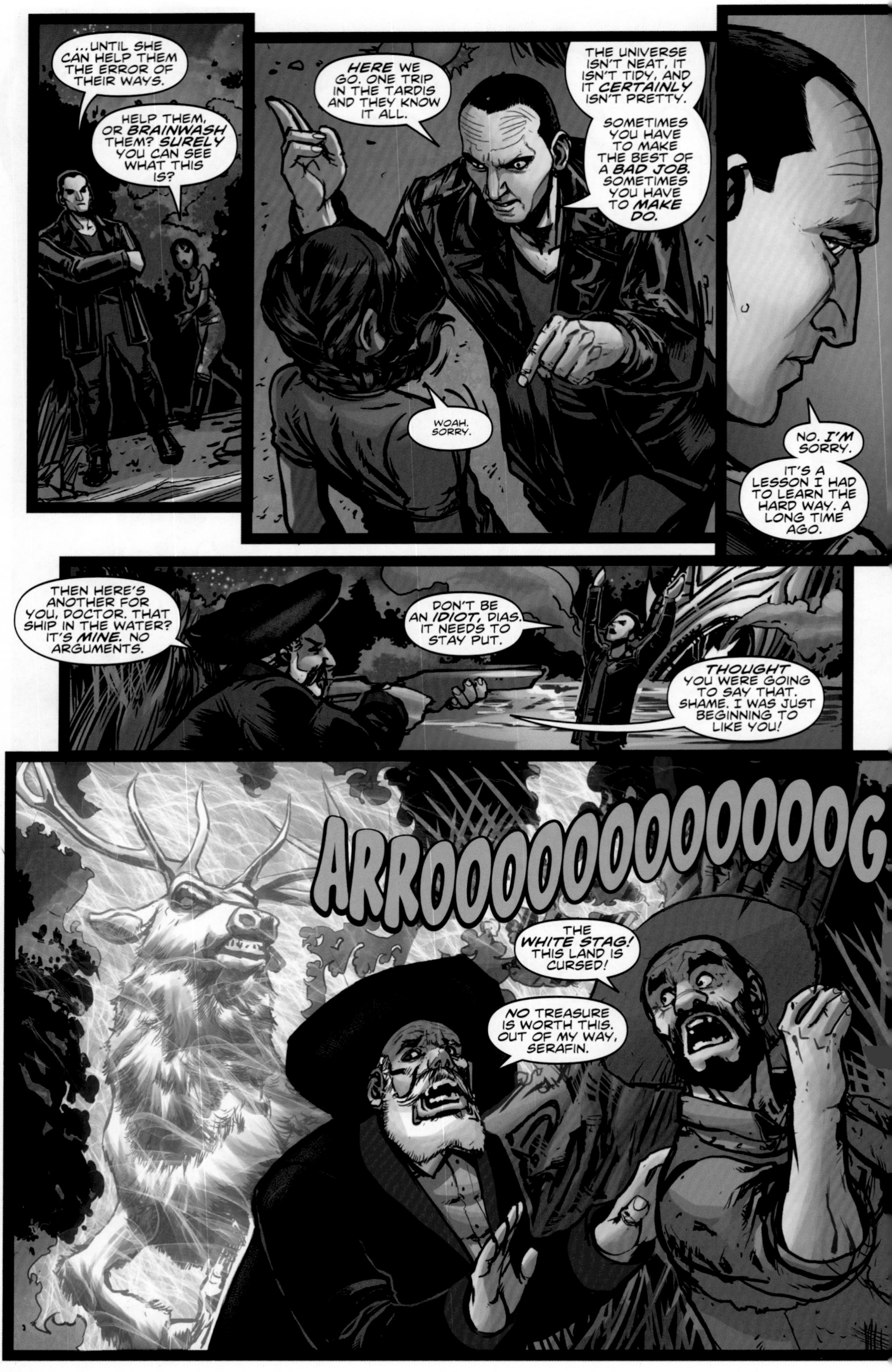
...UNTIL SHE CAN HELP THEM THE ERROR OF THEIR WAYS.
HELP THEM, OR BRAINWASH THEM? SURELY YOU CAN SEE WHAT THIS IS?
HERE WE GO. ONE TRIP IN THE TARDIS AND THEY KNOW IT ALL.
THE UNIVERSE ISN'T NEAT, IT ISN'T TIDY, AND IT CERTAINLY ISN'T PRETTY.
SOMETIMES YOU HAVE TO MAKE THE BEST OF A BAD JOB. SOMETIMES YOU HAVE TO MAKE DO.
WOAH. SORRY.
NO. I'M SORRY.
IT'S A LESSON I HAD TO LEARN THE HARD WAY. A LONG TIME AGO.
THEN HERE'S ANOTHER FOR YOU, DOCTOR. THAT SHIP IN THE WATER? IT'S MINE. NO ARGUMENTS.
DON'T BE AN IDIOT, DIAS. IT NEEDS TO STAY PUT.
THOUGHT YOU WERE GOING TO SAY THAT. SHAME. I WAS JUST BEGINNING TO LIKE YOU!
ARROOOOOOOOOOOOG
THE WHITE STAG! THIS LAND IS CURSED!
NO TREASURE IS WORTH THIS. OUT OF MY WAY, SERAFIN.

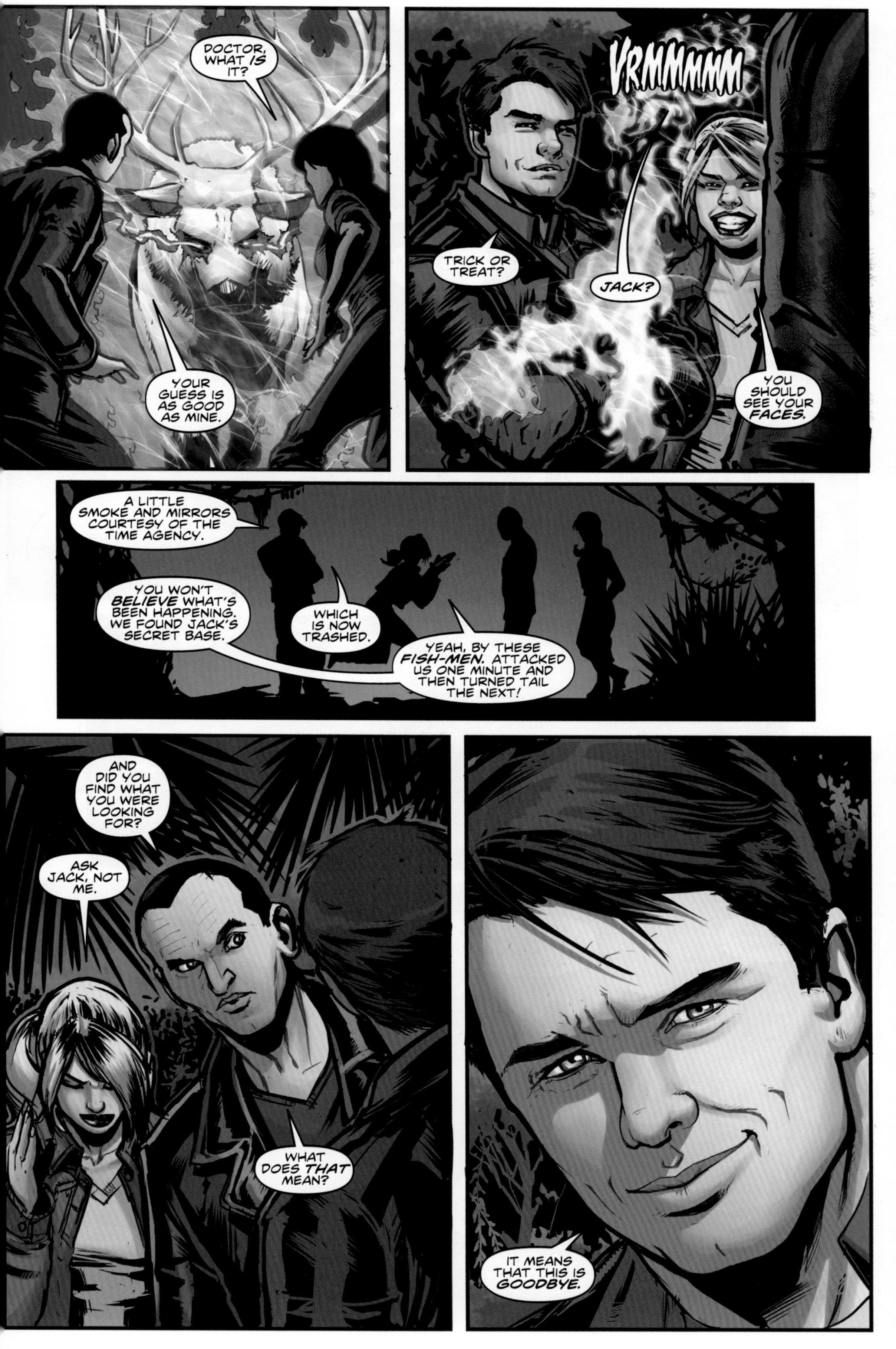
DOCTOR, WHAT IS IT?
YOUR GUESS IS AS GOOD AS MINE.
VRMMMMM
TRICK OR TREAT?
JACK?
YOU SHOULD SEE YOUR FACES.
A LITTLE SMOKE AND MIRRORS COURTESY OF THE TIME AGENCY.
YOU WON'T BELIEVE WHAT'S BEEN HAPPENING. WE FOUND JACK'S SECRET BASE.
WHICH IS NOW TRASHED.
YEAH, BY THESE FISH-MEN. ATTACKED US ONE MINUTE AND THEN TURNED TAIL THE NEXT!
AND DID YOU FIND WHAT YOU WERE LOOKING FOR?
ASK JACK, NOT ME.
WHAT DOES THAT MEAN?
IT MEANS THAT THIS IS GOODBYE.

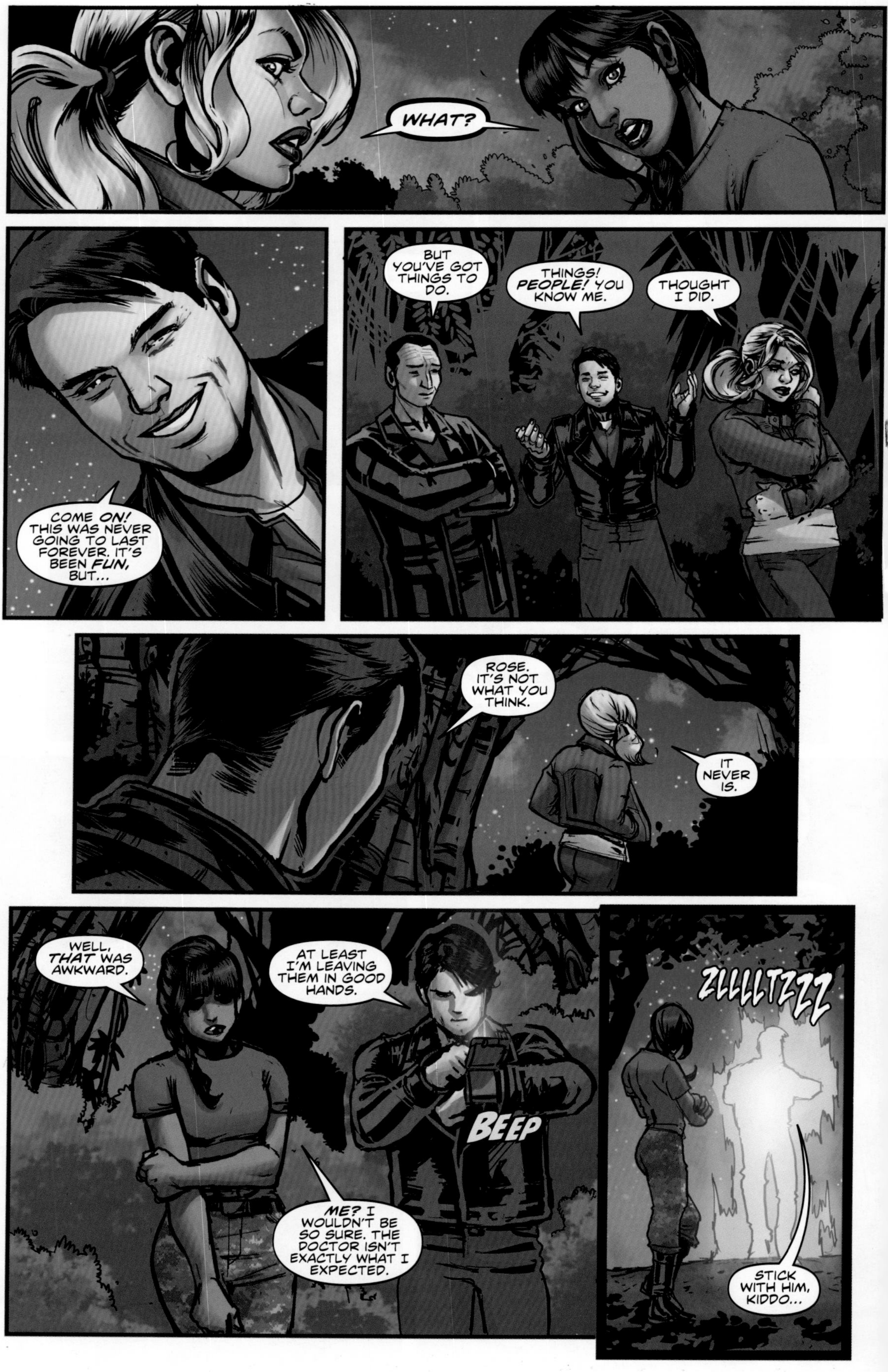
WHAT?
COME ON! THIS WAS NEVER GOING TO LAST FOREVER. IT'S BEEN FUN, BUT...
BUT YOU'VE GOT THINGS TO DO.
THINGS! PEOPLE! YOU KNOW ME.
THOUGHT I DID.
ROSE. IT'S NOT WHAT YOU THINK.
IT NEVER IS.
WELL, THAT WAS AWKWARD.
AT LEAST I'M LEAVING THEM IN GOOD HANDS.
BEEP
ME? I WOULDN'T BE SO SURE. THE DOCTOR ISN'T EXACTLY WHAT I EXPECTED.
ZLLLLTZZZ
STICK WITH HIM, KIDDO...

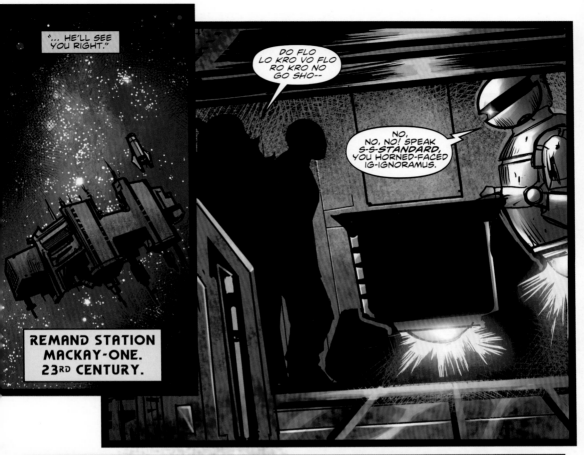

"... HE'LL SEE YOU RIGHT."

REMAND STATION MACKAY-ONE. 23RD CENTURY.

DO FLO LO KRO VO FLO RO KRO NO GO SHO--

NO, NO, NO! SPEAK S-S-STANDARD, YOU HORNED-FACED IG-IGNORAMUS.

DELIVERING PRISONER 280 FOR IMMEDIATE INCARCERATION.

THEN W-WHY DIDN'T YOU S-S-SAY THAT IN THE F-FIRST PLACE.

STATE RE-RE-REASON FOR ARREST.

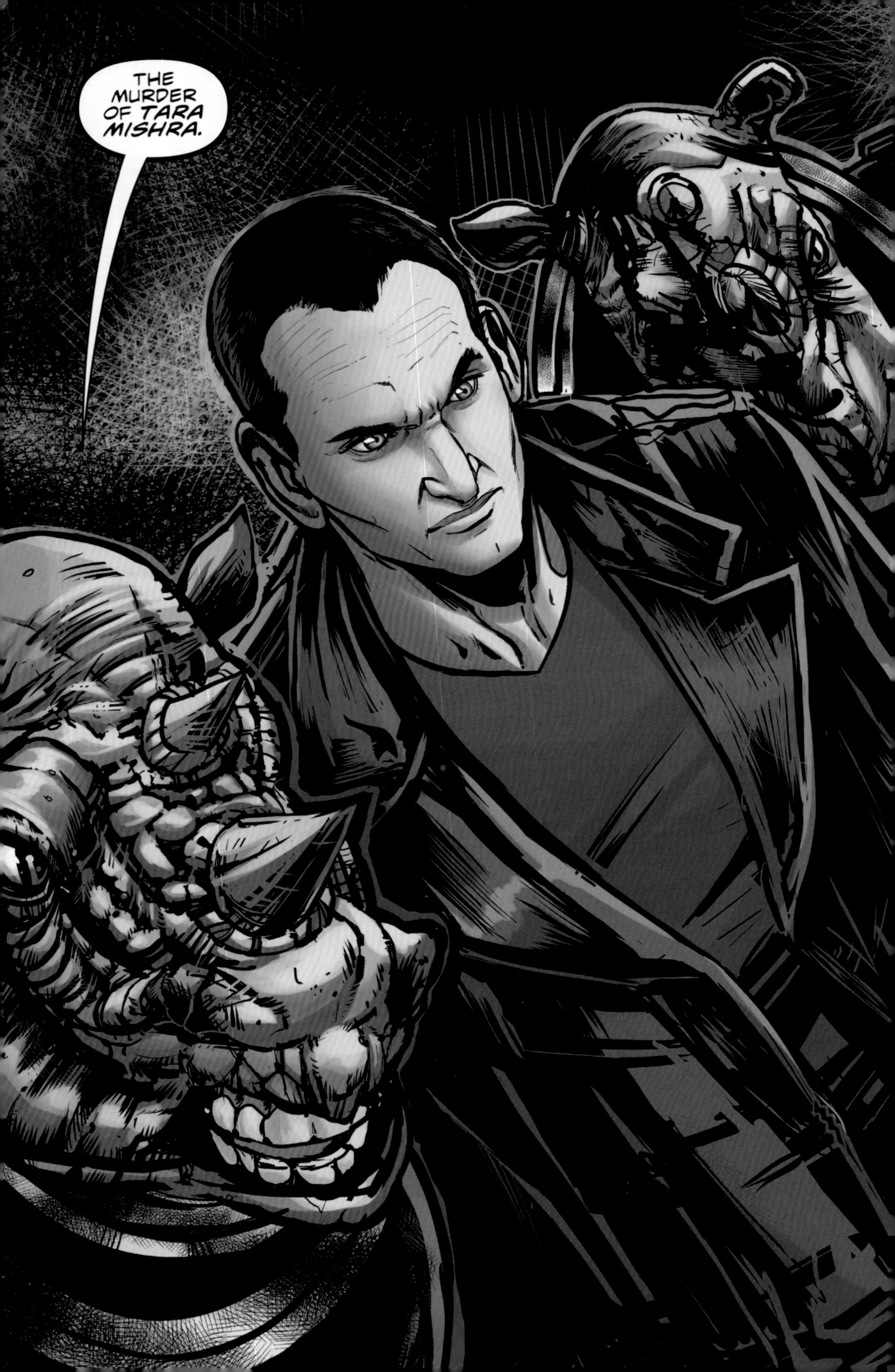
THE MURDER OF *TARA MISHRA.*

BBC DOCTOR WHO THE NINTH DOCTOR

COVER GALLERY

A

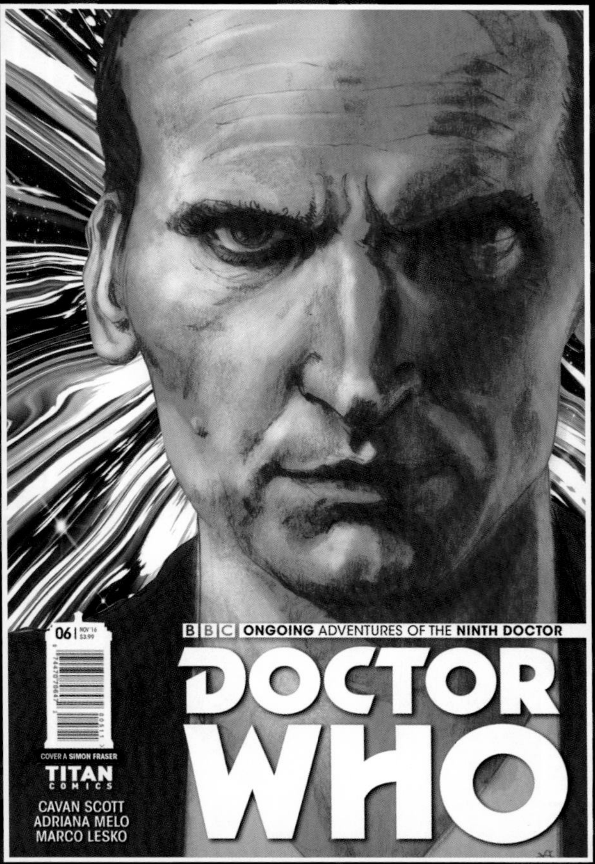

06 | NOV '16 $3.99
BBC ONGOING ADVENTURES OF THE NINTH DOCTOR
DOCTOR WHO
COVER A SIMON FRASER
TITAN COMICS
CAVAN SCOTT
ADRIANA MELO
MARCO LESKO

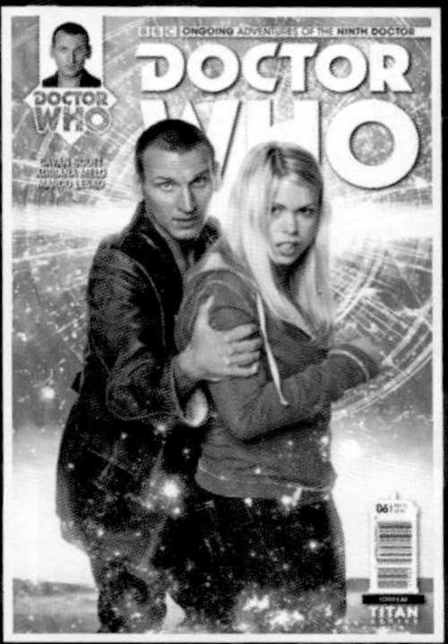

BBC ONGOING ADVENTURES OF THE NINTH DOCTOR
DOCTOR WHO

B

C

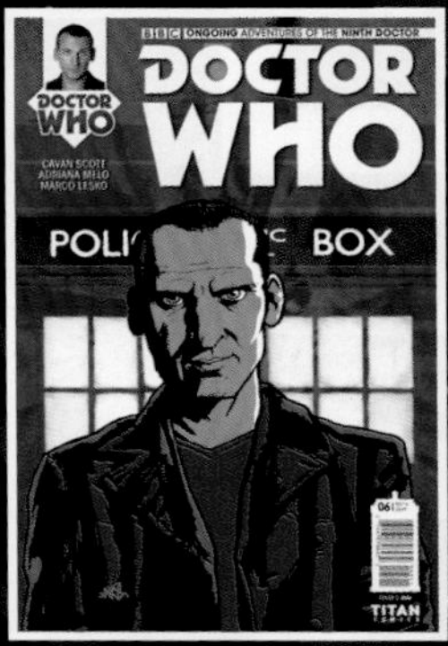

BBC ONGOING ADVENTURES OF THE NINTH DOCTOR
DOCTOR WHO
CAVAN SCOTT
ADRIANA MELO
MARCO LESKO
BOX
TITAN

D

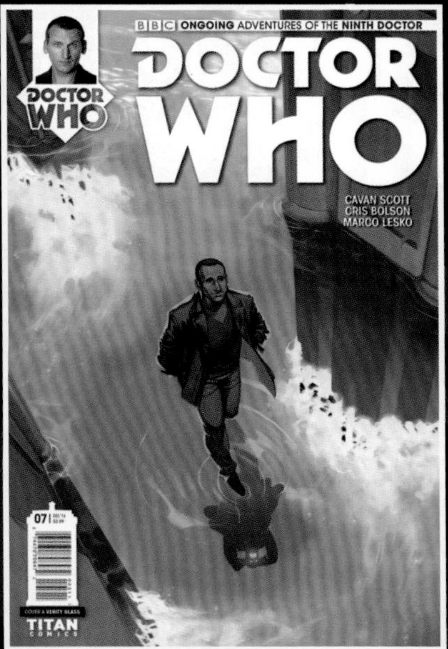

BBC ONGOING ADVENTURES OF THE NINTH DOCTOR
DOCTOR WHO
CAVAN SCOTT
CRIS BOLSON
MARCO LESKO
07
COVER A VERITY GLASS
TITAN COMICS

E

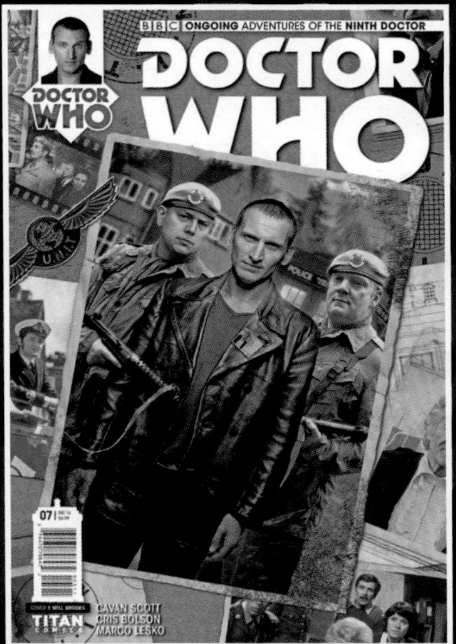

BBC ONGOING ADVENTURES OF THE NINTH DOCTOR
DOCTOR WHO
07
COVER B WILL BROOKS
TITAN COMICS
CAVAN SCOTT
CRIS BOLSON
MARCO LESKO

ISSUES #6-7

A. #6A - SIMON FRASER
B. #6B - **PHOTO** – AJ
C. #6C - JAKe
D. #7A - VERITY GLASS
E. #7B - **PHOTO** – WILL BROOKS

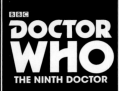

BBC DOCTOR WHO THE NINTH DOCTOR

COVER GALLERY

A

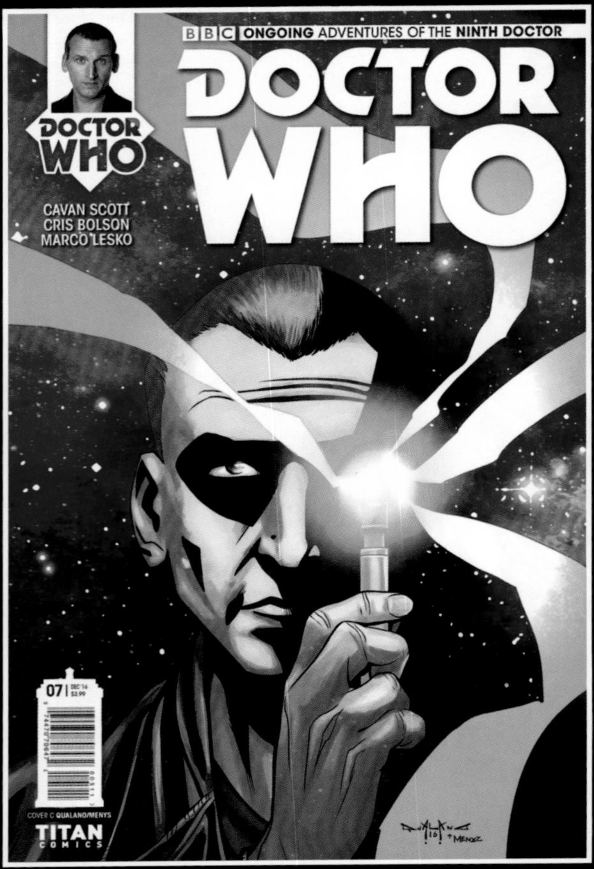
BBC ONGOING ADVENTURES OF THE NINTH DOCTOR
DOCTOR WHO
DOCTOR WHO
CAVAN SCOTT
CRIS BOLSON
MARCO LESKO
07 | DEC '16 $3.99
COVER C QUALANO/MENYS
TITAN COMICS

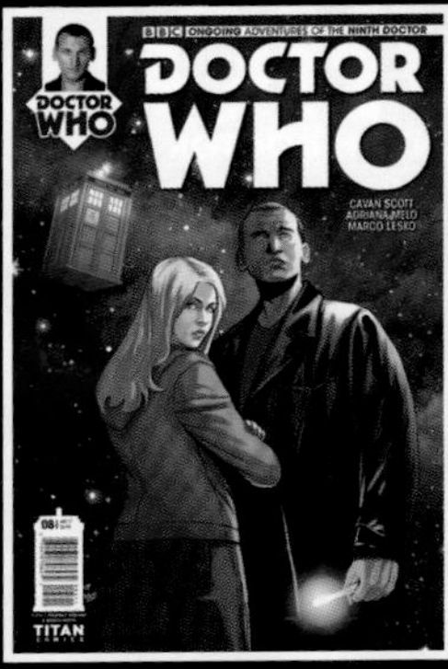
BBC ONGOING ADVENTURES OF THE NINTH DOCTOR
DOCTOR WHO
DOCTOR WHO
CAVAN SCOTT
ADRIANA MELO
MARCO LESKO
TITAN COMICS

B

C

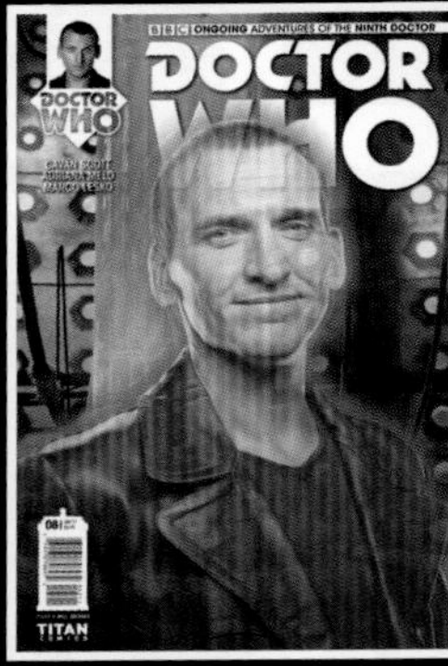
BBC ONGOING ADVENTURES OF THE NINTH DOCTOR
DOCTOR WHO
DOCTOR WHO
CAVAN SCOTT
ADRIANA MELO
MARCO LESKO

D

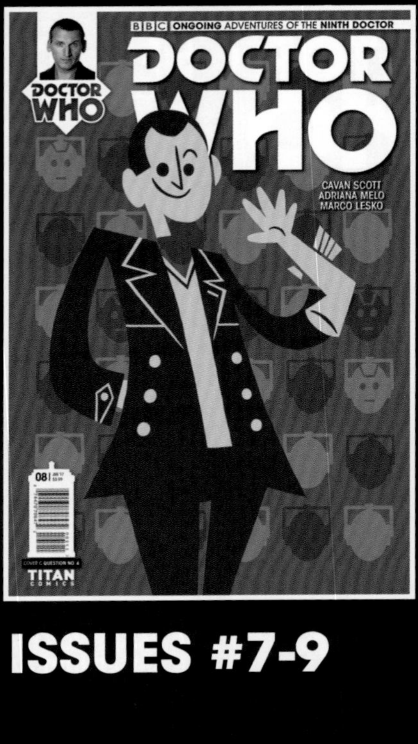
BBC ONGOING ADVENTURES OF THE NINTH DOCTOR
DOCTOR WHO
DOCTOR WHO
CAVAN SCOTT
ADRIANA MELO
MARCO LESKO
08
TITAN COMICS

E

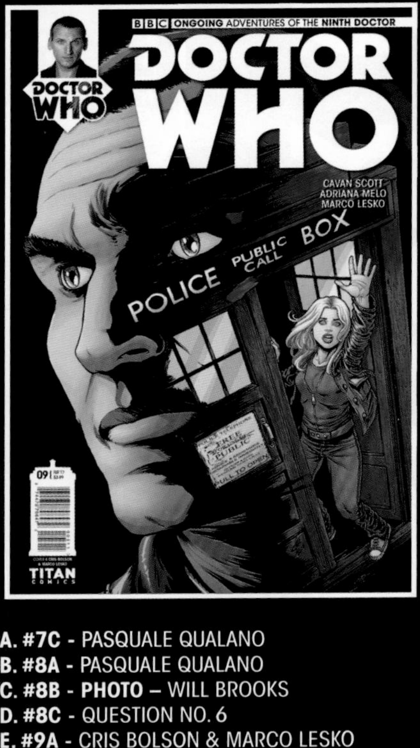
BBC ONGOING ADVENTURES OF THE NINTH DOCTOR
DOCTOR WHO
DOCTOR WHO
CAVAN SCOTT
ADRIANA MELO
MARCO LESKO
POLICE PUBLIC CALL BOX
09
TITAN COMICS

ISSUES #7-9

A. #7C - PASQUALE QUALANO
B. #8A - PASQUALE QUALANO
C. #8B - **PHOTO** – WILL BROOKS
D. #8C - QUESTION NO. 6
E. #9A - CRIS BOLSON & MARCO LESKO

A

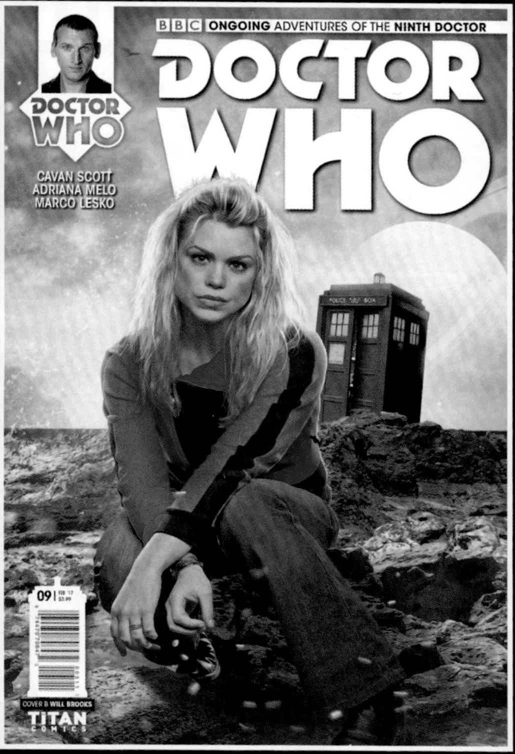
BBC ONGOING ADVENTURES OF THE NINTH DOCTOR
DOCTOR WHO
DOCTOR WHO
CAVAN SCOTT
ADRIANA MELO
MARCO LESKO
POLICE BOX
09 | FEB '17 $3.99
COVER B WILL BROOKS
TITAN COMICS

B

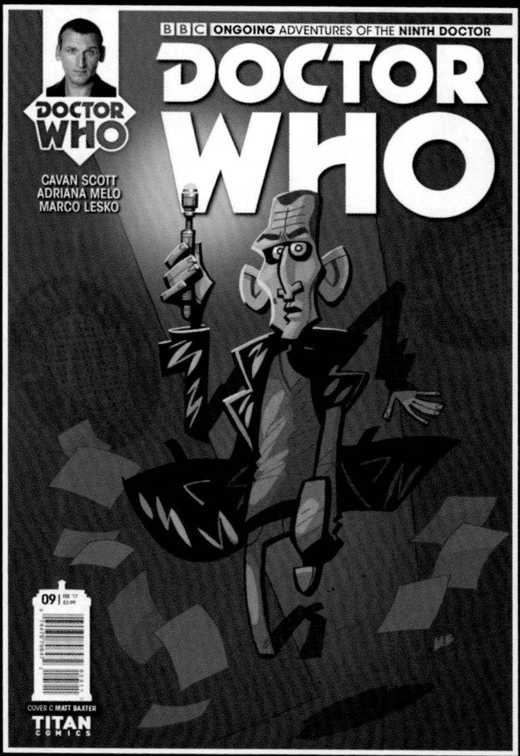
BBC ONGOING ADVENTURES OF THE NINTH DOCTOR
DOCTOR WHO
DOCTOR WHO
CAVAN SCOTT
ADRIANA MELO
MARCO LESKO
09 | FEB '17 $3.99
COVER C MATT BAXTER
TITAN COMICS

C

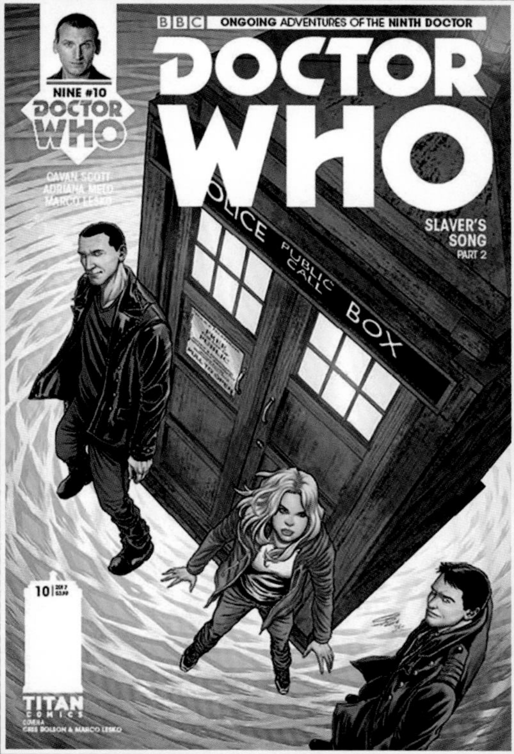
BBC ONGOING ADVENTURES OF THE NINTH DOCTOR
NINE #10
DOCTOR WHO
DOCTOR WHO
CAVAN SCOTT
ADRIANA MELO
MARCO LESKO
SLAVER'S SONG PART 2
POLICE PUBLIC CALL BOX
10
TITAN COMICS

D

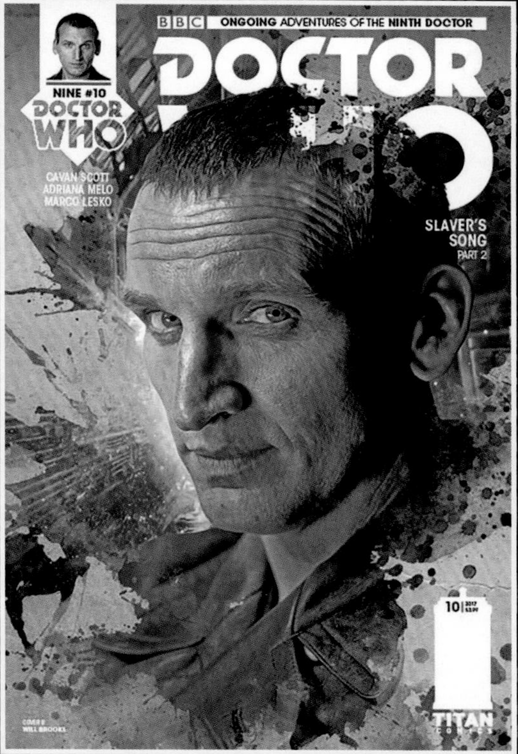
BBC ONGOING ADVENTURES OF THE NINTH DOCTOR
NINE #10
DOCTOR WHO
DOCTOR
CAVAN SCOTT
ADRIANA MELO
MARCO LESKO
SLAVER'S SONG PART 2
10
WILL BROOKS
TITAN COMICS

ISSUE #9-10

A. #9B - PHOTO – WILL BROOKS
B. #9C - MATT BAXTER

BBC

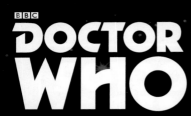

DOCTOR WHO

READER'S GUIDE

With so many amazing *Doctor Who* comics collections, it can be difficult know where to start! That's where this handy guide comes in.

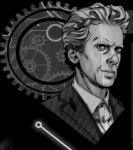

THE TWELFTH DOCTOR – ONGOING

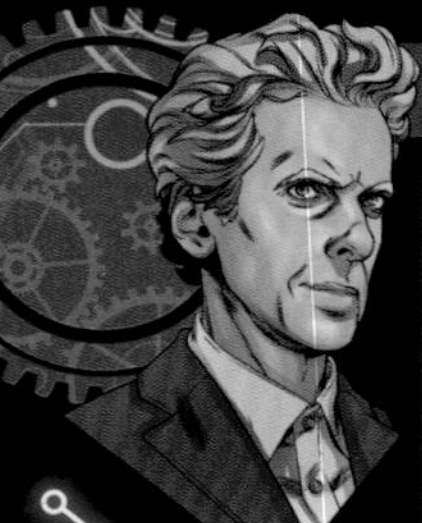

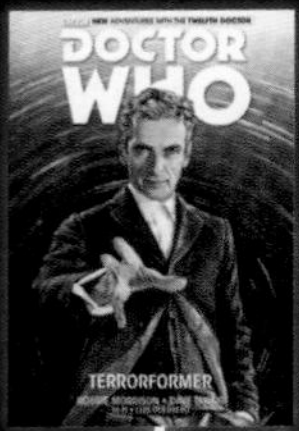
DOCTOR WHO
TERRORFORMER

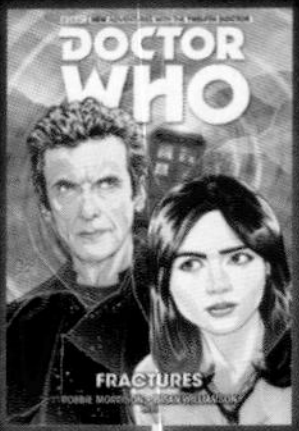
DOCTOR WHO
FRACTURES

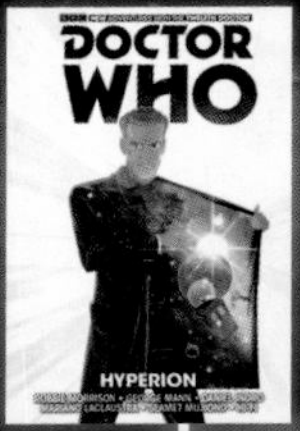
DOCTOR WHO
HYPERION

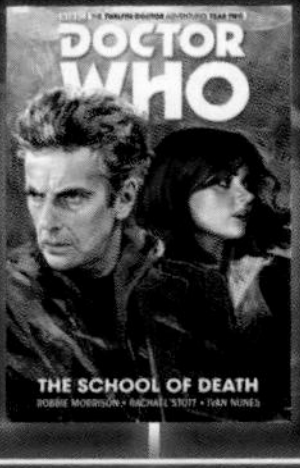
DOCTOR WHO
THE SCHOOL OF DEATH

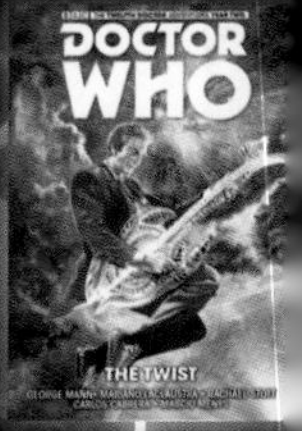
DOCTOR WHO
THE TWIST

VOL. 1: TERRORFORMER

VOL. 2: FRACTURES

VOL. 3: HYPERION

YEAR TWO BEGINS! VOL. 4: SCHOOL OF DEATH

VOL. 5: THE TWIST

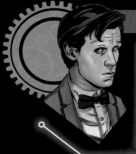

THE ELEVENTH DOCTOR – ONGOING

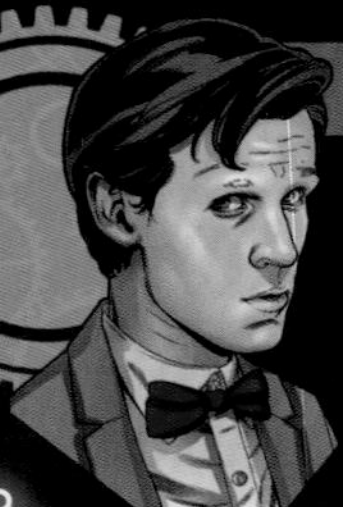

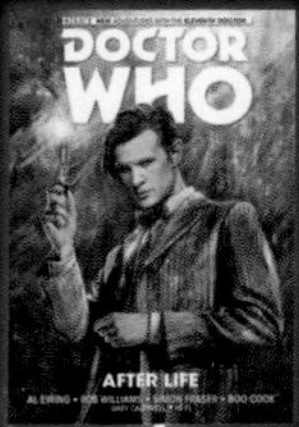
DOCTOR WHO
AFTER LIFE

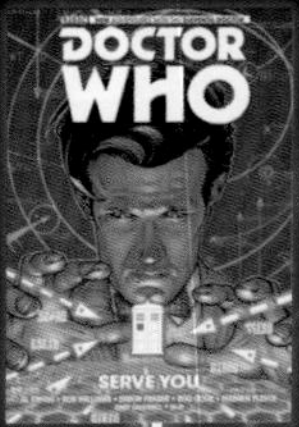
DOCTOR WHO
SERVE YOU

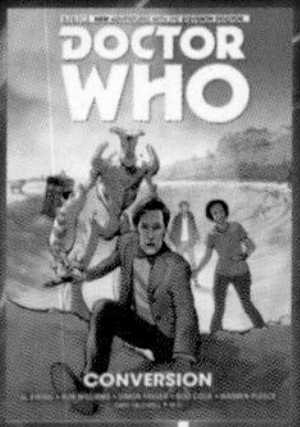
DOCTOR WHO
CONVERSION

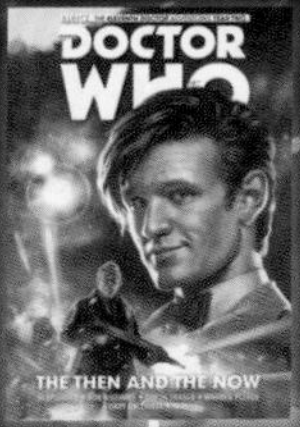
DOCTOR WHO
THE THEN AND THE NOW

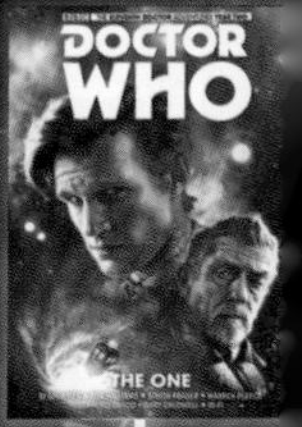
DOCTOR WHO
THE ONE

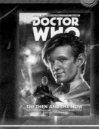

VOL. 1: AFTER LIFE

VOL. 2: SERVE YOU

VOL. 3: CONVERSION

YEAR TWO BEGINS! VOL. 4: THE THEN AND THE NOW

VOL. 5: THE ONE

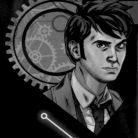

THE TENTH DOCTOR – ONGOING

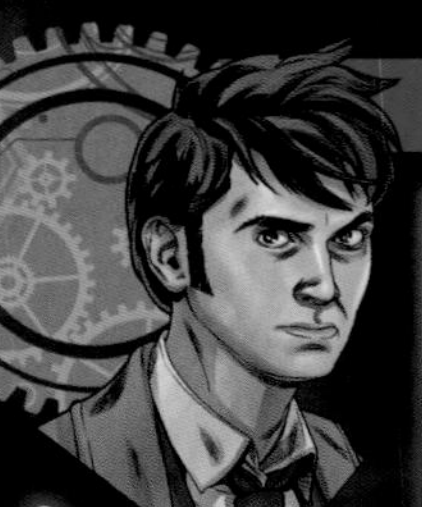

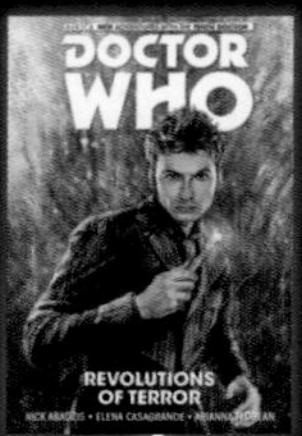
DOCTOR WHO
REVOLUTIONS OF TERROR

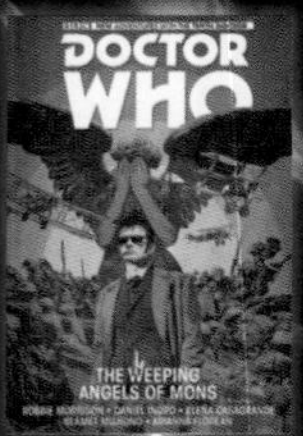
DOCTOR WHO
THE WEEPING ANGELS OF MONS

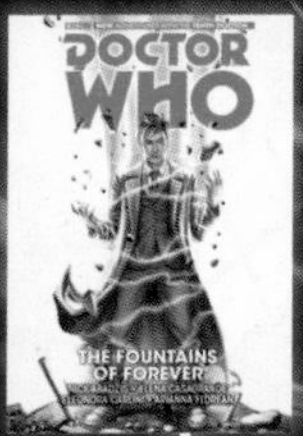
DOCTOR WHO
THE FOUNTAINS OF FOREVER

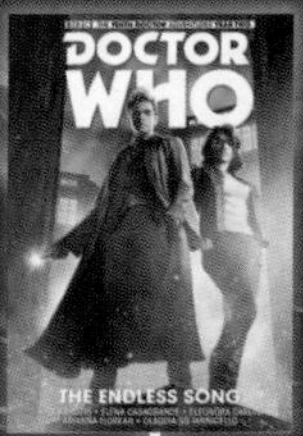
DOCTOR WHO
THE ENDLESS SONG

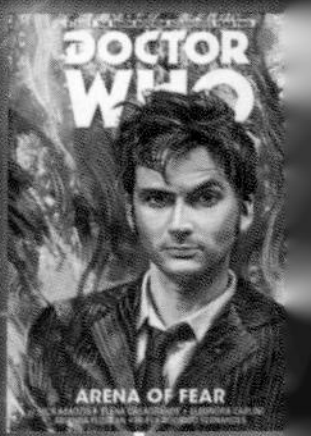
DOCTOR WHO
ARENA OF FEAR

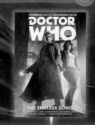

VOL. 1: REVOLUTIONS OF TERROR

VOL. 2: THE WEEPING ANGELS OF MONS

VOL. 3: THE FOUNTAINS OF FOREVER

YEAR TWO BEGINS! VOL. 4: THE ENDLESS SONG

VOL. 5: ARENA OF FEAR

THE NINTH DOCTOR – ONGOING

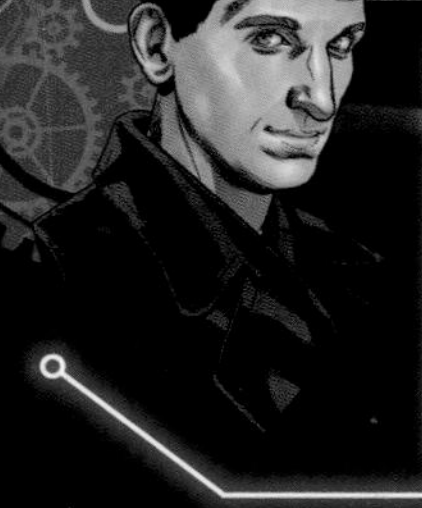

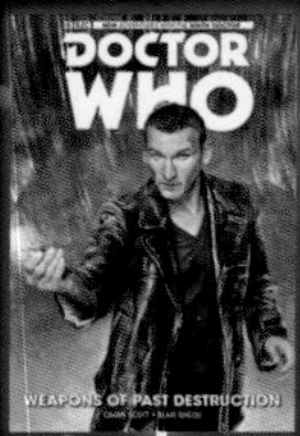
DOCTOR WHO
WEAPONS OF PAST DESTRUCTION

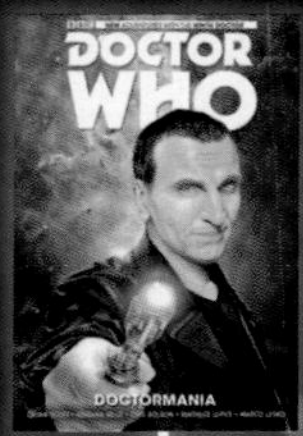
DOCTOR WHO
DOCTORMANIA

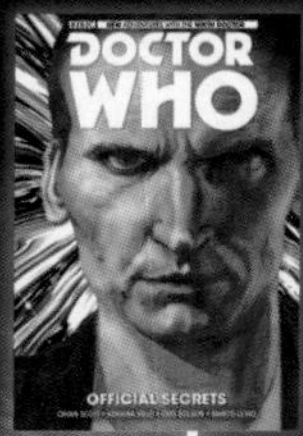
DOCTOR WHO
OFFICIAL SECRETS

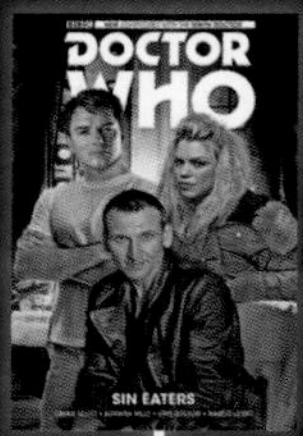
DOCTOR WHO
SIN EATERS

VOL. 1: WEAPONS OF PAST DESTRUCTION

VOL. 2: DOCTORMANIA

VOL. 3: OFFICIAL SECRETS

VOL. 4: SIN EATERS